Books by Ruth Bell (co-author)

OUR BODIES, OURSELVES
OURSELVES AND OUR CHILDREN
CHANGING BODIES, CHANGING LIVES

Books by Leni Zeiger Wildflower (co-author)

CHANGING BODIES, CHANGING LIVES

TALKING WITH YOUR TEENAGER

TALKING
WITH YOUR
TEENAGER

A BOOK FOR PARENTS

RUTH BELL
and
LENI ZEIGER WILDFLOWER

Random House/New York

All rights reserved under International and Pan-American Copyright
Conventions. Published in the United States by Random House, Inc., New
York, and simultaneously in Canada by Random House of Canada
Limited, Toronto.

Library of Congress Cataloging in Pubication Data

Bell, Ruth.
   Talking with your teenager.

   1. Youth—United States. 2. Youth—United States—Social
conditions. 3. Adolescent psychology. 4. Child development—United
States. 5. Parent and child—United States. 6. Child rearing—United
States. I. Wildflower, Leni Zeiger. II. Title.
HQ796.B355   1983   305.2′35′0973   83-42770
ISBN 0-394-52773-9
ISBN 0-394-71605-1 (pbk.)

Manufactured in the United States of America
9 8 7 6 5 4 3 2
First Edition

THIS BOOK IS DEDICATED TO

SAM AND IRENE DAVIDSON,
MY WISE AND WONDERFUL PARENTS,
WHO, FORTUNATELY FOR ME,
KNOW THE DIFFERENCE BETWEEN
WHAT IS IMPORTANT AND WHAT ISN'T

BEA AND IRV ZEIGER,
MY DEAR MOTHER AND FATHER,
WHO TAUGHT ME THE PRECIOUSNESS OF FAMILY
AND THE VALUE OF STANDING ON MY OWN

PREFACE

Everyone with children knows there is no such thing as stress-free parenthood—and living with teenagers and preteens can be especially difficult. During these years parents face the challenge of raising responsible, healthy young adults in a society that often seems to sabotage their best efforts. It can feel like an awesome task. We hope this book will make the task a little easier.

As health educators who have taught and counseled adolescents and their families for more than twelve years, we know that good communication between parents and teenagers depends to a large extent on parents being informed about what their children are experiencing during adolescence. This book gives detailed information about puberty, adolescent emotional health, sexuality, drug and alcohol use, and eating disorders, so that parents can discuss these issues knowledgeably and compassionately with their teenagers.

But our book is more than simply a compilation of facts. It is also designed to give parents support and recognition for what they themselves are going through during their children's adolescence. As our own children have entered their teenage years, we have become aware of how limited the position of the "experts" can be. It's fine, for example, for a professional to urge parents to keep open the lines of communication with their children but we know from our own experience how difficult it can be to try to hold a conversation with an adolescent who is disdainful of everything you say or do.

Being parents has taught us that the best support and advice for improving communication with teenagers often comes from other parents in similar situations. For this reason, we interviewed scores of parents and have directly quoted their stories and observations. In the pages that follow, these people describe how they are dealing with the changing family dynamics created by adolescence. They share with us their frustrations, and offer suggestions for making the parent-teenage interaction work more smoothly.

Our intention was to present readers with a primary resource, one to which parents could turn for reassurance and basic information about adolescence. We know, however, that some circumstances call for more specific reading. A number of problems require person to person involvement. Consequently, at the conclusion of most of the chapters you will find a bibliography and list of resources pertinent to the topic discussed in that section. We have listed only those books that should be relatively easy to find and those organizations that should be easy to contact. In all probability, once you begin the search you will uncover a network of many additional fine resources from which to choose.

We invite you to share this book with your teenagers. Adolescence has to do with separation, and the process of separating can be difficult for both sides. It helps when we can each appreciate what the other is feeling and experiencing. Our hope is that this book will be useful in that process of mutual understanding.

ACKNOWLEDGMENTS

The authors owe special thanks to a few people without whose help this book would never have been completed.

CHARLOTTE MAYERSON, our editor at Random House, who with unflagging determination helped us keep this project on schedule—almost. We thank you for your advice, your encouragement, your insight, and above all your perseverance.

DAVID ALEXANDER, whose sense of humor carried us through the most difficult moments and whose willingness to walk the baby—for however long was necessary—allowed us to continue typing. Thank you for your ability to remain level-headed throughout this long process.

And from your wife—my deepest thanks for your good nature, your understanding, and your love.

PAUL POTTER, whose continued graciousness, even in the face of frantic midnight phone calls, helped us stay sane. Your wise suggestions, your fine skills as writer and editor, and your sensitivity to the adolescent experience were invaluable aids to our work. We are grateful that you agreed to join us in this project.

SARAH, ZACHARY, JESSE, and CASSIE, our children. We thank you for being patient with us while we've been absorbed in writing this book. You have taught us many lessons, not the least among them to be humble about what parents can and cannot do.

NATHAN REYNOLDS and the students and parents at Westlake School. Your enthusiastic response helped this project become a reality. Thank you for lending us your support.

We want to thank all of the parents we interviewed for their warm and open generosity in sharing with us their family experiences. This book could not have been written without them.

We also want to thank the following people who were of enormous help:

Gail Abarbanel
Tom Adams
   Pacific Institute for Research and
   Evaluation
Andra Akers
Sarah Alexander
Bill Ames
   Center for Living Skills
Deanne Belinoff
Zachary Bell
Miriam Black
   Focus Center for Evaluation and
   Development
Richard Borofsky
Boston Women's Health Book Collective
Bryan Breen
Joe Broido
Michael Casey
   Beverly Glen Hospital
Nancy Cooperstein Charney
Judy Chason
Stuart Chason
Kim Connell
Gordon Davidson
Irene Davidson
Judy Davidson
Sam Davidson
Bea Davis
Anders Diamant
Kit Dreifus
Gary Drum
Jim Dunnigan

Carole Edelstein, M.D.
Donna Evenhuis
Ron Fine
Dick Flacks
Mickey Flacks
Darcy Gelber
Patricia Giggans
Sharon Gillin
Mike Goldstein
Vida Goldstein
Marge Gordon
   Focus Center for Evaluation and
   Development
Julie Goudie
Tony Greenberg, M.D.
Janet Gross
Sally Hamilton
Linda Harris
   Santa Monica Alternative School
Brad Harter, D.C.
Nancy Highiet
Debbie Hilliker
Philip Himberg
David Hoffman, Ph.D.
Sonia Hoffman
   Center for Health, Behavior and
   Nutrition
Dawn Hummer
Judy Joyce
Metta Julian
Antra Kalnins
Helen Katz

Rebecca Katz
David Katzin, M.D.
Bob Kimmel
Oliver Kuzma, M.D.
Regina Kuzma
Jeanne Leach
Elizabeth McGee
Deena Metzger
Louise Miller
Michale V. Miller
Gaye Nelson
Mary Owen
Michael Peck, Ph.D.
Cathy Pomponio
Jesse Potter
Gerda Range
Laura Schiller
Lee Smith
Adele Starr
Scott Stolnitz, D.D.S.
Hal Strick, M.D.
Sally Sussman
Diane Tessler
Richard Torregrossa
Craig Weisman
Barbara Wellisch
Mark Wellisch
Cassie Wildflower
Bonnie Winston
Madelyn Winterbourne
Bea Zeiger
Irv Zeiger

Credits:

Graphics were drawn by Leslie Stone. Los Angeles, California.

Bibliographies were prepared by Laura Schiller of the National Child Labor Committee. New York, New York.

Resource Lists were prepared by Mary Owen of the Centinela Valley YMCA. Inglewood, California.

Thanks to these people who were especially helpful with the preparation of the bibliographies and resource lists:

Toni Liquori, Nutrition Education Resources Project
Sue Rosenzweig, The Center for Early Adolescence
Leigh Hallingby, SIECUS Library
Elizabeth McGee, National Child Labor Committee
Claudia Ockerman, Centinela Valley YMCA

CONTENTS

I

WHAT IS ADOLESCENCE?

The reason we have written this book—and the reason you are reading it—is that parents and their children need help in getting through adolescence. These can be difficult years for everyone. Teenagers can be awkward, sullen, arrogant, and rebellious, and the way they behave arouses all sorts of conflicts and reactions in us.

Yet most of us also know the extraordinary qualities of our teenage sons and daughters. Our children's physical development is a wonder to behold; they are making great strides in the things they know and understand; and they are becoming more confident in themselves and their abilities.

The tendency in our society is to see teenagers as "the problem." It's easy to forget that adolescents have problems of their own. They have to cope with radical body changes, with big life decisions, with peer pressure, and with a changing identity. Whether we approve or not of the way our children are handling these issues we must remember that adolescence is a major life challenge, which many children face feeling frightened and alone.

Every culture recognizes the period of transition from child to adult that we call adolescence. However, how adolescence occurs, the way it is valued in the society, its duration and tempo, vary enormously. In many primitive cultures there are formal rites of passage that mark the transition from child to adult. And although the tests a child encounters in going through these rites may be severe, few if any fail. That is because they all have been well prepared. Children live close to the lives of their parents and other adults. Their school is their daily life of observation, participation, and play. Their games emulating adult activities become quite literally their apprenticeship. The ceremony and respect with which they watch older children successfully cross into adulthood gives them deep assurance that they can do it too. They are not expected to fail.

In our own society adolescence does not have such an integrated focus. Formal rites of passage do exist, especially among certain ethnic groups, but for most of our children becoming an adolescent is marked only by getting a driver's license, by the first date, first sex, drinking alcohol, experimenting with drugs, getting a part-time job. Our children's and our own attitude toward these rites can range from enormous enthusiasm and pride to humiliation and fear. The values and importance we attach to a particular rite (experimentation with drugs, for example) may differ from our children's. Our own desire to confer status on and give recognition to a particular passage—for example, first menstruation—may conflict with our daughter's desire to keep this event secret or private. The point is that there is no established way to say, "This is it. Now you are a grown-up."

Neither is there a direct way for a child to learn exactly what is required in order to become an adult. The way parents provide their families with food and shelter is hard to understand and harder to imitate. Adults go off to work at offices and factories where children are seldom allowed. It is one thing to watch your parents hunt or garden to provide food; it's quite another to realize that your parents put dinner on the table by selling insurance.

Nor is it easy in our society to learn from older children. Age groups are segregated from one another. Special institutions, like day-care centers and after-school programs, are created to deal with children. Younger children are separated from older children.

It is hard for us to know how to guide our teenagers in this society. We know that what was "right" during our own adolescence may not hold true for our children's. Kids may learn more about what "life" is like from advertising, movies, TV sitcoms, and their peers than from us.

When adolescence works well it helps to form an authentic individual, a creative person who has both the ability and the desire to take responsibility for his or her actions in the world. Challenging authority, taking risks, and expressing powerful feelings are part of a successful passage through adolescence. These are qualities that create an independent person. They can be a sign of our teenager's health and growth, and yet they can be difficult for us to accept.

Passive resistence, sullenness, withdrawal, defiance, delinquency, and other forms of antisocial or self-destructive behavior are also part of the adolescent arsenal. Parents are understandably upset or alarmed by many of these patterns. We don't want to be abused by "adolescent behavior." However, it helps to keep the larger picture in mind—that all this arises from our children's need to separate from us and assert their independence. It is an important struggle.

One of the major problems adolescents face in coming into their own is that they often have little self-esteem. They are, almost by definition, in an extremely vulnerable state. When they go out in the world they are often treated as if they were a lesser class of humans, seen not as individuals but as a group to be controlled. At home their struggles with us can produce tension and distance between us. Alone, they have anxieties about how they look, what they've said, whether they're popular, or lovable. They frequently feel unappreciated and unseen, yet they are afraid to show people who they really are and how they really feel. Teenagers are terrified of being "different" at the same time they want to be recognized as individuals. They are self-conscious and easily embarrassed or humiliated. Even their bravado, aggressiveness, and apparent poise and sophistication—the "cool" of some of them—can cover the same feelings of insecurity.

Teenagers need allies and most often they turn to their peers for help and understanding in this period. They enter a subculture where they can find support for being different and growing apart from us. Paradoxically this often requires their slavish adherence to new norms—eccentric hairstyles, outrageous clothing, "loud" music. This conformity is really a teenager's expression of wanting to belong *someplace*.

As we've been told so many times, the major job of the parents of teenagers is to help our children leave us. To do that we have to help them acquire the skills and the self-confidence they will need to be out on their own. They need us as their advocates at home and in the community. It is a great help to them to see us on their side in some of their struggles. Though to adults, a household with teenagers doesn't often seem like a peaceful place, in fact, for many of our adolescents their home is their only place of refuge. It is a place where they can let down, where they don't always have to act "together" or appear sophisticated, where they can still show their ambivalence about becoming adults.

II
OUR OWN ISSUES

Many parents experience their children's adolescence, at least at times, as an assault on their own identities. And in a sense they are right: one of the main tasks our teenagers have is to assert themselves as separate and distinct from us. In their need to do this they often reject our attitudes, our behavior, and our way of life. This can really hurt.

During adolescence our child prepares to leave home. He or she must pull away and we must begin to let go. Whether we're ready for it or not, whether we like it or not, the kind of parenting we did for over a decade is ending. We have to wean ourselves from *active* parenting now, and this shift precipitates periods of sadness for many parents. We mourn the loss of our baby, the one we carried so easily over one shoulder. We miss the little child who once fit so comfortably in our lap.

We may sense that we are not loved in the same way we used to be and we are right. Our adolescents are often more distant, less demonstrative, more defensive. Their desire not to be with us, to have experiences outside the family, to make decisions or formulate plans independent of our influence demonstrates that we're less important in their lives than we were:

> Watching my teenage son fills me with much joy, but also sadness. He's so surly and private now. So many things are awkward between us, and more strained.

It may help to remember that though this behavior is hard to accept at the moment, much of it will pass. As they enter their late teens and early twenties, children are more able to love their parents, to see them simply as people, not as the enemy. A mellowing generally takes place in which our teenagers are apt to want to renew their relationship with us and appreciate us again for our best selves:

> My son is in his second year at college and he has started to say things to us like, "I'm so glad you and dad made me

do this when I was younger." I honestly believe everything good you put in comes back—if you live long enough.

Since Karen turned nineteen she's become so much more appreciative of her mother and me. She's always telling us how lucky she is that we're willing to pay for her college and be there for her when she needs us and that she knows she can always come home if she wants to. It makes all those years of struggling worthwhile.

Not only are our children changing; we are too. Their changes are more visible, more dramatic; ours are usually more subtle, but they are equally powerful. This chapter is about our side of the parent-adolescent drama and about the importance of identifying and separating our issues from our children's. It isn't easy to do, because for one thing our children's adolescence inevitably takes us back to our own. Being parents of teenagers reminds us of how our parents treated us during those years. Our children's emerging sexuality, their youth and vitality, their arrival at center-stage of a youth-oriented society, forces us to face our own transition into middle age. Virtually everything they do—dating, relationships, experimentation with drugs or alcohol, sports, school work, career, friendships—prods us to think about our own behavior and feelings:

> The other night I was watching Julie get ready for a date. She spent what seemed like hours in the bathroom and then she changed her clothes at least five times. Then she got all hysterical when her makeup didn't go on right and she had to do it over. She was so nervous. Suddenly it hit me: "Oh my God, that's exactly what I used to do."

When we can distinguish our own memories, expectations, fears, and desires from those of our children, we get the perspective to stand back a little and say: "My child and I are two separate individuals. There are things about her I like and things I wish were different. But I can see and appreciate her for what she is.'' Being able to do this makes parenting adolescents easier.*

LOSING CONTROL—LETTING GO

When children are young a parent's role is quite clear-cut. They need to be diapered and fed, hugged when they get hurt, disciplined when they get out of line, and protected from the many dangers in life that they do not yet comprehend. Our responsibility is to control their environment and protect them from harm, without so overprotecting them that they cannot develop. Over the years we learn that we can safeguard them to a point, but that there are dangers and risks our children must face on their own. There is no way to learn to walk without falling. There is no risk-free way to grow.

Adolescence takes the issue of parental control and protectiveness and sets it squarely in front of us. Parenting becomes more complicated now because the factors we must deal with are no longer skinned knees but rather pressure to try drugs, experimentation with sex, serious sports' accidents, driving, rejections and loneliness, decisions about career, college, and lifestyle, and other problems for which there are no easy solutions.

We live in a fast-paced, sexually exploitative, drug-oriented society. In many cases our fears for our teenagers are justified, despite their protestations to the contrary. The chances are extremely good that the world our son or daughter experiences at fourteen or fifteen or sixteen *is* objectively more dangerous than it was when we were growing up. It is less safe to go out alone, to hitchhike; there are more murders, rapes, and suicides. More teenagers are getting pregnant and taking drugs than when we were young.

Our ideas change when we become parents. As teenagers, we may have valued adventuresomeness; as parents we view it with mixed emotions. As young people we may have wanted to try everything and push ourselves to the limit. A part of us admires our teenagers' spirit and identifies with their fearlessness. Another part of us is petrified that they're going to get hurt:

> My fifteen-year-old doesn't seem to be afraid of anything. I get so angry with her because I'm afraid she will get herself into some dumb situation and it will be terrible. I will sometimes tell her horror stories just to shock her into being more careful.

> Friday night Emily is going to see the Styx concert and she's going with a bunch of her girlfriends. They want to go to the eleven P.M. show. When she told me this I thought to myself: ''Am I crazy to let my sixteen-year-old daughter do this?'' You really have to remind yourself not to be too overprotective, but there's no way I'm not going to worry when she's out that late in the middle of the city.

*Please note: we are using the verb ''to parent'' for want of a simple alternative.

LENI WILDFLOWER

How can you know in advance that you're going to have all these anxieties about the welfare of your kids? You know it's important to have growing experiences and make mistakes and even get hurt. But you just want to make sure they're not going to get irreversibly hurt.

By the time our children reach adolescence we've been watching out for them for so many years it's like a deeply ingrained reflex. Now we have to unlearn with full consciousness what we so conscientiously learned when they were infants. Obviously it doesn't come easily. It takes tremendous courage to let go. We can't help wondering to ourselves: Are they going to make it without my help? But in spite of that worry we have no alternative because breaking away is what adolescence is all about.

Our concerns cover more than physical danger. There's a very natural tendency to want to protect our teenagers from painful emotional experiences too. We feel the responsibility to make our children's growing up less turbulent and less traumatic than ours may have been. If we have pleasant memories of adolescence, we want the same for our children. When things go well for them, when they are happy, we can feel glad for them and relax. But most of us know that there is nothing quite so heartrending as seeing our own son or daughter caught in the same problem that trapped us in our youth:

> My son is so shy. My heart aches for him when I listen to him talk to a girl on the phone. I remember being the same way. He seems to have inherited all my insecurities.

> My daughter doesn't make friends easily and now that all the kids are going off to parties and getting together on the weekends I just know how lonely she feels. I was so much the same when I was a teenager, it makes me just want to die for her.

If our kids go through similar unhappy experiences, it can fill us with guilt that our weaknesses or inadequacies have somehow been transferred to them—and guilt that we can't make life better for them. It can also make us angry that our child isn't doing it differently to keep us from having to re-experience the pain ourselves.

There's also a tendency to want to shape our children's lives—to help them succeed, to give them all the things we never had, to provide them with opportunities we consider important. This works when their behavior meets our expectations. When what they want is different from what we want for them, we naturally feel frustrated and disappointed:

> I played sports all the time when I was growing up—sand-lot baseball, basketball, football. I loved any physical activity, still do. John is just the opposite. It makes me sad. He's not very interested or very coordinated, for that matter.

> I love to read. Reading has always come easy to me since I was a little kid in school. So it has been quite a shock to discover that my daughter not only can't read very well, but also is not at all interested in reading. I had saved all the classics from when I was growing up to give her and there they are just sitting on the shelf.

DOING IT BETTER

As we parent our adolescents we can't help remembering how our own parents reacted to us during our teenage years. No matter how different we think we are from our parents, we invariably experience moments when we hear their voices coming out of our mouths. A good deal of the parenting we do comes directly from them:

> Debbie keeps telling me that I am nagging her and that I expect too much from her, that I'm too critical. I don't really see myself that way, but I certainly remember leveling the same criticism at my mother when I was fourteen.

> I can hear my mother when I start offering food and no one's hungry. I do it almost by rote. It's like an echo coming back from my childhood: "Girls, are you sure? Did you eat enough?"

> My father was a pretty strict parent. I know I didn't appreciate it at the time, but as my kids are getting older and going out on their own, I find myself laying down the law like my own dad did with me.

Many of us have a pretty clear idea of what we would have liked from our own parents in the way of support or love, and though we may know intellectually our parents did the best they could, our efforts often center around doing better with our own children. If our parents were rigid and controlling, chances are we've tried to be more relaxed. If our parents were remote, then we are probably working at being more available to our kids. If they gave us too few or too many responsibilities, we may do the opposite:

> When I was growing up in New York our family had very little money. I was the oldest of four kids and I guess had the most responsibilities. When I think back to when I was a teenager, I was always feeling responsible—or guilty—that I wasn't doing more. With my own teenagers I've tried to give them less responsibility. We have a housekeeper, so they really don't have that much to do. But it seems to me that they don't even do the few chores that they have—like their room, or drying the dishes or cleaning up after the dog. I didn't want my kids to have all the responsibilities I did, so what I've got is kids who have *no* responsibility.

> The other day my daughter came to see me and said she wanted to take off school on Friday so she could go for the weekend with her friends. She said to me, "I don't know what to do. Will you let me?" I said, "I refuse to take the responsibility for whether you go to school or not. You have a certain amount of work to do. If you feel you can handle it, go ahead. You decide." So she decided she could afford to miss school and she did her homework in advance and then went. My parents never would have treated me with such reason. If I had said, "Can I take off school?" they would have said, "What's the matter with you?"

Since we're trying to be the best parents we can, our adolescent's rejection of us comes as a hard blow. It can help to remember how we felt as teenagers—to remember how we couldn't stand it if our parents intervened in our lives or tried to fix everything for us, to remember how we hated being criticized or judged or reminded to stand up straight or comb our hair. Now, as parents, we're coming at all of this from the opposite angle, but the game is the same. Reviewing our own teenage feelings and behavior can help us understand why our children are responding to us the way they are. It may not convince us to change our ideas, but at least it gives us a solid basis for communicating with them.

PHYSICAL DEVELOPMENT AND SEXUALITY

It is at adolescence that we see what our children will be like physically; they have come to resemble their adult selves. Our reaction to this is often complicated for, like their emotional and intellectual growth, their physical changes act like mirrors for us, reflecting an appearance that may be very similar—or very different—from our own:

> Andi is built quite petite. She usually wears a size five. My younger daughter is the same. I often tell them, "Thank God you girls inherited your father's hips and legs and not mine!"

> I hated having freckles as a kid. I thought they were very unattractive. The same freckles on my son look adorable, only he can't stand them.

> I had my nose fixed when I was a teenager partly because I wanted to and partly because my mother wanted me to. My daughter is eleven and hasn't started to develop yet. So her nose is still small and cute. But I'm terrified that in a few years she will get this big ugly nose like mine was.

We are forced back on our feelings about our own looks and bodies. We may be unhappy about our son's or daughter's physical appearance because it is difficult for us to accept our own bodies and the way we ourselves look. Almost all teenagers feel vulnerable about their looks, and precisely because they do have these feelings, they need our admiration and support. Having to give to our teenagers in this area can be helpful to us in making us less critical about our own appearance:

> Watching my daughter in anguish about her weight, memorizing the caloric content of every bite that goes into her mouth, and going on every crazy diet she can get her hands on has made me look at what I've been doing to myself for the last twenty years.

Our adolescent's body development in and of itself is no more dramatic than what happens to a baby during the first two years of life, but our attitude about it is usually very different. The media and society's ambivalent feelings about sexuality make it almost impossible to react to adolescent growth neutrally. Our children aren't just getting bigger; they're becoming sexual in an adult way. Some of the most successful, highly paid, sexiest models in this country are only fifteen years old, and this sort of emphasis puts pressure on our teenagers to look and act sexy at a very early age. A twelve-year-old girl may still feel like a little girl inside, but to the outside world she may look and dress like a fully developed woman. And in many instances she'll be admired as a woman by other adults. The same is true for well-developed teenage boys. It can make us "older folks" feel less sexually attractive than we'd like to feel:

> My daughter is so beautiful, and everywhere we go everyone says how beautiful she is. Sometimes I want to say, "Hey, what about me over here?"

> My son is a real hulk. Big and strong and terrific looking. He looks a lot like I did at that age. I know I don't want to be sixteen again, but sometimes I think I wouldn't mind having his body.

Having teenagers makes us more aware of the media's stress on youth and sex and also makes us sensitive to the value of creating a life based on more enduring qualities. Though it may be a personal struggle to come to terms with a middle-aged body, over and over parents told us that they would not want to be a teenager again. Age, along with sags and wrinkles, seems to have brought to most of the parents with whom we spoke a much greater self-acceptance:

> I have been having such a ball ever since the kids left home. My husband and I have traveled all over Europe and Asia. We have much more time for each other—and for life. I feel sexier and healthier and happier now than I ever did when I was thirty.

Of course, the other side of the coin is that adolescents *are* sexy. Acknowledging that may make us uncomfortable, because for one thing we're not used to thinking of our own children in that way:

> I felt peculiar when I found a *Playboy* magazine under my son's bed. I thought to myself, "You're too young for this. I still tuck you into bed at night."

> My fourteen-year-old played a French barmaid in a school drama production last year. When she came out on stage I was really thrown. She was dressed very provocatively and I found watching her unnerving.

We may also be aware for the first time of the possibility of feeling "turned on" by our son or daughter or, conversely, of turning our child on. Even when we know it's common to have those feelings, they can be very confusing:

> Last year my son had a party in our backyard. Later in the evening I joined the kids and I realized that I was attracted to some of Jeff's friends—and they were attracted to me! I was pretty startled by the discovery.

> I was driving my fifteen-year-old daughter to school the other morning. She had her feet up on the dash board and when I looked over she had her dress pulled up to her thigh and she was shaving her leg. I thought to myself: "Who is this gorgeous thing?" And then, more to the point I thought: "And who the hell am I? I'm not her date, but I sure don't feel like her father."

These kinds of sexual feelings between teenagers and their opposite sex parents in particular can be even trickier when only one parent is around. Mothers and sons or fathers and daughters living alone have unique problems to deal with:

> Sometimes I feel funny and have to watch myself. Here's this gorgeous body I'm alone with in this apartment. This gorgeous male body. And he'll come and start kissing me to the point where I get real nervous and I kind of pull away. Not that I don't love it because I do. And he's only thirteen. But the female part of me gets disconcerted! I'm really careful not to walk around undressed now.

I am a single father and have the primary responsibility for raising my daughter. I felt very close to Jessica when she was growing up. I used to come sit on her bed at night and rub her back and talk to her. She was very open and trusting with me. When she hit about twelve or thirteen I realized I had to stop some of that, that we just couldn't be that intimate. It wasn't right. I felt myself starting to get turned on and I knew I had to pull away from her. It made me feel sad.

Our tendency, especially with children of the opposite sex, is to push them away at this point, to limit or restrain much of our physical contact with them. This is potentially harmful for them and very sad for us. Validating our teenagers' sexuality, letting them know we think they are attractive and appealing, and staying physically close to them at the same time is difficult in the face of our own sexual feelings. Many of us feel ashamed or guilty about those feelings and we assume that putting distance between us and our adolescents is the best way to handle them. Actually that's not the case. Our adolescents need love and approval from us just the way younger children do. It's the fear of our sexual feelings that keeps us away, and we should try to remember that feelings are different from actions. Feelings are natural; many parents experience them. We don't need to pull away:

When I turned twelve I remember almost all physical contact ceased with my father. Except for a very swift kind of joking hugs and a peck on the cheek, we had no contact. He never acknowledged that I looked pretty or sexy, and ever since, I've felt awkward around him. My own daughter recently turned twelve and I have been telling her father that he needs to support her femininity and her sexiness—and not stop the hugging.

How is our own sexuality affected by having adolescents? For many of us forming and maintaining comfortable and satisfying sexual relationships is an ongoing process on which we are always working. Whether we have been with one person for many years, are in a new relationship, or have casual sexual encounters, the presence of teenagers can complicate the process. One mother said:

My husband and I work hard at making a good sexual relationship and having enough time for each other and not being so damned tired all the time. Meanwhile, my son walks around the house oozing sexual energy. There are times when I find it irritating.

With teenagers in the house it's difficult to have privacy. They don't go to bed at eight o'clock anymore. When we do manage to carve some special time for ourselves, our adolescents' knowing glances can make us feel like teenagers again ourselves:

I can't stand it. It's ten o'clock and Marc's still chatting away and Peter's on our bed watching TV, so my husband says, "Okay. Time to leave us alone." And Marc winks at me and says, "We know when we're not wanted. Have

fun you guys." I feel like we have to ask permission to have sex.

For single parents or newly remarried couples the situation is further complicated by having to deal with our children's jealousy and possible judgment of our lifestyle:

I am a divorced mother with a fifteen-year-old daughter and an eleven-year-old son. My daughter and I are going through some rough times. There have been several incidents where I am going out on a date and the man comes to pick me up—and my daughter will be all over him, flirting, hanging on his arm. This is without even knowing him! The first time it happened I was furious. I was also very embarrassed. I know that part of what she's doing is just trying out her womanliness (her father isn't very available). But some of it is also competitive and directed against me.

For a long time after my wife and I were divorced I made sure that if I brought any of my women friends home to spend the night that the kids were with their mom. Well, last year my wife moved out of state so now they're right there in the morning if anyone stays over. Neither of them has said anything yet—they're ten and twelve—but I'm waiting!

I've been dating this man for some time and last weekend I had him over for dinner. I was cooking in the kitchen and then I went into the living room to see what was going on. My twelve-year-old had decided this was the time to paste all the pictures she could find of me and my ex-husband in her photo album. She was sitting on the couch next to my friend showing him all of these pictures!

Arranging to have the time and privacy needed to enjoy our sexuality takes energy. We may feel embarrassed or uncomfortable when our teenagers recognize our sexual desires. Few of us have role models of parents who felt comfortable enough with us when we were adolescents to be open about the fact that they had a sexual side to their relationship. Indeed, most people say they can't imagine their parents as sexual. Many of us would like to be different. We'd like to be more honest with our children about our sexuality. We'd like them to know that sex is an enjoyable part of a loving relationship. On the other hand, it's disconcerting when they look at us as if we are nymphomaniacs or sexual perverts. Homosexual parents may have a difficult time explaining their feelings to their adolescent children.

It's important to remember that teenagers now are more sexually aware than most of us were as teenagers. Whether we approve or disapprove, television and sexually explicit movies have opened up to people of all ages what used to be the realm of adults only. So we may want to give our kids credit for being able to accept and even appreciate the fact of our sexuality—not by acting in their presence or being openly flirtatious or provocative, but simply by letting them know that sex is part of our lives.

Parents who are in homosexual relationships may feel especially reluctant to discuss their feelings with their children. Whether you tell your children or not depends on your personal circumstances and what you think the practical and psychological effects will be on your kids. The gay parents we interviewed said that "coming out" to their children was not an easy experience, but in the end it was a positive one.

Some teenagers will use our sexuality as an argument for their own. They say, "Well, you sleep with people you aren't married to, so why can't I?" or "You tell me sex is part of a loving relationship. Well, Billy and I love each other." It is valid to say in response, "I am an adult. You are not an adult yet. Sexual activity is part of my life now and I can handle the consequences of it. When you are old enough and mature enough to handle the consequences, it will be part of your life too." Parents do have a right to pull rank. We are older and we have been through more experiences. We hope we are more capable of making sound judgments about what we want for our lives than young teenagers are.

There's another side to this issue. When there is some strain in our relationship with a spouse or lover, there is a tendency to use the "ever-present" teenager as an excuse not to be more sexually loving with each other:

> I think sometimes Ron enjoys being with the kids more than he enjoys being with me. We've been distant from each other lately. We hardly spend any time alone together because one of our three kids always seems to need to talk or want to go some place, and we haven't made any effort to say no. I thought it was bad when they were little and I was exhausted all the time. But this is just as bad.

Tensions in our relationships often get exacerbated during these years. Particularly when teenagers have problems, the drain on us as parents leaves very little time for our relationship with each other:

> When Sandy went through a depression the first part of her senior year, there was a lot of strain on our marriage. We probably have one of the world's better marriages, but during that time we were fighting a lot. It was just that we were so tense worrying about Sandy all the time.

> I can't cope with keeping my son from flunking out of school and keeping my marriage together at the same time. It's too much.

We need to remember ourselves as people, especially during the most difficult periods. And if our intimate adult relationships are suffering from lack of attention or communication, it's important to try to make the effort to renew them.

BEING PARENTS TOGETHER

If we are fortunate enough to have a good relationship with our husband or wife, sharing the parenting of teenagers can be a very positive experience. We can support each oth-

er, fill in when the other is not around, and together enjoy watching our children develop into independent people. We can even spend more time together, since our teenagers don't need baby-sitters or our constant attention. As we have seen, we may have to make a conscious effort to find privacy for ourselves, but when that's something we really want to do, we can do it.

NANCY HAWLEY

However, it's inevitable that raising teenagers will create some stress in even the best of relationships. Differences in our style of being a parent can erupt into major issues during our children's adolescence because the things adolescents do can have such serious consequences. Differing ideas about discipline often become divisive at this time:

> My husband will let the kids do almost anything. He wants them to try everything he was scared to do or wasn't allowed to do when he was a teenager. So he almost pushes them into things. I get scared. I'm more strict. I don't want them staying out late and partying or going off alone on wilderness trips. It feels like part of what he's doing is making them live his life for him. But what gets communicated when I express my concern is that I'm just the uptight mother.

> I worked since the time I was a kid. We lived in a small town and we didn't have much money. My wife never had to work. When she was growing up she had everything she ever wanted. Well, I think our kids should know what it's like to work for something if you want it, but my wife thinks: "God forbid they should have to suffer and not get something they want right away."

When the kids were young and we had a disagreement with our spouse over how to proceed, we could talk it out between us when they were asleep. Once our kids reach adolescence they are aware enough and articulate enough to want to join in the fray, which can turn it into a major family event. At these times the parent who is taking the "hard line" position often is left feeling isolated and unappreciated. This can create more distance between parents, because the one who is labeled "bad guy" feels betrayed by the one who seems to be siding with the kids. Many parents say that some of the bitterest arguments between them start as differences of opinion about how to treat their teenagers.

Perhaps we are more vulnerable to our children's attempts to play us off against each other during adolescence. Many parents report that there is particular stress during these years between mothers and daughters, fathers and sons. And sometimes parents feel torn between their spouse and their child, believing that they need to be on the "side" of one or the other:

> My son knows that when he calls from a party and wants to stay later because he's met a great girl, he'd better talk to me and not his mother. She doesn't like to give in on curfew but he knows I will because I remember how important that stuff was for me when I was growing up.

> My daughter uses "sexual blackmail" on her daddy. If she's mad at him, she won't talk to him or be his little girl anymore and she knows he can't stand it. So if she wants something really badly, she knows who to go to.

The idea isn't to present a "united front" at all times, but simply to understand that these differences in approach to parenting adolescents can make us feel cut off from each other. It's important for our relationship with our spouse to make the time to air our feelings. Keeping communication open with your teenagers is important, but it is equally essential for parents to keep working on staying open with each other. Sometimes, in fact, a discussion of our feelings about particular issues can give us a deeper understanding of each other:

> When Donna wanted to go on this backpacking trip with two of her girlfriends, it set off a battle. I was all for it, but my husband, who's the big backpacker in our family, kept coming up with objections. I couldn't believe he was being so negative and petty. Donna finally said that she thought my husband's feelings were hurt because he wasn't needed to take the girls camping. He suddenly looked very sad and said, "You're right."

BEING A SINGLE PARENT

Many parents who are raising their children alone say that it gets harder when their children reach adolescence. Parents in "intact" families also have to deal with adolescent sexual experimentation, drug and alcohol use, ways to provide good role models. However, such concerns can feel more intense to single parents because they are facing them alone:

> I've been raising Joanie on my own since she was six. Her mother lives on the other side of the country and she only sees her for vacations. I think the hardest part of being a single parent is that there is only one set of eyes and ears instead of two. I feel like I've got half as much ability to figure out what's going on with her.

> For my son's sake I wish I could get into football but I just don't like it. He's always watching games on TV and he's

on the high school team. I think he really misses being able to discuss the games with his dad.

> When you're living alone and your kids finally get to be teenagers, in one sense it's easier. They can help out more, pick things up at the market for you, help with the cooking. You don't have to watch them all the time. But in another sense, it's harder. I feel at a loss when it comes to disciplining the boys now. They're both bigger than me.

During adolescence most children identify more closely with their own gender. As their bodies begin to develop sexually, they can benefit from discussing those changes with a same-sex adult. Many parents who live alone with their opposite sex children say this makes them feel somehow inadequate:

> My twelve-year-old is living with me. This year she's really beginning to develop and her body is changing a lot. I bought her some books and we talked, but I noticed when she really wants to discuss something, she'll call her mother long-distance.

> I think the times when I feel most inadequate being a male is when Stacey and I go shopping. She disappears into the dressing room and comes out telling me that nothing fits and she's fat and ugly and nothing looks good on her.

Adolescents are likely to be more vocal than younger children about their parent's divorce or the current custody situation. Their comments can make us feel guilty about the "deficiencies" caused by the "missing" parent situation. We can find ourselves working extra hard trying to be both mother and father to our teenagers. It's not possible to do that, of course, so many single parents make an effort to provide their children with outside same-sex role models by finding ways to include grandparents, uncles, aunts, or family friends in many family activities.

In some divorced families in which both parents participate in child-rearing, adolescence is the time when children go to live with the "other" parent for a while, quite often the same-sex parent. This can work out well when the estranged couple has good enough communication to arrange the necessary details to everyone's satisfaction.

Unfortunately, lack of communication is what causes many divorces in the first place, so it may be quite difficult to accommodate each parent's role expectations. In particular, differences in parenting style can lead to severe disagreements. It's hard enough when parents are living together and don't agree on what to do in a certain situation, but when they are living apart and not on the best of terms anyway, it can be much worse. Single parents say that having to accept the other parent's style of parenting—when that style is antithetical to their own—is one of the most debilitating parts of the entire experience. And this is especially true during adolescence when, as we've suggested, the stakes can be very high. If, for example, at one parent's house the kids are allowed to drink or smoke marijuana while the other parent is completely against those activities, it's easy to see how desperate the latter parent might feel. Similarly, if the custodial parent is lax about homework or school activities, while the other feels strongly about academic achievement, that too can be tremendously frustrating to the parent who is not there on a day-to-day basis.

Obviously there are no simple solutions, because to work through these differences requires respecting each other enough to listen to each other. Some divorced parents cannot do that. There can be so much fury and distrust still unresolved that coming together on *anything* feels impossible. In most cases, single parents have to let go of their desire to influence the parenting style of the other parent. However, as we discuss in Chapter V (see p. 55), there are times when it is essential for the health and safety of our children that we overcome our feelings enough to find a mutually agreeable approach to a particular problem. Sometimes adolescents need to know that both parents are working together to help them through a difficult situation—like drug abuse or trouble with the law or failure at school:

> My ex-husband and I can't be in the same room together without fighting. But when Kelly started running away and getting mixed up in a wild crowd I knew we had to be firm about a way to handle it. If I said one thing and then she could run to her father for the opposite, it just would never get better. I called Stuart and talked to him for a long time about my feelings, and he agreed. We decided that we both had to demand that Kelly abide by certain rules.

Another issue that comes up for single parents is companionship. If they are not involved in fulfilling adult relationships, single parents may become emotionally dependent on their adolescent children. This can also occur in two-parent families. However, when there is no adult partner we may find ourselves particularly susceptible to seeking the companionship of our teenager. Of course, as they get more independent our kids begin making their own plans for evenings and weekends, and they usually would prefer being with their own friends than with us. This can hurt a lot, and make us feel guilty for needing them so much. For parents who only see their children on the weekends anyway, it can be especially difficult:

> Last Saturday I had arranged to pick up the girls and go for a picnic at the beach, which I know they like. On Wednesday, Gail called and said she had some other plans with her church group. Then Adrian called, I think on Thursday, with some other excuse.

> I understand they're older now and they're both involved in a million activities, but it's hard when you only see them twice a week and that gets washed out.

> I've started to go by my ex-wife's house and pick up my daughter for school. It's not that I like taking her to school so much but if I don't do that, I don't know when I would see her anymore.

LENI WILDFLOWER

LIVING WITH TEENAGERS

Since it is a transitional stage, adolescence is characterized by ambivalence. As parents who must respond to their children's development, our position isn't too steady either. We have to let go of some of our parental control; we have to adjust to more grown-up, independent children; and we have to accept the fact that frequently our children will show us that really they're still children. Just when we get used to the fact that our teenagers are able to take care of themselves pretty well, they'll do or say something that lets us know they still need our support and attention. When we begin to enjoy the increased independence adolescence brings us, our kids make it clear they're not out of the house just yet. In fact, sometimes we may feel that adolescence is taking over our lives:

> My son is fifteen and he's *big!* When he and his friends are in the living room it feels like the Vandals have invaded. There's no place for us.

We look for a Coke; there's no Coke left. We crave a cookie or some ice cream or a piece of fruit and the cupboards are bare. We can't get at the telephone. The dining-room table is covered with homework. And not only that, now that they're our size our closets are ripe for their picking:

> I went to find my gorgeous new purple sweater the other day and where was it, in a crumpled up mess on Kathy's floor.

> My son uses my car. He takes my shaving cream; he drinks my beer; he wears my socks. He even beats me at tennis. If I were a little more uptight I'd feel like my position were being threatened.

The boundary between our world and theirs is fuzzier now that our children are older. Consequently, if it's important to us we may have to put some energy into maintaining a sepa-

JIM WILDE

rate space for ourselves. Otherwise we may end up feeling resentful.

Although this may sound like a contradiction, our ability to be "good" parents rests directly on our capacity to nurture ourselves. That means taking time for the parts of our life separate from our children—our career, our interests, our health, our relationships with other adults. When we nourish ourselves in those ways we are able to bring a renewed spirit to the task of parenting.

Classics for parents on being parents and bringing up children.

Faber, Adele, and Elaine Mazlish. *Liberated Parents, Liberated Children*. New York: Avon Books, 1974.
Easy-to-read narrative about parents who took a parenting class and how it affected their relationships with their own children over time.

Galinsky, Ellen. *Between Generations: The Six Stages of Parenthood*. New York: Quadrangle/The New York Times Book Company, Inc., 1981.
Describes the effects of the developing child on the parents themselves.

Julty, Sam. *Men's Bodies, Men's Selves*. New York: Dell, 1979.
Sensitively written book for men on sexuality, relationships, and health care.

Rubin, Lillian Breslow. *Women of a Certain Age: The Midlife Search for Self*. New York: Harper & Row, 1979.
A woman's description of life in the middle years and suggestions for how to make them the most fulfilling.

Spock, Benjamin. *Problems of Parents*. Westport, Conn.: Greenwood Press, 1978.
The old pro turns his pen to discuss the feelings parents have about their role.

Zola, Irving Kenneth. *Ordinary Lives*. Cambridge/Watertown: Apple-wood Books, 1982.
An anthology of beautifully written, sensitive, honest, very human essays on disability and disease.

Resources

For information about counseling, see Chapter V, "Emotional Health."

Single Parents:

Parents Without Partners (P.W.P)
International Headquarters
7910 Woodmont Ave.
Bethesda, Md. 20814
(800) 638-8078 toll free

Single Parent Network
Family Service Agency
1010 Gough St.
San Francisco, Calif. 94109
(415)441-KIDS (24 hr. "talk line")

Parent Resource Center
3896 24th St.
San Francisco, Calif. 94114
(415)821-7058

BOOKS AND RESOURCES

Recommended Reading

Boston Women's Health Book Collective. *Our Bodies, Ourselves*. New York: Simon and Schuster, 1979. 3rd Edition will be available 1984.
Written by women, for women, on relationships, sexuality, and health.

Boston Women's Health Book Collective. *Ourselves and Our Children*. New York: Random House, 1978.
Written by parents, for parents, on parenting.

Dreikurs, Rudolph. *Challenge of Parenthood* and *Children: The Challenge*. New York: Hawthorne, 1979 and 1964 respectively.

III

COMMUNICATION

Patterns of communication are built up over years within a family. We get used to each other and we come to expect certain responses from each other, but once our children become adolescents all that changes. Our familiar ways of being together—dinnertimes, family outings, holiday trips, our habits of interaction, rules and responsibilities—all take on new character to accommodate the changing character of our children. To the extent that they experience themselves as "older" and participate in the adolescent subculture, they force us to communicate with a new person:

> I can't believe how Danny's changed in the last six months. He's like a different person. Sometimes I feel as if I hardly know him. I don't even know what he likes to eat anymore—one week he's a vegetarian and the next week it's strictly protein.

> I've had to teach myself not to include the girls in everything these days because so many times I'll buy them a ticket or something to a concert or a play we're going to and they'll say, "Oh, sorry, I can't go because I have too much homework" or "I've got other plans."

First, what our adolescents bring to their interaction with us is a changing sense of who they are and a concurrent host of new characteristics: a new assertiveness, a new vocabulary, new interests, intensified demands, new experiences, definite opinions, and a strong need for privacy. By their very nature these qualities make communication more challenging. On another level, their growing independence and expanding capabilities make teenagers easier to live with than little ones:

> It's so much easier now that the kids are in their teens. God, what a relief! No more baby-sitters. Everyone takes responsibility for himself. I can walk out of the house and not have to worry about who will get them dinner, who will make sure they get to bed on time. They're just so much less dependent on me and I love it.

I get a lot of pleasure out of just sitting around the kitchen table with my fourteen-year-old and his friends. These kids have such an energy for life. They're so intense. They're so sincere. I have to say they energize me too.

Teenagers can be good companions to us now. We may genuinely enjoy having conversations and sharing experiences with them. If we're open to it, we can learn from them too. Whatever their new interests—computers, photography, sailing, sketching, politics, health—we're likely to hear all about them. If they're studying drama, they may read to us from a favorite play; if they have a passion for dirt bikes or cars or sports or rock music, they may try to spark in us some of their enthusiasm for those things:

> When Frank was thirteen and fourteen he was heavily into dirt biking. We always set aside Friday night to be family night where we'd take him down to the place where all the kids met and we'd all watch them. It was really a lot of fun.

> Now that the kids are teenagers we go to a movie together or watch a show on TV and it's amazing how much they know. They're like our in-house experts on popular music and the drug scene or even what certain words mean.

> I'm reviewing whether I should become a vegetarian because of my seventeen-year-old's influence. She's doing things I admire. Like saying she won't eat meat because she doesn't like to think of all those animals being killed. And I know myself, if I had to kill all the cows I eat, I wouldn't eat meat anymore. As much as I love pastrami I couldn't do it.

Not only do adolescents have new interests to share but their way of sharing is likely to present a refreshing contrast to our adult conversations. They can be shrewd and unmerciful analysts of character as they look beneath the surface that's presented by teachers and friends and parents. They compare notes about different teachers, about how different parents treat their children, about each other's behavior.

There are those times, though, when we'd just as soon they didn't talk with us so much. Who's going with whom, why so and so won't talk to his or her best friend anymore, and what everyone's wearing to the party Friday night can be interesting topics, but not as a steady diet:

> I often pick Diana up from school when I'm on my way home from work. She'll get in the car and start talking to me about all the things that happened at school that day— and some days I just don't have the energy to listen. I'm too exhausted and preoccupied with my own day's events to have patience for hers.

Unfortunately, a lot of the ways our adolescents express themselves can be exasperating. They challenge our rules. They test our limits and question our authority. They're likely to be highly critical of what we do and say, putting down our suggestions, pointing out our hypocrisies and condemning our opinions as self-righteous or unsophisticated. Seen in the perspective of what adolescence stands for—the time children separate themselves from their parents—that's actually appropriate behavior. But for parents, having to face that constant antagonism on a daily basis can be annoying and exhausting, even if we do understand why it's happening:

> Jenny was a perfect angel until the eighth grade then BOOM. All of a sudden nothing was good enough for her. Everything became a struggle between us.

> Our fifteen-year-old argues about everything. Like I wanted him to stay home tonight because he was out all day and he said, "How come I have to stay home if you two are going out?" How do you handle that? I say, "You have to stay home because I say you have to stay home." I feel like he forces me to be unreasonable.

They criticize us in ways that can feel devastating. They seem to know intuitively what can hurt or upset us:

> I remember telling my father I wished he were dead when I was thirteen or fourteen. Then I forgot about it. But it was so painful for him he brings it up to this day, twenty-five years later.

> I was having an argument with my husband last night and both my sons told me they wouldn't want to be married to me.

> My fourteen-year-old and I had a long talk the other day. She basically told me that she doesn't like who I am. She thinks I am superficial and weak, and that I let other people, particularly her stepfather, tell me what to do. I can't tell you how much it hurt to hear that. I know part of why she was saying that was just for the effect, but there was just enough truth in it to hurt me deeply.

Rules that our children used to take for granted, or would at least honor on threat of punishment, are now seen as challenges to their personhood. "You can't control me." "I have rights too." "Don't you trust me?" "You treat me like a baby." "Why don't you let me take responsibility for my own homework, room, curfew, friends, appearance, bed time?" To us it may seem that their need to assert themselves is getting in the way of any positive communication.

Frequently many of our teenagers go beyond what we consider tolerable defiance. They push us past our limits and huge scenes erupt. In these instances their behavior isn't simply annoying, it's enraging:

> One Sunday night about ten o'clock Ben, who's fourteen, got a call from a friend asking him to come over to a party down the block. I said, "No, Ben it's too late and you still have some homework to do." Well, he went back into his room and shortly afterward I went in to say good night to him and he wasn't there. He'd gone out the window. My wife and I threw our clothes on and went down to that party and told him in as dignified a way as we could that if he didn't leave and come home that minute we would drag him home. He left.

> We were on vacation and everybody was a little on edge anyway, Lisa started in on something and my husband said, "No we can't do that. I'm too tired." And Lisa stood up and told her dad to "fuck off." And I thought he was going to have a heart attack. He grabbed her and said, "One more word from you and I put you on a plane home."

A certain number of major blow-ups are, unfortunately, normal. It's hard to find a parent who hasn't lived through several. We talk more about this later (p. 30), but the point to be made here is that we can be understanding and reasonable—and still these scenes will occur. As a mother told us:

> It's part of adolescence to rebel. You have to rebel to break away. In fact, I always say, that's a good reason to have rules because if everything is okay with you, then your kids are going to do something wildly outrageous to make a dent.

Parents and teenagers are often under such pressure that we fall back on our ability to "beat up on" our kids verbally. All of us are guilty of this at one time or another, especially when our teenager is acting out or being unresponsive.

> I can remember one time when I'd had it with Angie. All week she'd been surly and talking back to me. That day I asked her to do something for me and she made some smartass comment back and I blew up. I started yelling at her, screaming at the top of my lungs, and I called her a bitch. I told her she was an ungrateful little spoiled brat . . . and a few other choice names too. I can't remember all of what I said, but it wasn't too terrific.

Knock-down, drag-out fights are common within families, and when they're over, most of us feel bad for what we said and how we behaved. The problem comes if we find ourselves abusing our teenager often, as some parents do during these years. After a while our attacks stop being effective because our children seem to become impervious to our insults.

If we do insult our teenagers in anger, we must at some point come back to them and acknowledge that we're aware of what we did. It's very important to apologize, not necessarily for our anger, which may have been justified, but for our way of expressing it.

Adolescents are just getting to know themselves. They're vulnerable because their idea of who they are and who they want to be is so easily shaken. Because of this, teenagers are usually extremely sensitive to orders or criticism, becoming offended, outraged, or deeply wounded by any comment or look from us that feels degrading or condescending to them.

During adolescence much of how our children think of themselves is tied up with their appearance, and that almost always becomes a big communication issue. The battles between parents and teenagers over hairstyles and dress are so universal as to have become a stereotype. But that doesn't neutralize their power. Most of us *do* care about what our teenagers look like, and if they're dressed so outrageously that we're ashamed to take them to a restaurant or to a relative's house, then it really can interfere with our lives:

> We were all going to dinner at my mother-in-law's last weekend and Debby was going out with some friends after dinner, which was okay with me. Except when it was time to leave she came down in this outfit I couldn't believe. She looked like a streetwalker and I told her so. A long V-neck sweater barely to her knees, no slacks, no bra, and a striped rag around her waist. I said, ''You are not going to grandma's looking like that.'' And we argued for fifteen minutes. She was screaming at me about how I didn't know what was in style and how I want her to dress like a nerd, etc. etc. Finally we compromised and she put on some jeans under the sweater.

> I don't think Richard has had a haircut in six months and I told him no more privileges until he gets it cut. He said, ''It's my hair and I have a right to wear it any way I want to.'' And I said, ''Like hell you do!''

Sometimes it seems as if our teenagers dress a certain way precisely to get a reaction from us. It can feel as if they deliberately design their outfits to push all our buttons:

> I just couldn't stand the hassling about clothes and hair anymore, so when Robin turned thirteen we told her that from then on she was in charge of her appearance. No more interference from us. It was working pretty well for the first few months and then one day she marched in with a homemade punk haircut the likes of which you've never seen—pink and yellow and completely butchered. And she had this look in her eye that said, ''I did this for you, Mom.'' I was so mad at her I said, ''Listen, if you think I'm going to do something to punish you, you're wrong. You're old enough to know how you want to look and if you want to look ridiculous that's fine with me.''

We can joke about teenage fashions or become frustrated

LENI WILDFLOWER

or angry over our kid's seeming inability to dress in a reasonable manner, but the meaning of clothing and appearance are symbolically very important to teenagers. The more we can accept their choices the less likely it is that our entire family communication system will break down over a haircut or a sexy blouse.

When our kids were young we bought their clothing for them; we dressed them in it. Even as they got older many of us helped them select which clothes to wear and told them what was appropriate dress for certain occasions—school clothes, party clothes, play clothes, holiday clothes. It was our job to remind them to wear sweaters or rain boots or to button up their jackets. In terms of their general appearance, it was we who took them for haircuts, made sure their nails were clean, asked them to wash their hands or take baths or shampoo their hair. In those ways we took responsibility for how our kids looked to the outside world, and we could also take part of the credit when they looked good.

As our children become adolescents, however, *they* become more concerned about how they look. They start showering and grooming themselves, not because we tell them to but because they want to look nice. They wash their hair because they care how it falls or shines or curls; or they let it grow long and shaggy or cut it severely short because that's the way they want it to look. Their clothes, too, are symbols of being in style or part of a certain group or of being a maverick. And though we ourselves may be partial to the preppie look, if our adolescents want to look punk, there's no way we're going to get them to put on a crew-neck sweater and a button-down shirt.

The conflicts we have with our adolescents over their appearance are prototypes of many parent-teen miscommunications. We want them to look "nice" by our standards; they want to look "nice" by their standards. When the standards are different, problems arise. It's almost as if we went into a foreign country where everyone was tattooed all over their bodies. Even if we hated tattoos, in that culture we wouldn't feel comfortable saying how ugly they were. In fact, within that culture they might not even seem ugly to us, since that was the style:

> The other day I told Paul his underpants were showing through his shorts and he screamed at me about how I didn't know anything! Apparently that's the style these days, to have your underwear showing. I only wanted to tell him so he wouldn't be embarrassed by someone else noticing it.

With teenagers, it's probably best to concede that how they dress is their business. This is an area where we can do the accommodating, and in the process, spare the family a tremendous amount of strife.

Needless to say, appearance isn't the only problem area. Chores, money, school work, manners, participation in family events, respect for us, responsibilities toward other family members—all of these can be sources of contention. These issues have one thing in common: they all reflect our teenager's changing sense of his or her role in relation to us. Our nurturing and our desire to correct and shape our child is being challenged here, though with many contradictions and regressions. Even the way we talk to our adolescents has to be changed. We have to learn to talk to them not as children, but as the young adults who live with us.

More difficult subjects like sex, drugs, risk-taking, drinking, unacceptable friendships, need to be discussed. We have a responsibility to try to keep communication open around those issues. That means we can't afford to let our kids back us into a corner. Neither do we want to lay down arbitrary rules, which are broken when our backs are turned. Potentially dangerous issues can't be allowed to be lost in continual bickering or in out-and-out battle.

Obviously, here and elsewhere, it's urgent that we keep talking despite the fighting that is sometimes involved.

OPENING COMMUNICATION—
HOW TO DO IT

In this section we'll discuss some specific suggestions for how to open or keep open communication between parents and adolescents. We do so with the obvious reservation that there is no formula for success. Goals and techniques help, when they do help, pretty much to the degree that they are compatible with who we are and what our family history of communication has been up until now.

Interaction doesn't take place in a vacuum. Our years of living together have created well-established patterns of communication: how we handle crises; how we approach problems; whether or not we deal openly with issues before they come to the surface; how much we are able to say to each other. Patterns already exist, but they are not written in stone. They can change if we make an effort to change them, and they will change during adolescence no matter what.

RUTH BELL

GOALS—BETTER COMMUNICATION
WITH TEENAGERS

The primary goal is to take the changes that inevitably occur in our communication with our teenagers and make them positive. In order to do that we have to recognize our own part in the process. It's pretty easy to blame our kids for the breakdown in interaction; their increased demands and defiant attitude do disrupt family life. There's no way to force people to change their behavior. The only thing we can do is change *our* part of the interaction to set the stage for more open communication.

LISTENING WITHOUT JUDGMENT

The first goal is to try to hear more clearly what our children are saying to us. As they get older, many children become acutely sensitive to when they are really being listened to versus when they are merely being tolerated. They're very aware of the difference between being understood and simply being talked "at." Consequently, if we want to communicate better with our adolescents, the first step is a commitment to open listening.

What does that mean? It means trying to hear our children without making judgments or having preconceived ideas about what they are saying. It means trying not to defend against their statements or to figure out ways to convince them that they're wrong. We can't turn off our minds; what we can do is make the effort not to let our judgments, conclusions, ideas, or need to talk interfere with our ability to hear what our children are telling us.

That is particularly difficult to do when our adolescents tell us about their pain or unhappiness. Here's what a sixteen-year-old said:

My parents really are wonderful and I have a very close relationship with them but I think they can't handle it when I'm not happy. Like this summer I went away to camp and it wasn't fun for me. I had a hard time making friends and, the one big event I was looking forward to—an intercounty swim meet—was cancelled. So when I came back I was pretty low and I tried to talk to them about it. But they didn't want to hear, so I just pretended I was okay.

A mother said:

My daughter is going through a lot of pain just now because her first serious relationship just ended. She's away at school and she's been calling me a lot. If it's been a good day for me, I can usually just hear her out, but it all depends. When I'm impatient or preoccupied I end up directing the action, telling her how to make things better, telling her what she ought to do. I can always tell afterward when I've blown it because she clams up and gets off right away.

Listening without judgment means we allow what our kids are saying to get through and make a dent on our consciousness, whether we like it or agree with it or not. And even if our judgments are sympathetic, it's important to hear our children out, to resist the urge to jump in with helpful advice or reassurance:

It's so painful for me when Luke's upset. The other day he was near tears because he'd had a fight with his girlfriend, and when he finally started telling me about it I kept wanting to tell him how he could have made everything okay. I was offering advice and trying to get him to see the bright side when all he wanted was to tell me about how he was hurting.

But what about when they tell us things that scare us? If they're doing something that we think is dangerous or may lead them into a bad situation, we may have a hard time listening patiently. The impulse is to tell them immediately what we don't like about what they're saying and why, but too often when we say no without hearing their side of the story they get resentful and react automatically with "My parents won't let me do anything."

Sometimes our kids tell us things because they want us to react. They want us to know they feel they are in a dangerous situation even if they don't say that directly. Here again we're being asked to listen to the meaning behind their words. We can let them know we think the problem is serious and let them know we want to help them do something about it, but we need to do that without overreacting, making them feel that they're stupid or wrong or naïve for having gotten into that situation in the first place:

Jess and I were in the car and out of the blue he says, "Johnny's been arrested." He was our neighbor up the street and Jess was a good friend of his brother, Ronny. It turned out that Johnny had raped a girl and was part of this gang that was terrorizing a group of girls. There may have even been weapons involved, Jess wasn't sure. Well I freaked out and Jess said, "See, I knew I shouldn't have told you." But I calmed down and told him he was absolutely right to have told me. I told him how frightened it made me to think he'd been around a group of kids like that with weapons. After we talked some more I said, "Listen. I think from now on you and Ronny should hang out at our house not his house, I don't want you going up there anymore until this thing gets cleared up." I was prepared for a fight, but Jess didn't say anything except, "Okay." I think he was relieved that I'd laid down the law because I think he's been pretty worried about the whole thing himself and couldn't see any way out of it without looking like a sissy.

READING INDIRECT MESSAGES

Another aspect of good listening involves decoding our teenagers messages. Many adolescents approach their parents cautiously about the important things in their lives. They may act supercasual about something that's really bothering them. They may spend a lot of time in their room, staying out of our way, so as not to be asked what's wrong. Or they may send up trial balloons (consciously or not) to see whether we are receptive to listening to them about a particular issue and to test our reactions. These trial balloons may come in the form of jokes, or anecdotes about friends, or through nonverbal "statements" delivered within sight or sound of us:

Matthew sounds us out periodically. Like "What do you think of such and such." And if we hit the ceiling, he doesn't bring that up again for a while.

We can err in the other direction, though, assuming that if our kids want to talk they will come to us. Sometimes that just isn't the way it works as this situation illustrates:

A mother:

I think kids make it clear when they want to talk and when they don't. And I think you just have to go with that. I can't see prying into their lives just because I think it's healthy for them to talk. I don't think it necessarily is.

A few weeks later we talked to this woman's sixteen-year-old daughter, who said:

You know I really wish I felt I could talk to my parents. They always make me feel like they don't want to hear about what's bothering me. I wish my mom would just say, "You know I see that you look upset. Want to talk about it?" or something like that. Mostly I just keep my feelings to myself.

That's not to suggest that parents should begin to psychoanalyze everything their teenagers do, reading deep meaning into every move or mood. Sometimes an anecdote is just an anecdote; a mood just a passing mood; a joke simply a joke. If our kids look upset, it doesn't hurt to give them the option to talk. If they open a subject, even indirectly, it doesn't hurt to give them the opportunity to pursue it more thoroughly. If they don't want to, that's okay, too.

EXAMINING OUR CATEGORIES

It's almost impossible to live with someone for years and not categorize them. We develop insights into our childrens' character and come to expect certain patterns from them:

My youngest has always been a challenge. From the day she was born she was more demanding than the others.

One of my boys is a real problem. He's cantankerous and needs to prove himself all the time; while the other one seems so self-sufficient and composed. It's been that way from as far back as I can remember.

My middle child has always been lazy. She would rather go out of her way to avoid doing a job than spend time doing it and getting it out of the way.

Being handicapped has really made Billy more determined than a lot of kids. He has such stick-to-itiveness. Give him any job to do and he'll find some way of doing it.

Since children are different, one from the other, forming these expectations about them is quite natural. They're based on our observations and they can be useful. We know who will need a little extra help or attention and when.

The problem is that our expectations can be self-fulfilling. When we expect our child to be angry or rebellious or lazy or disrespectful, we prepare ourselves subconsciously for battle, and even small incidents can turn into main events. And by preparing for certain behavior in advance, we have a much harder time seeing what may really be there.

One would think this would be more of a problem with negative categories and it usually is. But "good" kids can

feel boxed-in, too, feeling the pressure always to be happy or do the right thing:

In my family it was always my brother who was seen as the problem child and troublemaker. I could do no wrong as far as my parents were concerned. But even though I was a classically good kid, I know I would have felt better about myself if my parents had acknowledged that I was an emotional mess or a rotten brat sometimes.

My mother is so damned understanding. She thinks I'm so terrific. Sometimes I just want to scream at her, "Stop thinking I'm so great. I'm not."

LENI WILDFLOWER

OPENING UP OUR EXPECTATIONS

One of the most significant obstacles to open communication is our expectation that our child will turn out a certain way. When they're little, most of us fantasize about who our baby will become as an adult. But when they reach adolescence, our kids begin to develop some expectations for themselves. Communication becomes complicated when our expectations clash. If we're dreaming about our child becoming a doctor and instead he or she is interested in race cars or poetry, we won't be able to talk to her until we open up to *her* idea of who she is. It won't get us anywhere to keep giving him books about open heart surgery when he'd really like a ticket to the Indianapolis 500.

The adolescent cry of "My parents don't understand me" often is a direct reaction to our misperceived expectations of who our children are. When we're able to loosen our grip on these expectations, we give our children the opportunity to blossom in their own way, and the communication between us can get a lot better:

> My son gave me this Father's Day card with these aging hippie parents on the cover and a son dressed with a mohawk haircut and the parents are looking at each other as if to say, "Where did this kid drop from" and inside Don wrote, "Don't worry Dad, I think it's all going to work out for us." I was so moved I started to cry.

> All my ideas about who Jenny should be are being radically changed. She doesn't like school. She'll be lucky if she passes all her subjects, so there's really no point in even considering college at this point. It's been tremendously disappointing for me and her mother, but the other day she came to me and said, "Listen. I want my life to work out. I want to make something of myself and I will. You watch." Well, I said, "I believe in you." And she said, "I'm glad, but I never would have known it." The big breakthrough for me is that I really do believe in her now.

BEING HONEST ABOUT OUR FEELINGS

We don't want to imply that our goal should be to become saintly, nonjudgmental figures who watch understandingly on the sidelines of our children's lives. There are things we have to say to our teenagers and things they have to hear. Most of the parents we interviewed want to set standards for their adolescents about drug use, drinking, sexual activities, appropriate behavior. It's really important for us to discuss those issues with our children, since they are coming face to face with them and having to deal with them every day.

We have opinions and values we want to communicate with our children. It is certainly appropriate, for example, for a mother who has deep feelings about sexism to express those feelings to her children, forcefully if necessary:

> My son came home talking about this girl he likes and he was telling his dad about her—the usual, about how great-looking she was. Then he said, "She's got a great body. Fantastic ass." I was listening and I got very upset. I couldn't stop myself. I said, "It makes me so uncomfortable to hear you talk about a girl's body that way." He got real angry, but when he calmed down I explained to him how it bothers me to feel like women are still judged as if they were a body and nothing more.

Since the goal is to make our communication more loving and more effective, we may have to revise our approach, especially about things that really mean a lot to us. Many of us speak in terms of shoulds and oughts and rights and wrongs. We talk to our teenagers about acceptable and unacceptable behavior. During adolescence this may not be enough.

When we can tell them about the experiences that shaped our values, the personal decisions we had to make to accept certain beliefs, the reasons behind our feelings—the chances are much greater that not only will our children hear us, they may understand and respect our values too. This applies even to the most mundane of our interactions with our teenagers. When they come in two hours late, it's pretty natural to want to shout and punish them, but it's also important to tell them how scared we were for them. We don't want their lives to be ruled by our fears, but it makes a much deeper impression when we allow our teenagers to see how much we care about them and want to protect them in the best way we know how:

> I picked up my son from a punk rock concert and I went inside to look for him. It was like Dante's Inferno in there. I'll tell you the truth, I was scared. The air was full of violence and it seemed like everything was on the brink of chaos. So the next morning I said to Danny, "You're never going to another one of those unless you're carrying a submachine gun." He knew I was kidding, but we did have a real conversation about how scared I'd felt and how worried I was about it being a dangerous environment.

There is another side: adolescents need to hear the reasons behind our statements, but they also deserve to have their opinions heard. They may not agree with what we have to say. They may have reasons of their own for feeling different from the way we do on a particular issue. In order to have good communication with them, we have to be willing to listen to their position:

> The other day my daughter was telling me about the new boy she's interested in. I have my own ideas about why I think she's interested in him. It would be so easy to get into a fight about that but she's already so much of an adult she really has a right to choose her own friends. If I were to tell her what I don't like about him she'd say, "It's none of your business." And she's right.

GETTING HELP FOR OURSELVES

Particularly in times of crisis, translating these suggestions into action may be very difficult. Being a parent can be a lonely experience. It's hard to know whether what we're doing is helpful or harmful, too strict or too lenient.

The idea is to find someone or a group of people with whom we can discuss our questions and concerns about parenting teenagers. These people need not be "experts." It isn't necessary to get formal counseling or even advice, although that can be helpful at times. Often all we need is a sympathetic ear, someone who can listen to us without judgment, and who is sensitive enough to give us compassionate feedback about what we are saying. It can be very comforting to talk to other parents experiencing similar problems, but if that isn't possible, your confidante can be spouse, friend, relative, another child, or even a child's friend. It's obviously helpful if the person knows you or your family, but even that's not essential.

A single father said:

Once or twice I've thought to myself, ''Well if I feel so strongly about this, why don't I call up so-and-so's parent to find out what they think.'' It really is a benefit to talk to another parent, since your child is always telling you that everybody else's parents are letting them do it . . . whatever IT is.

Julie, my fourteen-year-old, was running away and being completely disrespectful when she was home. I was baffled. I felt like I was losing her. And I felt alone since my ex-husband doesn't want to hear about it. Finally I called my co-worker, who is very sympathetic, and he was wonderful to talk to. He gave me some very helpful advice. And I was so relieved to be able to talk to somebody who was willing to hear my side of it.

There are some specific techniques that help us communicate and show our children that we really want to meet them halfway.

Giving Praise

Many of us routinely acknowledge our children's accomplishments, but some of us find this kind of praise hard to offer. Maybe we simply assume that our kids know when we are pleased or proud or impressed with them. Even if that's true, it's important to tell our children openly and without reservation our positive feelings about them.

Spending Special Time Together

Parents frequently and guiltily commit to ''doing something'' with their kids as an appeasement for some real or perceived neglect. For a variety of reasons this ''appeasement time'' almost never has particularly beneficial effects. We want to distinguish it here from what we call ''special time.'' ''Special time,'' as we hear parents talking about it, is something that both parent and child can commit to with enthusiasm and optimism. It represents an important kind of communication in itself:

On two or three occasions, starting when I was about fourteen, my father took me with him on overnight business trips. I loved it—riding in the car with him, seeing places I'd never been before, eating at the restaurants and staying at the motels he went to on his travels. I don't recall him giving me any instructions about how I was to behave when he was actually doing business. I knew the fact that he'd asked me to come with him showed his confi-

dence in my maturity, and there was no way I was going to let him down. When he introduced me to his regular business associates or the motel and restaurant people he knew, they already knew about me and the rest of the family. I began to appreciate more how much my father carried his family with him everywhere he went. I don't think my father and I ever felt closer to each other than we did on those trips.

Nonverbal Communication

Certainly there are times when there is no substitute for ''putting it into words.'' However, as the experience of many parents indicates, it may be that too much emphasis is placed on verbalizing, that most of us talk too much and say too little, and that much that is most profound in our lives gets communicated without words. Sometimes nonverbal communication eliminates the need for talking it out. Other times it makes it easier to talk later or say what needs to be said simply and without elaboration:

My daughter and I went camping together at the beach. At one point we were walking along in silence and she looked at me and smiled. I smiled back. I felt wonderful.

Touching

As we have seen, most or all physical contact between parents and children can cease during adolescence. The children usually pick up first the attitude that ''big kids are acting like little kids if they ask for hugs and holding,'' and later the taboos associated with their sexuality. The result is that at the very moment when our children are likely to feel the greatest uncertainty about their physicality and their connection to us, they lose the deep, nurturing reassurance of our holding and touching. Our loss can be just as profound. It's important to try to retain or regain that connection.

A father said:

My five-foot-eight-inch, hundred-and-fifty-pound son will grab me and hold me by the hand as we're walking down the street. It's like Gargantua holding hands with King Kong. I love it!

My daughter and I touch a lot, we hug each other a lot, because I think that's so important. When I was a teenager I remember two significant experiences that were difficult for me. Once when I broke up with my first boyfriend and the other when I accidentally burned a large hole in my mother's favorite cashmere sweater. Both times I felt terrible and both times my mother hugged me and told me how much she loved me and ultimately that was so much more important than any sweater—or even a boyfriend at age thirteen.

Family Meetings

Family meetings are a way to reorganize family life and deal with the issues raised by the changes everyone is going through. They create a mechanism through which everyone can participate on an equal footing. And although the formality of a meeting (in some families including motions, minutes, rules of order, etc.) may seem intimidating at first, it has the virtue of setting this communication apart and designating this as a time when serious and difficult topics can be discussed. At a very practical level, a formal, regular meeting means that there is at least one time in the week when everyone in the family gets together to attend to the business of a family:

> Once a week my daughters and I meet together to talk about things that need to be done in the house. It works well. It's a way for my daughters to get out what is bugging them about each other. We'll also say things like, "We need more toilet paper." It keeps the house functioning.

Using Books and Other Written Material

Books also can facilitate communication. Particularly where subjects are difficult for us or our children to broach comfortably or where we feel uninformed, books, pamphlets, newspaper and magazine articles can be just what we need to initiate discussion.

We have included suggested readings at the end of each chapter. However, once you start looking for it, an abundance of material on all sorts of subjects can be found in everyday sources—including some we might not normally consider:

> My twelve-year-old daughter found a copy of *Penthouse* magazine. She showed it to me and I wasn't exactly delighted, but I realized when I thought about it that this was probably as good a chance as I'd get to monitor her introduction to this kind of pornography before she started reading it on the sly. I also remembered how interested in this kind of stuff I'd been as a boy of about her age. We looked at some of the pictures and cartoons together and talked about the sexploitation involved in the stories. Basically, she seemed to find the whole thing to be sort of weird/funny/interesting. The net result of the whole episode was that I felt my communication with her about sex was opened up.

Using Movies, Plays, Lectures, and Other Community Resources

Going to a movie or play with your teenager can be fun and also can provide a time and a context for talking about an issue we are concerned about. Finding the most useful resources may be no more complicated than being aware of what you're looking for and then tuning in to what's around—reading the entertainment and calendar sections of the paper, checking bulletin boards, or making a few calls to get on the mailing lists for such things as community or college lecture series, church and youth organizations, parenting networks, etc. A willingness to take what comes our way and use it—helps too.

Look for a movie that deals with your teenager's problem. Go together—or separately—and then bring the film up and use it as a springboard:

> A good friend of the family is gay and I could see how upset our son was when he found out. There was a rerun of *Sunday, Bloody Sunday* playing and we all went together. Afterward Jim brought it up himself and I think that cleared the air.

Watching TV Together

Often children and parents watch different TV programs at different times of the day. Changing this pattern, finding programs to watch together with our teenagers or dropping in on their TV scene to watch their programs and find out how they feel about what they watch can open up a lot of discussion about the things that are bothering us. We think this technique is particularly important since TV *itself* turns out to be an issue of some contention in almost every household.

Role Playing

We have discussed repeatedly the dangers of getting stuck in the rut of old roles with our children, and we have also noted how difficult it is not to. Role playing, in which parents and children "play each others' parts," can be a particularly effective technique for pushing us out of those ruts. Some of us have observed or participated in role-playing exercises in therapy groups, school courses or training programs. Others who want to try this technique need only find the right moment, usually in the midst of one of those "going-no-place arguments," and say, "For the next five minutes, let's trade places. You be me and I'll be you." There are several good books that will help you do these exercises in your family (see Resources, p. 31).

Talking with Other Teenagers Around

Many parents find that sometimes it is easier for them to talk to their teenagers' friends than to talk to their own children. It's not hard to understand: we're not so "uptight" about what other children do. We're not stuck with the family's specific history and problems as we are with our own kids'.

Some parents deliberately raise sensitive or difficult subjects when their children's teenage friends are visiting. By initiating the discussion with another child, we give our own a chance to stand back for a while; sometimes we can depersonalize and desensitize the issue—take the sting out. We are also likely to learn how other parents deal with the problems we are confronting and how their children react.

Another advantage of this approach is that it tips the balance of power in the direction of our children. Usually adolescents have to deal with the collective authority of their parents—one against two. And even when we are one on one with our children, they still confront the historic and symbolic odds of adult power over them: "I'm your father and you'll do what I say." When our children have the support of their friends in one of these discussions the power is more evenly balanced. We, in turn, are more likely to tolerate and appreciate adolescent qualities that we might otherwise reject when we see that "it's not just our kids."

Talking with Other Adults Around

Talking to our children in the presence of other adults whom our children like can have many of the same effects. A favorite aunt or uncle, a mutual friend who likes and appreciates your child, or a friend whose age is midway between yours and your child's can ease, facilitate, and arbitrate discussions. In particular, the young adult who is still close to his or her own adolescence but is looking at it with greater experience and detachment is likely to be a sympathetic and creative participant in your discussions.

Communicating About Limits: When and How to Intervene

With all we've said so far about communication there remains the most difficult question of all: how do we set convincing and effective limits for our teenagers? Where do we "draw the line" and how do we assure that our teenagers won't step over it?

It's a tricky issue. Our children are becoming more competent and independent. They spend much of their time out of our sight and therefore away from our supervision. They need our recognition of their developing maturity, and they need our trust in their ability to make sound judgments for themselves. At the same time, they are still children. It's difficult not to feel that they still require our protection, guidance, and discipline. To set effective limits we must remember both sides of this balance.

Establishing Rules That Work

The best chance we have of establishing effective rules is through discussion with our adolescents of what's going on in their lives, how able they feel to take responsibility for themselves, and what we as parents need to require for our own peace of mind. It's a difficult talk, but unless it's a collaborative effort it's probably not going to work. There have to be trade-offs. Our authority is limited. With a little cleverness our kids can break or get around nearly every rule we set. When we acknowledge that openly—to ourselves and to our children—we lay an important piece of groundwork for both good communication and effective limit-setting:

I was a very wild teenager. I know what you can hide from your parents. I would be out drinking at sixteen and seventeen and coming home ripped out of my mind. And my folks would be in bed and shout out, "You home?" And I'd say, "Yeah. Good night." Then I'd go throw up or pass out on my bed. I don't know how much they really knew, but as long as I was in by my curfew they were happy. That's why with my own kids I'm different. I expect them to let me know where they are and what they're doing, but I'm also smart enough to know you have to trust them.

Some rules are "bottom line." We make them because otherwise life would be unbearable. Knowing where our teenagers are when they're not at home, not allowing them to talk back to us, not allowing them physically to abuse another family member, making sure we know who they're out with and when they'll be home; these are examples of reasonable rules.

Other issues, while important, are of a different order. Allowances, curfews, household responsibilities, homework fall into this category. To keep ourselves sane and to avoid constant bickering we have to pick what we want to be firm about and what we're willing to let go of. This will be different from family to family:

LOUIS ALEXANDER

We cut out Tommy's allowance because we wanted him to learn that if he needs money he has to work for it. So I don't know how he does it, but he finds a way to get along for six months on two dollars. I watch my purse now because we have to believe he's been doing some pilfering and that's the issue with us. My husband told him, ''I don't ever want to catch you taking money. If you need any money I'll always give you an opportunity to earn it. But stealing is stealing, even from your parents.''

I've just had to give up on homework. My wife and I were spending all our time fighting and struggling with Sue to do her homework and she would always leave everything till the last minute. Finally we just said, ''Fine, it's your life. Your homework's your responsibility.''

My son's grandmother gave him a twenty-dollar bill for his birthday last week, and in three hours he spent the whole damn thing playing those video games down on the corner. I'm worried about his school work and it just doesn't seem normal to sit all the time in front of a machine. Anyhow, we told him we couldn't afford all that money going into computer games.

An important part of establishing sensible rules is our willingness to be serious about enforcing them:

We don't ground our children very often. I remember one time, though, when Sara came in very late, way after her curfew, without calling to tell us where she was, that's when we were very hard on her. We were frantic and we told her no weekend privileges for a month.

When Carolyn turned thirteen she became really unmanageable. She was talking back all the time and running away to friends houses when I wouldn't let her have her way. For a long time I was letting her have her way about everything because I think I felt guilty about divorcing her dad. Finally it came to a head and I had to do something. I locked her out of the house one time when she ran away and told her she would not be allowed back unless we got some rules straight. One was that she was absolutely not to speak disrespectfully to me. I said, ''I've let this get way too far and it's my responsibility to put things back in order.'' It's amazing, but it's been six months now and things are a lot better.

Certain rules are needed to guide our teenagers' activities when they are not with us. These are tough to enforce because they are based on the trust that our kids will follow them. Rules about drugs, sex, drinking, driving, and truancy apply here. We can't stop our kids from having sex. We can't stop them from taking drugs. The only way these rules have a chance is if our teenagers understand our reasons for setting them and agree that those rules are sound:

I think it's possible to get some rules and have them followed. But you can't have many. In our house we have two: Whatever our kids do when they're away from home,

they have to do with a buddy. Whatever it is, wherever they go, they have to go with someone else. And the other is never drive when you've been drinking or if you've had drugs. Now, we don't think our kids do drink or take drugs, but it's more important to us that if they ever were to be in that situation—they know never to drive. They can call us any time and we'll come for them. That's a hard and fast rule.

One essential element in reaching our teenagers is our willingness to respect them as ''older.'' It doesn't work to talk down to them or treat them as if they can't make a move without us. Even saying things like, ''Button your jacket'' or ''You look terrible, go get a haircut,'' undermines our communication. They are old enough now to take a lot of responsibility for their lives—for their appearance, for their grades, for their interests. We can encourage them but we can't set arbitrary rules that don't give them credit for being able to make some decisions themselves.

Another element in setting effective rules is to learn about our teenager's world. It helps to talk with our kids directly about what is really going on in their particular environment. How prevalent are drugs? Do their friends drink? Is there heavy sex? Which of their friends do they trust to be responsible?

Many of us make the crippling assumption that our teenagers aren't willing to share their world with us. It's pretty easy to feel that way, since during adolescence almost all young people become very private. Bathroom and bedroom doors get closed and locked now; conversations with friends or siblings may stop when we approach; telephone calls are made away from our earshot. And some kids make it a point to be as evasive and uncommunicative as possible. It's difficult not to get paranoid about this and not to assume that something terrible is going on.

Usually that's not the case. Our children's desire for privacy is a signal that their life is separate from ours, not necessarily that there's anything dangerous or unsavory going on. When we can respect their privacy and not insist on knowing all the details of their daily existence, we show them that we recognize their growing independence. In turn, they may be more willing to share important information with us when we do ask, especially if we're careful not to overreact:

I've had to learn to hold my tongue. Aaron will tell me something or start on some subject and if I even so much as look too interested, he'll back off.

My kids seem to tell me if there's been liquor or marijuana at one of their parties, but if I get too excited about it, they clam up. I've tried to watch my reactions because I think it's better to keep the dialogue open around those issues. I let them know when I think something's dangerous, but aside from that I just listen.

LENI WILDFLOWER

When All Communication Breaks Down

In all families with teenagers there are those times when communication falls apart for a while, when the only words between us are unfriendly. These periods can last for hours or weeks or even months depending on what our kids are going through and what's happening in our lives. For a variety of reasons, at these times our children choose not to share much with us and that can be very hurtful. As one mother said, "I feel so discouraged. My son and I used to be so close and now he'll barely say two words to me." Other parents report the same thing:

I think what's the worst for me is when my sixteen-year-old daughter won't talk to me. I thought my kids would talk about everything with us because we're so different from our parents—whom we didn't talk to of course—but my daughter puts me in that same position I used to put my mother in.

In these situations the best we can do is hang in there and try not to let their withdrawal upset us too much. We can make attempts at conversation; we can offer positive com-

ments about how they look or what they're doing. More than that we can let them know quite frankly that we miss talking to them. Some parents make it a point during times like these to invite their son or daughter to a special dinner or out to a movie as a way to reopen dialogue. But it helps to remember, if nothing else works, that time probably will. These episodes usually don't last too long.

When they do go on and on and when, in spite of all our efforts, we can't get through to our teenagers, some form of intervention may be called for. Children with very deep emotional, behavioral, or substance-abuse problems may not be able or willing to hear anything that their parents have to say. Sometimes communication between parents and teenagers becomes so strained as to require drastic measures. (These issues are discussed more specifically in the "Emotional Health" [p. 53) and the "Substance Abuse" [p. 103] chapters.)

In general, parents who find themselves with a teenager who steals or continually gets into trouble with the law; with a child who is a habitual runaway or one who refuses to attend school; with kids who are severely depressed or withdrawn; or with teenagers who are severely disrespectful to the point of violence, cannot rely on simple suggestions for making communication better. Many parents in this situation feel they can no longer reach their child by themselves. Some form of outside assistance is necessary.

Sending a child to live somewhere else with another family or actually making a child leave the house or having a child institutionalized or arrested are among the extreme methods these parents feel they have been forced to use:

Vicki had been running away pretty regularly during the seventh grade so finally I had the locks changed and when she returned I wouldn't let her in. Well, she broke into the house and I said, "Vicki, I'm calling the police." She didn't believe me and went in to watch TV. Well, I did call the police and I convinced them she shouldn't live at home any longer and that they would have to take her. I said, "She is incorrigible. I've tried. I can't take anymore." They called her father and he agreed with me. She had done this so many times that both of us were able to agree on this, even if we didn't agree on anything else. So finally the police said, "Well, we'll have to take her to Juvenile Hall." So I said, "Then I guess that's where she's going to have to go." And they said, "You don't want your daughter to go there." And I said, "You're right. I don't. But she can't live here until she's ready to abide by some rules."

At a certain point you have to say to a kid, "Listen, this is your life. You get to destroy your own life if that's what you have to do. I can't live it for you. I can't breathe for you. I can't keep you from being stoned."

These situations are extreme, however, and most of us have mixed and anguished feelings about how we would deal with them.

In most parent-adolescent communication there seems to be an anchor parents can hold on to:

> I interpret child-rearing as a contract. I've got a responsibility to my kids and they have a responsibility to me. We try to fulfill our end of it the best we know how. You negotiate and you bargain and you make trade-offs. You have to be willing to give in on some points because when the negotiations break down, that's when you really have trouble. So you hang in and somewhere along the line the contract changes and gets revised until one day you say to each other, "Okay, the contract's been discharged. You're on your way."

LENI WILDFLOWER

We Can't Expect to Be Perfect

Jenny wanted to have a slumber party and she wanted to have boys and girls over and they'd all sleep in the living room on the floor. She's fifteen now and her friends are all in the tenth grade. Well, it seemed okay to me because they're all nice kids, but to be honest it really worried me that some other parent would call and say, "What's going on over there?" Maybe my limits weren't strict enough. I didn't want to come off looking like a bad father.

Most important is that we don't have to follow anybody else's dictates in the matter of communication. We have to do and say what feels right for us. We have to trust our own intuition. Sometimes we get too bogged down in what we think we *should* be doing and how we think we *should* be responding:

> I think our whole society is without confidence in itself. There should be an antedote to our reliance on somebody else telling us what to do. The message to parents should be: Trust yourself.

BOOKS AND RESOURCES

Recommended Reading

Bayard, Robert T., and Jean Bayard. *How to Deal with Your Acting-Up Teenager: Practical Self-Help for Desperate Parents*. San Jose, Calif.: Accord Press, 1981.
Written by two psychologists who have experience working with families in crisis. This book presents guidelines for helping parents deal with their teenagers.

Delaine, John K. *Who's Raising the Family? A Workbook for Parents and Children*. Available from Wisconsin Clearinghouse, 1954 East Washington Ave., Madison, Wis. 53704.
Although this workbook specifically focuses on teenage drug and alcohol abuse, the author presents parenting techniques and practical guidelines for improving communication and laying the groundwork for responsible decision-making.

Dodson, Fitzhugh. *How to Discipline with Love: From Crib to College*. New York: Signet Books, 1978.
Practical book for parents that focuses on every stage of development from birth to twenty-one. See also, *How to Father* and *How to Parent*.

Farel, Anita. *Early Adolescence: What Parents Need to Know*. Chapel Hill, N.C.: 1982. Available from Center for Early Adolescence, School of Public Health, University of North Carolina at Chapel Hill, Suite 223, Car Mill Mall, Carrboro, N.C., 27510.
This handbook describes the physical and emotional changes experienced by children as they enter adolescence and the typical behavior accompanying these changes. Offers advice on ways to improve communication and clues about when parents should intervene.

Ginott, Haim G. *Between Parent and Teenager*. New York: Macmillan, 1969.
Suggests specific techniques for parents on how to deal with a broad range of adolescent problems.

Gordon, Thomas. *P.E.T.: Parent Effectiveness Training*. New York: New American Library, 1975.
Popular book that presents the P.E.T. philosophy and the specific skills parents need to raise responsible children. Uses case histories and examples to illustrate approach.

Gould, Shirley. *Teenagers: The Continuing Challenge*. New York: Hawthorn Books, 1977.
Helpful book for parents on how to develop better relationships with their teenage children. Gould also addresses some of the special issues divorced parents and stepparents face.

Satir, Virginia. *Peoplemaking*. Palo Alto, Calif.: Science and Behavior Books, Inc., 1972.
Very readable book about family dynamics, communication, and self-esteem.

For Teenagers

Talk to My Parents? Available from Planned Parenthood of Monterey County, 5 Via Joaguin, Monterey, Calif. 93940.
Easy-to-read pamphlet for teenagers on why and how to start talking to parents about sensitive issues. Designed to encourage parental involvement.

Resources

Parent Effectiveness Training (P.E.T.)
Effectiveness Training, Inc.
531 Stevens Ave.
Solano Beach, Calif. 92075
(610)481-8121—Ask for Diane Lucca—nationwide referrals
President: Dr. Thomas Gordon

Systematic Training for Effective Parenting (S.T.E.P.)
American Guidance Service
Publisher's Building
Circle Pines, Minn. 55014
(Write to ask for S.T.E.P. instructors in local areas.)

National Parent Teacher Association (PTA)
Program Department
700 N. Rush St.
Chicago, Ill. 60611
(312)787-0977
(Will give local referrals for Parent Seminars on Adolescent Sexuality.)

IV

THE CHANGES
OF PUBERTY

The physical and sexual changes of adolescence are inevitable; all healthy children go through them. In spite of that, most of us still marvel at the sight of our own child's changing body. Watching our children develop into adults is a profound experience for a parent.

In the chapter "Our Own Issues" (p. 9), we spoke about the way our child's growth affects our lives and our feelings. In this chapter we will be discussing what that physical and sexual development means to our children and what we as parents can do to make this time as positive for them as possible.

Primarily we are needed as educators. It helps adolescents tremendously to understand what is about to happen to them and why. Without preparation some of the changes can be quite frightening. Normal breasts may develop unevenly in boys as well as girls. Voices crack. Wet dreams can seem to come from nowhere. Sometimes girls who aren't expecting their period see the blood and panic, worrying that they're bleeding to death. Even with preparation many of the changes can be unsettling—for example, when a child shoots up six inches in one year and suddenly towers over all the other kids at school, or when a boy has an embarrassing spontaneous erection. At times like this it's hard not to feel that your body has gone completely out of control.

Many adolescents sleep long hours during this time. Their appetite can be enormous and insatiable:

I've always had this thing about wanting to keep a well-stocked refrigerator, but now that Kevin's fifteen he and his friends can go through it and clean it out in one afternoon. A gallon of milk, boxes of cookies, drawers full of fruit, cheese, bread. It's impossible—and very expensive—to keep up with them.

Ideally, we have been talking to our children about body parts and sexual development since they were little and first asked about penises and vaginas. If that has been the case, they are already more knowledgeable than many adolescents. But even if we haven't done much talking up till now, this is the time to start. There's a lot to learn about puberty: what menstruation is all about; why boys have erections and how ejaculation takes place; what breasts are for; how conception occurs. Preteens who go into puberty understanding why their bodies are changing have a much better chance of feeling good about themselves and their bodies than kids who don't know what's going on. Knowledge is powerful, and body knowledge enhances our ability to take care of ourselves and keep ourselves healthy.

Many American children will learn some of the basic facts about puberty at school. Usually in the fifth or sixth grade they'll see a filmstrip on physical development. Girls get a discussion of menstruation; boys hear about erections and ejaculation. This is certainly better than no sex education at all; however, it comes too late for many students. Some girls start their periods in the fourth or fifth grades. Many begin to develop breasts even before that. And although boys will for the most part develop after girls, a number of boys go through puberty early, having their first ejaculation at ten or eleven.

Aside from being offered too late, school sex education usually lacks depth. Rarely are students given an opportunity to discuss their feelings about body changes. They usually aren't encouraged to talk about their fears or concerns about what happens.

We can be particularly helpful to our adolescents by making sure feelings are discussed. If our children are reticent about opening up to us, we can share some of our own memories with them, telling them stories from our experience as a preteen or teenager. Most teenagers enjoy hearing how their parents felt when their breasts or penis or body began to grow, and about the first time they got their period or had their first wet dream or ejaculation:

I told my daughter about how when I first got my period I was so embarrassed to wear a bathing suit because in those days they only had those big clunky pads and I was sure everybody could see it bulging through.

I remember if I'd be out on a date and I'd get an erection in the car or during a movie I'd be so embarrassed that the girl might notice. I told Tommy about that and he said, "Hey I hate that."

Eloise had menstrual cramps. One time I remember talking to her about how I had bad cramps when I was a teenager . . . and how it was for me. She was really interested in that. I talked a lot to her about my feelings. Sometimes she wouldn't say anything back but I think she really heard me.

This is intimate stuff. Being able to talk this openly with our children requires a history not only of open communication between us, but specifically of open communication about sex. We may not have had that in our family, or there may be some personal issues we simply don't feel comfortable discussing with our children. That's okay. There are alternatives. The critical point is only that we make sure our children get the facts they need about both sexes and that we offer them the opportunity to ask questions and share their concerns with us.

Aside from, or in addition to, talking, we can give books to children. Some books are designed to focus on feelings; they quote teenagers and offer anecdotes from other people's experiences. Other books focus on physiology. The resource section at the back of this chapter lists several good books:

Annie's reaction to puberty was very matter-of-fact. She wanted a book with the facts and so that's what we gave her. Then when she did get her period it was no revolutionary thing. She came in and said, "Hey, Mom. Guess what. I got my period."

Another approach is to speak generally about the facts of puberty, telling stories in the third person about what happened to friends or acquaintances. It's sometimes easier to talk about other people's experiences than about one's own. But we need to remember that while an event may seem funny or cute to us now, it may be scary or embarrassing to a child who doesn't quite know what to expect for him- or herself. A twelve-year-old said:

My mom told me about periods when I was nine. She told me about how her sister got it when she was at a party wearing a white dress and it was a bloody mess.

Frequently, kids will bring up the subject themselves:

My thirteen-year-old came home from school the first day after Christmas vacation and said, "Man, you should see Joseph. His voice has changed and everything. I felt like a shrimp next to him."

My daughter was nine when she told me her friend had explained to her about what a period was. She thought it had something to do with dogs bleeding in the street.

Some adolescents don't seem to want to talk about their body changes at all. They act as if they know more than we do. Even so, no matter how "cool" your child appears, find ways to bring it up—without trying to invade his or her privacy. They need the information and what have you got to lose? The worst that can happen is that they'll hear it twice.

IRV ZEIGER

Some kids do seem to close off from us completely for a while. Privacy is a big issue with adolescents and it usually becomes important at just about the same time their bodies begin to change:

The minute our kids started to mature, the curtain went down and we never saw their bodies again! Everything was locked. We would joke about it. When they were younger they used to go nude outside, you know, running through the sprinklers. But the minute they started to develop, it all changed. They got very private. My wife was curious to see if everything was coming along okay, but she never got the opportunity.

I don't think my husband even knows that his daughter has periods. I mean of course he knows, but the minute she started her period, she became so private.

Above all, our children want to be reassured. They want to hear from us that what is happening to them is normal and natural. They need to know they aren't sick or deformed or "immature" because someone else is developing more quickly or at an earlier age.

When puberty is discussed it's almost always spoken of in terms of what is normal. "This is the normal age range for menstruation." "It's normal for a boy's voice to change between the ages of . . ." "Normal" used in these ways is misleading. It sounds like a tightly prescribed quantity when, in fact, it is a broad, loose term based on averages and extremes. For example, the average age girls get their period is twelve-and-a-half to thirteen, yet it's within the norm for someone to get her period between the ages of ten and sixteen. Some girls who are also normal physically, simply not part of the norm, menstruate at eight years old, while others don't start their period until they are seventeen or eighteen.

We will use the word normal in these pages as others have, to give you some idea of what to expect and when to expect it. However, we hope you'll keep in mind how imprecise the word really is, and also how vitally important the concept of normal is to an adolescent.

Being normal is a primary adolescent concern. Am I like everyone else? Am I a freak? Is everybody going to find out how different I really am? Being the first one to develop facial hair or breasts or to get one's period can be embarrassing. Kids may make fun of you or look at you strangely. A teenager who's the last of his or her friends to develop also can feel like a freak. He or she can't help wondering if he or she will ever be like everyone else. It can be a devastating feeling and we should be aware of it:

My daughter will be fifteen this summer and she still hasn't gotten her period. She's very upset about it and even told us that if she doesn't get it by the summer, she's NOT going to go to high school in this neighborhood. I feel terrible for her, she's so upset.

Johnny is only sixteen, but so many of his friends look like young men already and he still looks like a kid. I try to tell him that his time will come, but he's miserable. He feels like a failure. Like he's been left out.

My daughter was the first of her friends to develop breasts and she was very embarrassed about them.

Some kids, on the other hand, are proud of being "first":

My daughter practically started a club when she started to menstruate. She was only ten and it was like she was queen or something. She made such a big deal about the whole thing.

Our son has been parading around since he first started to develop. He'll come out of the shower and lie around indolently for twenty minutes or so without any clothes on, waiting for us to admire him.

You'll see as we discuss the various aspects of adolescent development that there is a wide range in the timing of these events. Share that information with your kids. Try to help them understand that they are normal even if their development isn't happening when other people's is. If appropriate, you can relate their growth to your own or that of your spouse, since the changes of puberty tend to occur similarly within families.

If for some reason, after reading the information that follows, you are concerned that there may really be something wrong with the way your child is developing, it is probably wise to take him or her to be checked by a physician who treats adolescents. It's a good idea to make sure your pre-adolescent and adolescent children visit the doctor or health practitioner at least once a year anyway. Some pediatricians now specialize in adolescents. Others have many teenagers in their practice. If your teenager objects to going to a pediatrician, and many do, you might consider taking him or her to a teen clinic or to your family doctor.

BOYS NEED TO KNOW ABOUT GIRLS; GIRLS NEED TO KNOW ABOUT BOYS

One of the major problems with in-school sex education is that it usually segregates boys and girls. Boys learn about what will happen to boys and only that, while girls learn only about girls.

By explaining to our boys what happens to girls and to our girls what happens to boys, we can undo many of the sexist attitudes that take hold during adolescence. We teach our kids to be more understanding of each other and help them learn to respect each other's bodies and feelings:

Edward was in the fifth grade when one of his friends got her period and he came home and told me how all the guys were whispering and pointing at her and he told them to cool it. He said to me, "I felt really bad for Diana because everybody was teasing her about getting her period."

My daughter wore a heavy jacket to school all spring. Finally I said, "Aren't you sweltering? Why do you need that jacket?" She finally told me, "I need to wear it because the boys make fun of my boobs."

My daughter is terrified of getting her period at school. She's mentioned several times how embarrassed one of her friends was when a little blood soaked through to her pants. Since then Amy has done everything she could to get me to keep her home the first few days she has it.

At Jimmy's junior high they have co-ed gym classes, and I've heard the kids talking about how they hate it because the girls are always commenting on how well developed the boys are . . . or aren't.

OUR ATTITUDE INFLUENCES THEIRS

This point is so important it's worth emphasizing: our adolescents do better when they feel good about themselves. High self-esteem leads to responsible decision-making and a positive attitude toward life. Liking yourself, liking the way you look, and feeling that others accept you as you are, are vital components of high self-esteem.

In spite of our teenagers' seeming disinterest in what we have to say, our opinion of them matters. When we can let our adolescents know that we think they are lovable, and sexy, and that they have wonderful bodies, we give them a solid foundation for feeling good about themselves and for developing into healthy adults. Parents do this by hugging their kids, telling them how beautiful or handsome they look, smiling when they look at them, and remembering to let them know when they've done something well. We also help them build self-esteem when we celebrate their growth and development during puberty. Many of us hesitate to say these things because we think it sounds too sexual, but it's really important to tell our daughter how womanly she's becoming and our son what a manly body he has.

The changes of puberty can be anxiety-producing, in part, as we've already said, because some of the physical manifestations can be frightening. Many teenage girls have severe menstrual cramps, for example, and need special attention and support during those few days each month:

> Marsha has lots of pain when she gets her period. The doctor checked her out and said there was nothing physically wrong, but getting those cramps makes her feel very angry about being a woman, I think. Like it wasn't fair; so her dad and I have been trying to give her extra attention and reassurance during those times.

Teenage boys need to be reassured by their fathers that their penises are not abnormally small, that they will grow like everybody else's. They want to hear that the myths they may have picked up about masturbation aren't accurate—in other words, that they won't go blind or lose their energy if they masturbate. Moreover, if they are having any particular problems, it helps tremendously to be told that they're okay:

> Richard had a problem when he started puberty because his nipples became swollen and he was very self-conscious about that. He was afraid that he was getting breasts. Luckily the same thing happened to me when I was a teenager, so I was able to tell him that it goes away after a while. He felt better but he still wouldn't wear shirts that clung to his chest.

Puberty can also create anxiety because children more or less develop their permanent features during this time. They, and we, get to see what they're going to look like from now on—how tall they'll be, what their figure will be like, how their facial features will look. Unfortunately, teenagers often bemoan the fact that their nose is too big or their breasts are too full or not full enough, that their shoulders aren't broad enough or they have too many pimples.

It is a particular ailment of adolescence to feel "ugly." Especially among girls, a lifetime pattern of being overly critical of their own appearance is set at this age. Here's a sampling of what four thirteen-year-old girls had to say about themselves:

> I can't stand my eyebrows.

> I've got crooked toes. I hate my toes.

> My thighs and my butt are terrible; I have such short legs.

> I hate my nose. I really want to have a nose-job.

> I think I look dorky with these glasses. My mom promised to get me contacts for my next birthday.

My boobs are disgusting. I'm so flat. Boys are always making fun of me.

Only after listing all her faults one girl did have something positive to say about herself:

> I really like my hair. It's just normal. Not too curly, not too straight. Just normal.

Boys, too, talk about how they wish they were different from how they are:

> I wish I were tougher. I have no muscles.

> My ass is so fat it's embarrassing.

> Look at me. Just look at me. Curly hair, braces, pimples, fat ass. Not exactly your typical sex symbol.

Where does this negative self-image come from? Probably from many different sources. But it is certainly accurate that the concept of some "perfect" human image against which we all measure ourselves is fostered daily and continually by media advertising and image makers. Everywhere we look, everywhere we turn, we're confronted by the "perfect" male or female with sweet breath, no perspiration stains, no ring-around-the-collar, immaculate skin and hair, sexy figure, and gorgeous face. It's not difficult to feel disappointed with yourself when you're being bombarded continually with this media image of what people are supposed to look, smell, taste, and be like.

Help your children understand they're being sold a bill of goods. Criticize the messages they're getting while you're together. For example, while you watch TV or see people in the street, point out the men and women you think are beautiful or sexy who don't fit the media image:

> My daughter and I were watching TV when this commercial came on with a girl who was about five foot ten and couldn't have weighed more than ninety five pounds. My kids are big tennis players so I said, "See that girl? She wouldn't have the strength to get a serve over the net." Susie laughed.

> Sometimes my sixteen-year-old son complains because he's so slight. He wishes he looked more "macho." But I said to him the other day how much he looks like his Uncle Randy, who may not be the Marlboro Man, but he sure has a string of girlfriends all the time.

DISCUSSING SEX WITH THEM

When our children reach puberty they become physically able to reproduce. As soon as a boy begins to ejaculate he can make a girl pregnant, and as soon as a girl begins to ovulate she can become pregnant.

We have a responsibility to talk to our children about how conception occurs and explain that unprotected sexual intercourse may very well lead to pregnancy. (See "Sexuality" chapter, p. 64.)

Two points are worth making clear. One is that a boy's penis need not completely enter the girl's vagina in order for conception to take place. Sperm that have been deposited near the vaginal opening can sometimes find their way into the vagina. The second point is that a girl is not necessarily safe from pregnancy simply because she hasn't started to menstruate. Usually menstruation occurs for a few months before ovulation is established, but in some cases ovulation occurs first, before any bleeding appears.

Boy's Development

For the most part, boys develop later than girls. However, their physical appearance isn't necessarily an indication of their sexual maturity. Some may have experienced ejaculation without looking ''grown up.''

Many boys accept the changes of puberty in a very matter-of-fact way. Their genital development remains hidden under clothes most of the time, and they don't have monthly periods to worry about. However, puberty does bring some concerns. Boys feel uncomfortable when their development comes later than their friends. They may be self-conscious in locker room situations if their genitals haven't started growing or if they have no body hair while other boys their age are hairy and developed.

CONCEPTION

Conception occurs when sperm and egg join within the fallopian tube. If a couple has had sexual intercourse using no birth control, if birth control failed to work properly, or if sperm were deposited outside the vagina but close enough to swim inside, and if an egg has just been or is about to be released from the ovary, conception may occur.

Sperm enters a woman's body through the vagina. They swim up the cervical os (the opening at the tip of the uterus) and enter the uterus. Once in the uterus some sperm find their way into the fallopian tubes. If a healthy, receptive egg is in the tube at the time, a sperm will fertilize the egg and a pregnancy will be started.

After fertilization (conception) the sperm-egg unit, which is called a zygote, travels through the tube to the uterus. That journey takes approximately six days. When it reaches the uterus, the zygote attaches itself to the lining and grows for about nine months.

During pregnancy, hormones keep the uterine lining thick and nourishing for the developing fetus. No menstruation occurs during pregnancy for that reason. After childbirth the uterus sheds its lining, and begins to prepare for the next pregnancy.

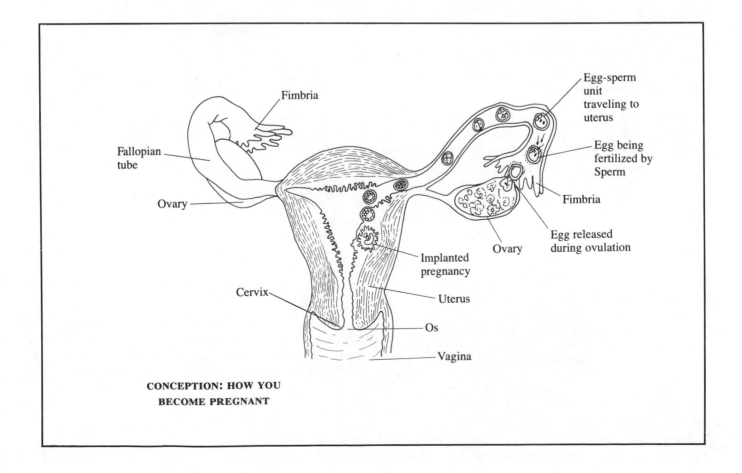

CONCEPTION: HOW YOU BECOME PREGNANT

We should try to be sensitive to our sons' feelings and reassure them that there is a wide range in the age at which boys develop. It doesn't mean there's anything wrong with them if they are late starters.

Penis size is a common concern. Here, too, we can reassure our boys that sexual fulfillment has little to do with penis size. Just like breasts, penises come in a variety of sizes and shapes.

Growth of penis and testicles: The first sign of puberty in a boy is growth of his sexual organs. On the average this begins between age ten and a half and fourteen and a half. Testicles may begin to grow first, before the penis gets bigger or longer.

Erections: Boys have erections throughout their lives, as newborns, even *in utero*. During puberty, erections tend to occur with regularity, especially when the boy is sexually aroused. Erections are caused when nerve impulses trigger the flow of blood into the blood vessels and spongy tissue inside the penis. The muscles at the base of the penis tighten, so the extra blood doesn't easily drain out. Because of the extra blood, during an erection the penis usually looks darker, and it becomes longer and wider than in its flaccid state.

General growth spurt: While genital growth is occurring, a boy's body goes through a general growth spurt, during which he may become many inches taller within a relatively short period of time. This growth usually starts later and goes on longer than does that of girls. It's not unusual for a boy to continue getting bigger and taller well into his late teens and even early twenties, while girls usually reach their full height by the time they are fifteen or sixteen.

According to the charts, boys will begin their growth spurt between the ages of ten and a half and sixteen. However, we always hear stories about kids who barely started growing until they were seventeen and then grew six inches in one year.

Height is an inherited characteristic. With good nutrition and good health the maximum height will be reached, but that will only be in relation to one's genetic program.

Pubic hair: Pubic hair begins to develop between the ages of ten and fifteen, usually around twelve to fourteen. It first appears as bumps or pimples that erupt into a soft fuzz and then becomes darker, coarser hair. This happens at approximately the same time the penis grows. The development of pubic hair is a sign of approaching ejaculation, which may follow in just a few months after the first curly pubic hair appears.

Ejaculation: Sperm development and the ejaculation of sperm and seminal fluid most often begin between ages thirteen and fourteen, although anywhere from eleven to eighteen is within the normal range. Ejaculation may first happen during a wet dream (nocturnal emission) when the boy becomes sexually aroused in his sleep. This occurs spontaneously and may be a cause of concern to a boy who isn't prepared for it. Boys may wake up and worry that they've urinated in their bed.

THE PROCESS OF SPERM PRODUCTION: SPERMATOGENESIS

Each testicle houses between 500 to 750 tubes, called seminiferous tubules, whose walls are lined with sperm-producing tissue. As a boy grows and develops, the number of cells inside the seminiferous tubules increases. These are called ''primitive'' sperm cells and they represent the first stage of sperm development.

The primitive cells divide producing spermatids. These mature into fully formed sperm cells during a nine-week period. Once this process of sperm production begins it renews itself continually throughout a man's life. Men do not ''run out'' of sperm.

While they are maturing, the sperm cells are nourished by the lining of the seminiferous tubules. Some sperm die. The ones that survive are transported into the epididymis (see illustration), which acts as an incubator, allowing the newly formed sperm to ripen for another six weeks. Again, the less healthy sperm die in the epididymis.

Sperm themselves are immobile. It's only when they mix with fluid from the prostate gland that they can travel with the speed and stamina required to reach the egg in the woman's fallopian tube. The mixture of sperm and prostate fluid is called semen. The chemical make-up of semen is designed to help sperm survive in the vagina.

In order to join with prostate fluid, the sperm are propelled from the epididymis by wavelike movements of the vas deferens (the connecting duct). During this journey to the prostate gland, the sperm pass through the seminal vesicles, where they are stored for a while and where they mix with another secretion, which enhances their ability to swim forcefully.

Once the sperm mix with the prostate fluid, the resulting semen waits to be ejaculated. If ejaculation doesn't occur through masturbation or sex play, the boy will eventually ejaculate in a spontaneous nocturnal emission (wet dream).

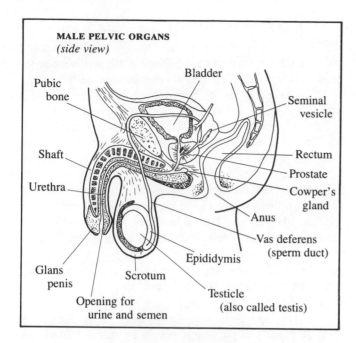

MALE PELVIC ORGANS
(side view)

- Pubic bone
- Bladder
- Seminal vesicle
- Shaft
- Rectum
- Prostate
- Urethra
- Cowper's gland
- Anus
- Vas deferens (sperm duct)
- Epididymis
- Glans penis
- Scrotum
- Testicle (also called testis)
- Opening for urine and semen

A boy may also experience his first ejaculation while masturbating. Almost all teenage boys masturbate. It is natural and nothing to be alarmed about. In fact, it helps children learn about their own sexuality and sexual pleasure. Parents who have religious scruples against masturbation need to share those feelings with their sons—if possible without being punitive.

Breasts: Many boys experience temporary breast growth during the early stages of puberty. This may take the form of a lump on the breast. This condition is called *gynecomastia*. It occurs in a high percentage of boys and its cause may be a very small amount of female hormone produced by the testicles normally. It disappears quickly, often within six months to a year, but can be a major source of embarrassment and concern to boys who worry that they may be developing female breasts. Reassure your sons that this breast growth is normal and will soon disappear.

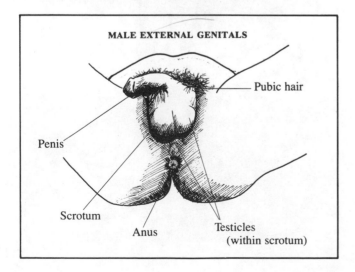

MALE EXTERNAL GENITALS

- Pubic hair
- Penis
- Scrotum
- Anus
- Testicles (within scrotum)

Voice change: Boys voices may deepen within the same year as their first ejaculation, usually a few months after that event. The reason a boy's voice cracks and squeaks during this time is that as the rest of his body experiences rapid growth, so does his larynx, or voice box. The stress of this growth, along with the relatively sudden distension of the vocal chords creates a cracking and squeaking effect for several months or longer, until the voice adjusts to its new capacity. This can be a source of embarrassment, especially if people ridicule the boy for it.

On the average, the voice of a mature man is about an octave lower than that of a woman. But this, too, is only an average. Some men have relatively high voices and others have very deep voices. Some boys have a very wide range, others a more limited range.

Body hair: Boys develop body hair on the chest, arms, legs, and underarms. The amount of hair varies widely from boy to boy and man to man, and it is genetically determined. Whether a boy will have a lot or little hair depends on the genes he has inherited. The amount of hair he has is in no way related to how "manly" he is. Some boys worry about that.

Skin changes: During puberty a boy's skin may become oilier and he may get pimples. Some boys develop severe acne. If this happens, it's important to have the condition treated by a competent dermatologist. Permanent skin damage can result, but these days there are many good treatments and products available that help. This condition usually disappears by the time the boy reaches his twenties.

Sweat glands: A boy's sweat glands become more active during puberty. He will sweat more and a strong body odor may develop.

Facial hair: Face hair usually appears between the ages of thirteen and eighteen, at around fourteen or fifteen in most boys. Depending on heredity again, a boy may have a lot of hair or relatively little. Some ethnic groups have almost no facial hair.

Taking care of the genitals: Until a boy starts having sexual partners, the only special care needed to take care of the penis and testicles is washing them with soap and warm water every day or two. Tell the boy to clear away any smegma (a secretion) that collects, especially if he is uncircumcised. Also, it's good to get in the habit of checking the testicles for any changes or lumps.

Of course, things may come up that a doctor should look at. Some of the signals that should send you to a clinic or doctor are:

— an open sore or persisting sore spot around the penis
— a burning feeling during urination
— an undescended testicle
— discharge (pus or whitish fluid) coming from the end of the penis
— a pain in the testicles that doesn't go away
— a lump that wasn't there before

Many of these things are more likely to happen once a boy is sexually active. They may be a sign of an STD—sexually transmitted disease (see p. 84).

Discharge from the penis: This is a common problem, which may have a number of causes. Always have it checked by a doctor, because a discharge might be a sign of gonorrhea (if sexually active) or urethritis, which is an infection in the urethra. Both these diseases require antibiotic treatment.

Also, if a boy stops himself regularly from ejaculating during masturbation or sex play, he may develop a condition known as retrograde ejaculation. That means that the semen has gone back down the urethra into the glands and is building up there. That buildup can cause pain and a discharge from the penis.

Pain in the genital area: Pain in the groin or genital area can be caused by many things. It might be a swollen lymph gland or a hernia or an infection. If it lasts more than a day or two, have it checked by a doctor.

Undescended testicles: Ordinarily a boy's testicles descend shortly before or just after his birth. Sometimes, especially in the case of premature babies, the testicles do not descend for several months. When they have not descended by themselves, the condition can be corrected by surgery or hormone treatment.

When one testicle has descended only partway, it can become twisted and cause a great deal of pain. An operation is called for to untwist the cord that supplies blood to the testicle. If there is pain in the testicles that hasn't been caused by an immediate injury, or if a boy was hit in the testicles and the pain lasts for a very long time, take him to see a doctor.

Testicle cancer: It is very rare for teenagers to have a problem with cancer. But since cancer of the testicles can occur, it is a good idea for them to get into the habit of examining the testicles, just the way a girl has to learn to examine her breasts. (See diagram.)

If you took the hormone DES during your pregnancy with your son, be sure to have him checked by a doctor. There is a link between DES and testicle cancer (also between DES and vaginal cancer in girls).

Jock itch, or jock rot: Itching and a damp feeling in the genital area, may indicate jock itch. The skin will be sore and red around the testicles and on the inside of the thighs, and it can hurt a lot.

Jock itch can be caused by wearing clothes that are too tight or that are made of fabrics that don't let the air circulate.

Lightly rubbing cornstarch on the area will often be enough to cure it, but the boy may need to use a fungicide. If the condition doesn't go away, he may want to see a doctor, especially to make sure nothing more serious is involved.

The area should be kept clean and dry, clothes should be washed well, and jeans or other pants that rub or irritate avoided.

Girl's Development

Girls generally go through the changes of puberty about two years before boys of the same age. It's not unusual for girls to get their periods and develop breasts while they are still in elementary school, in the fourth or fifth grades. This can be upsetting or confusing for girls, depending on how the people around them feel about their development. It can also be a source of pride. It all depends on what's "in" at the time. If you're sixteen and small-breasted, and Marilyn Monroe is the style, you're in trouble. If you have big breasts, and tall, skinny fashion models are the measure of beauty, you're not going to be happy with your figure.

Girls who develop late, when they are already in high school for example, can feel left out. It may seem to them that everyone else looks like and is being treated like a woman, while they are still regarded as a little kid. They need reassurance from us that they will catch up soon.

We can help our daughters put their changing bodies into perspective. Tell them why the changes occur. Celebrate their entrance into puberty if you think that would please them. Some girls enjoy being congratulated on getting their first bra or having their period for the first time. Others don't want it mentioned at all. We have to be sensitive to who our daughter is and respect her feelings.

LENI WILDFLOWER

These days teenage sexuality is used to sell everything from jeans to perfume to television shows, and more often than not these ads use sexy young girls. This kind of exploitation makes girls even more self-conscious than they already are about their bodies. Our input is needed to balance that. We can help them be proud of their development without feeling like they're constantly on display as simply a female "object."

Breast development: On the average, at around ten or eleven, girls' breasts begin to develop, first with enlarged nipples, then with growth around the nipples. It takes about three or four years or more from the first sign of development until the breasts are fully grown, and there may be changes in the size and shape of breasts throughout a woman's life.

The size of a girl's breasts depends on heredity. Overall body weight has little to do with it: there are thin girls with large breasts and heavy girls with small breasts. Many girls spend a lot of time wishing their breasts looked different from the way they do, mainly because breasts have special significance in our society. It helps when we can reassure our daughters that their breasts are beautiful exactly as they are. It also helps to let them know that the size of one's breasts doesn't influence one's sexual feelings, nor does it affect a woman's ability to breast-feed her baby.

Monthly swelling: Many girls and women have swelling and tenderness in their breasts just before their period arrives. The tissues tend to hold liquid before menstruation; this often makes breasts feel heavier than usual. Encourage your daughter to wear a well-fitting bra and to cut down on salty foods at this time.

Getting hit in the breasts: Breasts are sensitive. But the body is able to handle bruising and minor accidents, so unless breasts are badly bruised there is probably no cause for concern. If you are concerned, check with a doctor.

Hair: Lots of women have hair on or around their breasts. This also can be caused by birth control pills.

Secretions: Sometimes a discharge will come from the nipples. This is normal and occurs naturally as the body's way of keeping the nipple ducts open. The discharge may look like very thin milk, or it may be clear or green, gray, or yellow. Women who take birth control pills may have this discharge. It can come during sexual arousal and at certain times in the menstrual cycle. Washing the nipples with warm water and soap keeps the discharge from drying and accumulating. If it has pus or blood in it, or if it is brownish in color, it might be a sign of illness. Have it checked by a doctor.

Infections: If she has an infection in or near her breasts, a girl may feel soreness and see swelling or redness. This should be checked by a doctor.

Inverted nipples: Some nipples turn in instead of out. Sometimes, as breasts continue to grow, the nipples will be pushed out. Special nipple shields are made especially to help women with inverted nipples breast-feed. Lots of women have inverted nipples. If a nipple has been normal and suddenly becomes inverted, see a doctor right away. It might be because of a tumor.

Lumps: Breasts can be very lumpy. Some girls and women find changes in breast tissue throughout their monthly menstrual cycle. If a lump stays in one place for several weeks, see a doctor. Most lumps, in young women particularly, will be benign (noncancerous). For instance, if a lump hurts, if it is tender or sore, then it's most likely benign, but a doctor should be seen.

Teenagers of both sexes get a kind of lump called an adolescent nodule, a sore swollen spot right under the nipple. It will disappear by itself. See a doctor to make sure. Teens very seldom have breast cancer. Occasionally, though, a lump can be a sign of cancer.

THE MAMMARY GLANDS

From the time of puberty onward, mammary glands are ready to change elements of blood into milk for childbirth.

A mammary gland is made up of areas that make milk called alveoli, and passageways, called ducts, through which the milk travels to the nipple.

INTERNAL VIEW OF THE FEMALE BREAST

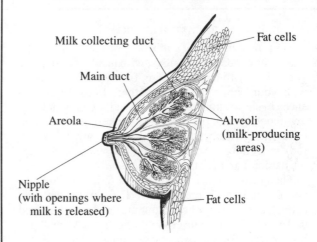

Milk collecting duct — Fat cells

Main duct

Areola — Alveoli (milk-producing areas)

Nipple (with openings where milk is released) — Fat cells

While a woman is pregnant her mammary glands get bigger as hormones make them ready to produce milk. Hormones released during birth trigger the milk-making a couple of days after the baby comes. When a mother holds her newborn to her breast, the baby sucks instinctively on the nipple. This sucking pulls the milk through the ducts and out. Since the baby's sucking stimulates the production of milk within a few hours, there will be more milk for as long as the mother wants to keep nursing, no matter how big or small her breasts are. If she doesn't want to breast-feed her baby, the first milk will dry up and no more will be made until another birth.

Parents should be sure to teach their daughters how to do checks for lumps after the monthly menstrual period. (See Breast Self-Exam box below.)

Pubic Hair: The second major change to occur is the growth of pubic hair. It usually begins to appear around one or two years after breasts start to bud and about one or two years before a girl gets her period. It may start as light fuzz or bumps; then a few longer, darker hairs will appear. More hair grows and it becomes thicker, coarser, and usually curlier, until it covers the entire area around the vulva.

Growth Spurt: On the average, girls experience a growth spurt between the ages of nine and a half and fourteen and a half. They usually reach their full height within a year or two after their period begins.

Reproductive Organs: Many internal changes are taking place. A boy's sexual organs are outside his body, so growth can be readily seen. Girls need to be taught about the growth and change that's taking place inside them.

Their ovaries are getting bigger, and the egg follicles within the ovaries are growing as well. Their uterus and fallopian tubes are maturing and increasing in size, getting ready for their role in ovulation, menstruation, and pregnancy.

THE PROCESS OF OVULATION

Baby girls are born with two ovaries, and within each ovary are approximately 200,000 to 400,000 follicles, each containing an immature egg (ovum). This number diminishes steadily throughout a woman's life. By the onset of puberty about one to two hundred thousand egg follicles remain in each ovary.

As the ovaries grow during puberty, some of the ova begin to ripen and mature. The first ovulation occurs when one fully ripe egg breaks out of its follicle, pushes through the ovarian wall and enters the woman's body. It is caught up in the fingerlike hairs (fimbria) of the fallopian tube and is pushed through the tube by wavelike contractions. The egg is receptive to sperm while it is in the first third of the tube. Whether fertilized by a sperm or not, the egg journeys through the tube and into the uterus.

After the first time, ovulation generally occurs monthly, although most women go through times of irregular ovulation during their fertile years. Sickness, travel, weight loss or gain, emotional upset, and stress can affect the cycle. At the beginning of puberty, many teenage girls ovulate irregularly.

BREAST SELF-EXAM

First stand in front of a mirror. Look at your breasts, with your hands at your sides; with hands raised above your head; with hands pushing firmly on your hips; or with your palms pressed together. Look for differences in shape, not size. Look for a flattening or bulging in one but not the other; for puckering of the skin; for discharge from a nipple when it is gently squeezed; for a reddening or scaly crust on a nipple; for one nipple harder than the other.

Then lie down on a bed or couch, or in a bathtub. As you examine each breast, raise the arm on that side above your head. Or bend your arm and put your hand under your head, your elbow lying flat. (A small pillow or large folded towel placed under your shoulder will distribute breast tissue more easily.) Feel your breast gently with the flat of the fingers of your opposite hand. Move them in small circles or with a slight back-and-forth motion, being sure to examine the whole breast. Pay special attention to the area between nipple and armpit, for most tumors are located there.

Breast self-exams should be done frequently at first (every few days) so that you can learn about the different ways your breasts feel during the course of a month. Later, examine them once a month at the same time each month. A few days after menstruation is good, as they will be less full then.

If you feel a definite lump that doesn't go away after a week or so, see a doctor.

External organs: Naturally, the external organs, the area called the vulva, can be seen and its growth can be noticed. The lips (labia) protecting the vaginal opening develop more fully. The vagina also gets larger during puberty. The clitoris, a pea-shaped bump above the urethra, grows too. This organ has only one function: sexual arousal. It is full of nerve endings and erectile tissue which make it extremely sensitive to touch.

The hymen: This membrane partially covers the vaginal opening. It almost never blocks the opening completely, since there must be a way for the products of menstruation to be released from the body. If, in fact, the vagina is totally closed, a girl will have to have her hymen stretched or opened by a doctor to allow an outlet for the menstrual flow.

Despite traditional beliefs, the hymen is not a reliable symbol of virginity. Many girls are born with almost no hymen and others have large openings in their hymen naturally. The hymen can also be stretched during normal childhood play.

Figure Changes: Another change that can be readily seen is the shifting distribution of weight during puberty. Hips become wider, waists smaller. Thighs and buttocks also become fleshier. These changes, like most of the changes of puberty, relate to reproduction. They give a woman a natural cushion during childbirth.

Body Hair: Girls develop body hair, first on their legs and arms, and then under their arms. Some girls also get some hair on their face and around their nipples. The amount of hair a girl has is based on her inherited characteristics.

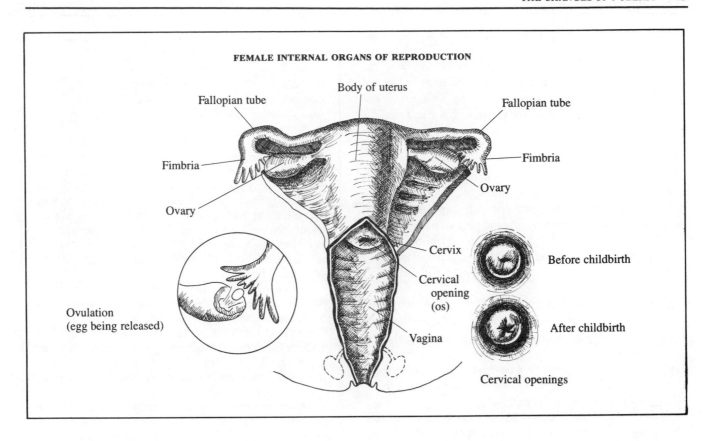

FEMALE INTERNAL ORGANS OF REPRODUCTION

Body of uterus

Fallopian tube

Fallopian tube

Fimbria

Fimbria

Ovary

Ovary

Cervix

Cervical opening (os)

Before childbirth

After childbirth

Vagina

Ovulation (egg being released)

Cervical openings

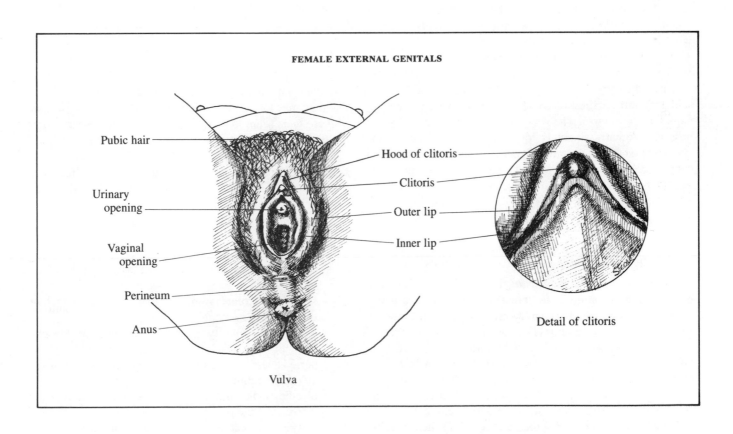

FEMALE EXTERNAL GENITALS

Pubic hair

Hood of clitoris

Clitoris

Urinary opening

Outer lip

Vaginal opening

Inner lip

Perineum

Anus

Detail of clitoris

Vulva

Some ethnic groups have a lot of body hair, others have only a little.

Menstruation: About three-quarters of the way between the beginning and end of her growth spurt and sexual development, a girl will start menstruating. This usually occurs between twelve and thirteen, although the age range is very wide. Some girls start their period as early as eight or nine, and others don't begin menstruation until their late teens.

Menstruation is the most significant event of puberty for most girls. Without preparation, the sight of blood can be extremely upsetting to a girl, but even with preparation the onset of her period is momentous. Some girls wait eagerly for it to arrive. Some girls are unhappy when they begin to menstruate. By talking with our daughters and preparing them for this natural, healthy event, we can ease their transition considerably.

Our attitude about menstruation will influence our daughters. We can give our girls a positive or negative outlook on the process simply by our choice of words in talking about it with them. Referring to it as "the curse" or "being on the rag" does little to encourage a positive attitude. Menstruation can be celebrated as a sign of womanhood; and that's what our daughters need to hear.

In our culture the tradition has always been not to talk about one's menstrual period, to keep it secret. Many teenage girls feel so shy about the onset of menstruation that they don't even tell their parents about it for a while. This can hurt us, but we don't have to take it personally or worry too much. The damage comes when this secrecy gets equated with shamefulness. Lots of girls and women are embarrassed about someone finding out that they are having their period. Women worry about being caught without a tampon or bleeding through to their outer clothes. Teenage girls have said they are terrified of some boy discovering a sanitary napkin in their purse. The way around these feelings of shyness and embarrassment is for mothers to be more open about periods with their daughters and their sons. It helps even more when fathers, too, can talk naturally with their daughters about it. A woman remembered:

> When I first got my period my dad was the one who took me to get the Kotex. And that was really nice for me. I think it helped me feel more comfortable about the fact that it wasn't any big deal to menstruate, even though I probably wasn't consciously aware of that at the time.

What to use for the menstrual flow: There are a number of different products designed to catch the menstrual flow. Most women in this country use some form of tampon. Recently, however, tampons have been associated with a serious disease called toxic shock syndrome, which seems to affect young women under thirty in particular. A few died from this disease. For this reason we may hesitate to recommend that our daughters use tampons. You might want to check with your daughter's doctor or a local clinic.

Some parents don't recommend tampons to their daugh-

THE PROCESS OF MENSTRUATION

As the egg matures within the follicle (or egg sac), the follicle releases the hormone estrogen. Estrogen causes the uterus to begin building up its inner lining (the endometrium). The endometrium grows, gets thicker with blood vessels and tissue, and forms glands that will nourish the potential fetus. After the egg is released, the follicle fills with new cell growth (corpus luteum). The corpus luteum produces progesterone, which causes the glands in the endometrium to secrete nourishing fluids. It also increases the blood flow to the uterus in preparation for a possible pregnancy, should the egg be fertilized. If conception were to occur, the egg-sperm unit (called a zygote) would travel through the tube to the uterus and implant in the thick, nourishing lining.

If, as is most often the case, there is no conception, the egg disintegrates and the corpus luteum begins to degenerate after about twelve or thirteen days. This cuts off the supply of progesterone, which causes the endometrium to cease secreting. The lining then begins to break down. It is sloughed off by the uterus and discharged through the cervix into the vagina during menstruation.

Menstruation is a woman's body's response to an unfertilized egg. The uterus cleans itself out and starts over, building up its lining to get ready for the next egg and potential pregnancy. The process is cleansing. It is a sign of health, indicating that a woman's body is functioning well.

---

ters for a different reason. There is a feeling that girls shouldn't put anything into their vaginas and also a feeling that they may lose their virginity by using tampons. Neither of these fears seem to us to be appropriate. (See discussion under hymen.)

Sanitary napkins come in a variety of widths and thicknesses, and most teenage girls find them quite comfortable. Some require a belt and others simply fit inside a girl's underwear.

Some problem signs: Some signs that mean a checkup is in order are:

— a very heavy menstrual flow that lasts more than four or five days
— severe menstrual cramping or pain that lasts more than three days each month
— a sudden irregularity in the cycle that isn't due to sickness, travel, or weight gain or loss—if suddenly the period doesn't come one month and there's no reasonable explanation
— bleeding in the middle of the cycle or at any time other than during the period
— severe cramps at times other than when a period is due

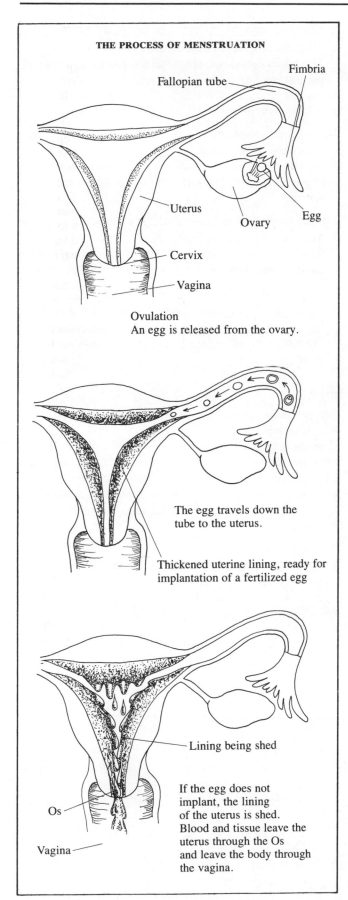

THE PROCESS OF MENSTRUATION

Fimbria

Fallopian tube

Uterus

Ovary

Egg

Cervix

Vagina

Ovulation
An egg is released from the ovary.

The egg travels down the tube to the uterus.

Thickened uterine lining, ready for implantation of a fertilized egg

Lining being shed

Os

Vagina

If the egg does not implant, the lining of the uterus is shed. Blood and tissue leave the uterus through the Os and leave the body through the vagina.

Those five symptoms are warning signs that something might be interfering with the normal functioning of a woman's body, and they mean you should see a doctor.

Endometriosis: When the tissue that usually grows in the lining of the uterus begins to grow in other places, such as the vagina, urinary tract or bowel, it is called endometriosis. Its symptoms are very painful periods that may last a long time and be quite heavy. Periods may also come more frequently than usual—for example, every twenty-four days or less. Endometriosis is more common among twenty-, thirty-, and forty-year-olds than it is among teenagers. Treatment for this disorder varies according to the particular case. If a doctor advises surgery to remove the extra tissue, you should check the diagnosis with another physician.

Pelvic Inflammatory Disease (PID): PID is a general name for different infections in the pelvic area, the area around the uterus and vagina. Symptoms of PID are extreme cramping with periods, irregular bleeding, cramps at times other than during a period, general pelvic pain and sometimes chills and fever. Gonorrhea is a major cause of PID, but other infections cause it as well. Sometimes PID is a problematic side effect of using an IUD for birth control. Treatment for PID is a heavy dose of antibiotics, lots of rest, and no sexual intercourse for at least two weeks after treatment. PID can cause scar tissue to form in the fallopian tubes, which may result in ectopic pregnancy or infertility (inability to get pregnant). Seek medical help at once.

Fibroids and other cysts: Fibroids are growths in the uterus. Cysts and tumors can develop in the ovaries, too. These growths can affect one's period by either blocking the flow altogether or causing extra bleeding during menstruation or at some other time during the month. Usually fibroids don't occur in teenagers, but if they do, they are almost always benign (not caused by cancer). However, they should be regularly checked by a doctor. He or she can usually tell fibroids by feeling them in the uterus. Since fibroids usually stay rather small, they don't always cause problems, and some women live with them for years. They usually disappear during menopause. If they get large enough to create pain or heavy or irregular bleeding, they can almost always be removed by surgery without removing the uterus.

Cancer: Teenagers get cancer very rarely. Most important, the best chance of cure is early discovery of the disease. So it is crucial to have symptoms checked by a medical person as soon as you suspect something may be wrong. (For example, symptoms may be irregular vaginal bleeding during the month or a breast lump that doesn't go away.) Some cancers effect a small percentage of teens. One type is vaginal cancer, which has been appearing recently in some teenage women whose mothers took DES (diethylstilbestrol) during pregnancy with these daughters. DES is a synthetic estrogenic hormone now known to be linked to cancer.

Write to the DES Action Group in New York to get more information about what to do. Their address is: DES Action

National, Long Island Jewish-Hillside Medical Center, New Hyde Park, New York 11040. Be sure to take your daughter for a complete checkup if you took DES during your pregnancy.

BOOKS AND RESOURCES

Recommended Reading

Bell, Ruth, et al. *Changing Bodies, Changing Lives*. New York: Random House, 1980.
Facts and feelings about teenagers' lives, relationships, and body development.

Changes: You and Your Body. Pamphlet, 1978. Order from CHOICE, 1501 Cherry St., Philadelphia, Penna. 19102; $2.50; bulk rates available.
Easy-to-read and informative booklet for teens about puberty. Available in Spanish.

Gardner-Loulan, Joann, and Bonnie Lopez and Marcia Quackenbush. *Period*. (1979) Volcano Press, 330 Ellis St., San Francisco, Calif. 94102; $6.00 paper; Spanish edition, $7.00.
Cleverly written and illustrated book about menstruation for preteens.

Gordon, Sol. *Facts About Sex for Today's Youth*. Fayetteville, N.Y.: Ed-U Press, 1979.
Short, direct discussion of anatomy, reproduction, love, and sex.

Pomeroy, Wardell. *Boys and Sex* and *Girls and Sex*. New York: Delacorte Press, 1981.
These two books present basic information about body changes and sexuality for teenage boys and girls.

Schowalter, John E., M.D., and Walter R. Anyan, M.D. *The Family Handbook of Adolescence*.
This book discusses the physical and psychological development and problems of adolescence.

For Teenagers

Betancourt, Jeanne. *Am I Normal?* and *Dear Diary*. New York: Avon Books, 1983.
Popular books with teens that deal with the emotional and physical changes of puberty for boys and girls respectively.

Blume, Judy. *Are You There, God? It's Me, Margaret*. New York: Yearling Books, Dell, 1974.
Reassuring story about preadolescent girls facing both the physical and emotional changes that usually accompany puberty.

Blume, Judy. *Then Again, Maybe I Won't*. New York: Yearling Books, Dell, 1971.
Story of a thirteen-year-old boy and the feelings he has about growing up.

Resources

Society for Adolescent Medicine
P.O. Box 3462
Granada Hills, Calif. 91344
(818)368-5996
This society will refer parents to doctors and clinics throughout the country that specialize in adolescent health care. Write to them enclosing a legal-size, stamped, self-addressed envelope.

DES Action National
Long Island Jewish-Hillside Medical Center
New Hyde Park, N.Y. 11040
Mothers who may have taken DES during pregnancy, write for information about health care for your teenager.

V

EMOTIONAL HEALTH

For some children adolescence is a period of fairly steady emotional growth and integration, but that is the exception. For most teenagers and preteens it is a time of emotional up-heaval. Children who have seemed easygoing and well-adjusted may become edgy and easily upset. Those who have been open and communicative may turn reticent and moody. Adolescents with previously recognized problems (for example, sleep disturbances, bed wetting, eating disorders) may reach a point of crisis.

For parents these changes are likely to be unnerving. We see our children anxious, depressed, unhappy or belligerent and we feel concerned. Are they all right? What's gotten into them? What can or should we do? It helps to try to understand the reasons behind their emotional turmoil and to recognize that our children are facing very real and important challenges during adolescence.

First, as we described in the previous chapter, they are confronted with enormous physical and biological growth occurring over a relatively short period of time. Everything about them is changing, and while many young people welcome these changes, for others it can be upsetting. Events such as budding breasts, voice changes, menstruation and wet dreams may be difficult to accept, or even frightening. Hormonal changes can result in increased sex drive, new sleep habits, huge appetites, and, for girls, the monthly emotional fluctuations of the menstrual cycle. All this can be confusing:

An eleven-year-old girl: I'm not looking forward to getting my period at all. I'm still a kid. I don't want to be a woman yet.

Our twelve-year-old is quite big for his age and he told us he didn't want to grow any more. He said, "I hate being taller than everybody else I know. It's disgusting."

Second, our children have to separate from us and develop an identity all their own. Of course, this has been going on since birth, but during adolescence independence becomes a more serious issue, since our children know that by the end of this period they are expected to be "adults." The process is not clear-cut. There is much ambivalence involved: at the same time adolescents want to shake off our authority and control, they also want the loving comfort that can come from family:

My fifteen-year-old just made the basketball team and at his first big game he was up for a game-clinching foul shot and he missed. He didn't say anything when he got home that afternoon, but that night he came into our room and watched television on our bed and just happened to fall asleep there between us.

A third characteristic of this period is that now, unlike the earlier years of childhood when we were responsible for most of the big decisions in their lives, our teenagers have to make complicated choices for themselves—what crowd they'll go with; what style they'll choose; what school they'll attend; whether or not they'll take drugs or have sex; what they're going to be when they grow up. As they try to figure out their own standards and values they tend to resist ours, and this in turn causes its own anxieties. They're thrown back on themselves at a time when they have little life experience and even less self-confidence:

If everybody's going to drive home with somebody who's high and you're the only one who says, "Well, I can't go because my parents told me I should never drive with anyone who's high"—well, how can you say that? You don't want to be a dork, but you also don't want to be dead.

My seventeen-year-old is in love. It's his first love and he's so serious about this girl I'm afraid it's really going to affect his life. He's talking about not going away to college because he doesn't want to leave her.

Considering all this, is it any wonder that adolescents go through the mood swings they do? Can we blame them for being rebellious at the same time they are needy? They experience many contradictory feelings all at once, and they may be confused, ashamed, or upset by their own feelings. If, for example, our son is feeling lonely, and he is ashamed and embarrassed because he doesn't have more friends, then our observation, "You look like you're hurting," no matter how caring, can feel like a painful intrusion. And his reaction to us may be anger or deeper withdrawal.

BRYAN BREEN

Clearly, adolescence is a stressful time and stress can erode self-esteem. Teenagers are, as a general population, the most self-conscious of all people: they doubt themselves and their abilities in every area. They have a very shaky sense of who they are, since, in fact, they are in the process of becoming something else. As a result, they may react strongly to anything that brings that into focus, and our efforts to reassure them about their looks, their intelligence, and about how worthwhile they are often backfire. As a mother told us:

> I tell my daughter: "You're not fat, you're beautiful. You're not dumb, you're very intelligent." And her response to me is, "What do you know, you're only my mother."

Adolescents also have lovely qualities. Teenagers can be remarkably intense, especially about issues like morality, honesty, politics, loyalty. They tend to be very romantic about love, and they are often idealistic about people or about the way the world works. As a result, however, they see many things in black and white—absolutes, without any gray areas:

> I'm never going to get married when I get older. I've never yet seen a good relationship.

> My daughter accuses us of being hypocritical and bourgeois. She says things like, "Don't you realize that three quarters of the world is starving? How can you live this way? Don't you care about anybody besides yourselves?"

The point is, for the most part, these sorts of reactions are normal ways of playing out the teenage scenario. Even things like experimenting with drugs, alcohol and sex; staying out all night; cutting school occasionally; starving or "pigging out"; driving fast; challenging the law—can be normal too, however hard they may be for us to deal with. We may remember doing many of the same things when we were teenagers. Unfortunately, that rarely keeps us from feeling victimized by our own teenagers' moodiness and defiance.

In these situations there may be little we can do directly to help our teenagers or ourselves. The best we can hope for is to remain available to them without getting caught up in their extremes. Our perspective in the face of their ups and downs can be reassuring to them:

> During the time that my son was breaking up with his ninth-grade girlfriend I almost never saw him. He was in his room most of the time, and when he wasn't he gave off a vibe that made it very clear that he did *not* want to talk. I knew he was dying inside and I really felt for him—but I respected his need to be alone and his ability to handle it. Somehow I knew he knew I knew.

> The best way to describe Kathy when she was fifteen is to say she was totally off the wall. Every day it was a different trauma—tantrums, testing, love affairs, fantastic sulks—you name it. If I tried to talk to her, she accused me of controlling her life. If I tried to ignore her, I was accused of not caring about her. It was very stormy for a long, long time—until I finally realized there was no way I could win, no way I could keep up with her. When I accepted that, I felt a lot more able to relax and just let her get through it.

One of the most important roles parents can play during this time is that of "builder-upper." As we've said before, in order to come through adolescence as healthy, functioning adults, our teenagers need self-esteem and self-confidence. When they are going through their angriest, most self-hating periods, that's when they need our support the most. Of course, those are also the times when they're likely to be mistreating us the most, so it's hard to give them what they need.

We asked several parents what they do on a day-to-day basis to help their teenagers through this rocky period:

> I think you need to keep telling your kids that they are terrific human beings. I'm not sure they hear it all the time, but over the long run I think it sinks in.

> I don't get home until six o'clock, so my daughter has to watch her younger brother and get dinner started. She's only thirteen, and at first I was afraid it was going to be too much for her to handle. But she actually seems to enjoy having the responsibility for the house. And she really responds when I tell her what a great job she's doing.

> My wife and I both feel that when we have the chance to sit down with our boys and really listen to them talk about school, their friends, their games—they're very involved

with sports—that makes them feel like we're really interested in them. We try to go to as many of their games as we can.

My older daughter has a lot of trouble thinking she's smart. The other day she wrote this poem which was just brilliant and I told her to just try to keep remembering when she went off to school what a beautiful poem she'd written.

I think my kids feel pretty good about themselves because they know we trust them and respect their opinions about things. We try to include them in our discussions at the dinner table and we really listen to their point of view.

SERIOUS EMOTIONAL PROBLEMS

It is when our teenagers' behavior gets out of control, when it brings danger, illness, or encounters with the law that it becomes alarming and serious. How can we guide ourselves so that we don't overreact to the ordinary, if unsettling, behavior of our kids and yet stay alert for signs of more serious trouble?

The answers, though tough to implement, turn out to be pretty straightforward: if a problem goes on for a long time, gets in the way of the rest of the child's life, if no one or nothing seems to help, if his or her behavior is self-destructive or destructive to others—that's the time to act:

My son's always been a challenge. He always had trouble at school. But then in the seventh grade he got all D's on his report card and I was getting calls from teachers every day. That's when I decided it was more than I could handle alone and that I needed help.

We knew Jennie was cutting classes once in a while but we thought it was no big deal. It took a couple of months for the principal's office and us to get it together and figure out that she almost never went to school. What happened was that she was living most of the time with an older guy who works at the hot-dog stand near the school.

When Jeff first got his license he got into three car accidents in a row. We were very upset—terrified that he was going to get killed. His school counselor suggested that we all go in for therapy and we agreed.

Though it doesn't always happen, certain life situations can act as triggers for severe emotional difficulties. Divorce, the family having to move, parental illness or death, serious marital difficulties, alcoholism in the family, provocative parental behavior, all increase the stress on teenagers and can tip a child from the edge of emotional trouble into crisis. Within their own lives, the triggers include breaking up with a girl- or boyfriend, being seriously ill, pregnancy, failure at school, the death of a beloved pet, severe pressure at school or in other areas of performance.

Recognizing certain symptoms of serious emotional disturbance—alcoholism, for example—may take a while, but once you're alert, the signs are available to you. (See "Drugs and Alcohol" p. 100.) What is harder to deal with, more subtle and also, often, more threatening, are the symptoms of serious depression. We all know or have read about teenagers who were so driven by difficult emotional problems that they did others grave injury or even killed themselves:

Some boy was at the school my daughter Louise went to and offered her and two of her friends a ride. They didn't realize he was drunk, but right after they got in the car, he speeded up and began spinning the wheel so the car went from one side of the road to the other. The girls were pleading for him to stop and screaming but he didn't—until they crashed. I know all these details because Louise's friend Allison survived. Louise and Cindy were both killed. It turned out another girl had been killed in an accident with the same boy two years before.

My son always had a health problem and had to take drugs for his condition. Pretty soon he was just taking drugs—and one day we found him on the bathroom floor, dead of an overdose. We'll never know. Did he do it on purpose? Was it a mistake?

What Are the Symptoms of Serious Depression?

Changes in sleeping habits: Most teenagers sleep a lot. (Sometimes it only seems that way. If you go to bed at three in the morning, it's natural that you're going to need to sleep till eleven.) However, when anyone is sleeping, regularly, more than ten hours a day, that's an "alert signal," as is a lot of sleeping during the day—or if someone complains of always being tired. Similarly, though occasional sleepless nights are nothing to worry about, it is a problem when a teenager is regularly insomniac, asks you for sleeping pills or regularly needs a beer or marijuana to go to sleep. Another signal is the erratic show of these patterns. Of course, teenagers keep what looks like crazy hours, but sleepless times interspersed with periods of almost constant sleeping can also be the sign of severe problems:

Our son never seems to sleep. You pass his room anytime during the night and the TV is on or he's walking back and forth. He always seems like he's wired. Finally, we had to talk to the doctor about it and now he takes pills. I hate it, but we don't know what else to do.

Eating: (See p. 113.) Teenagers, as a group, are not known for their sensible eating habits. However, dramatic weight loss or gain, signs of vomiting (see Bulimia, p. 115), severe loss of appetite, bizarre food fetishes, are of a different magnitude than the hamburger and pizza pattern we all know. Make sure your child has a thorough medical checkup by a knowledgeable physician and then explore the emotional background of the problem and the resources to deal with it. (See p. 118.)

Persistent and marked withdrawal: If a teenager withdraws from school, family and/or friends in a dramatic way, he may be signaling a grave difficulty. Occasionally cutting a class is no big deal, but when a teenager stays out of school or misses classes more than once in a while, when school work suffers, when no one knows his whereabouts, attention must be paid.

All young people have periods of feeling that they're not popular and of wanting to move away from the company of their peers. All people have periods of wanting to be alone. However, a teenager who never has friends, who shuts him- or herself away from the family for long periods of time, who seems to have no close personal relationships, is probably in trouble.

Another sign of difficulty occurs when a teenager seems to lose all interest in life, gives up the things that used to give him or her pleasure, seems not to react emotionally to anything; in other words, seems to "shut down":

My daughter went through a year when she never smiled. Whatever we did, we couldn't break through. She didn't seem to care about anything or do anything or make any plans for herself. She sat around watching TV all summer.

RUTH BELL

Not any one of these symptoms separately is necessarily a matter of life or death. Some teenagers seem to reject their families completely but they have found people outside their homes to be close to. It is those children in whom we see a combination of these withdrawal patterns who need help.

Acting out: Up and down is, as we have seen, the way of teenage life. These changes are alarming when they are disruptive, stubborn, and out of the child's ordinary pattern.

How do we identify which kids fall into this group? A good student who suddenly is failing most of his courses. A child who loved animals and is found to be abusing a pet. A teenager who seems to be sexually out of control: a boy who is a Peeping Tom, a girl who picks up men in the street. A child who shoplifts more than once. A child who runs away. A child who is severely accident prone. A child who blindly commits himself to joining a cult. A child who mutilates herself or threatens suicide. A child who often gets into bad physical fights or constantly abuses others verbally. A child who is afraid of everything. A child who is always seeking dangerous thrills.

Sometimes severe emotional trouble also manifests itself as physical illness such as frequent and severe headaches, stomach trouble, dysmenorrhea, backaches, feeling ill enough not to function a lot of the time, unexplained illnesses with no apparent cause.

When our children are showing these danger signs, we want to intervene effectively enough so they do not irreversibly injure themselves or anyone else physically or emotionally. This is when we have to spend more time with our child. Parents may have to change their working hours if that is possible, or even consider bringing their son or daughter to work on occasion if that can be arranged. If a career demands long hours away from home, either the mother or father may choose to take a leave of absence from work until the child is over his or her crisis.

We should try to talk to our child about the trouble, even if that means forcing the issue and going up against our child's resistance. Lovingly, but with perseverance, we have to let our child know that we care about him or her.

We should also be in touch with other people who have contact with our child—friends, teachers, close relatives— to see if they confirm our perceptions and can support our efforts to intervene. Many parents seek out professional help, too, in the form of counselors, therapists, or psychiatrists who can provide individual therapy for their child. Sometimes therapy groups are effective as an adjunct to or instead of individual therapy.

Another way to approach the problem is to think about what in our environment could be contributing to our child's trouble and to try to change that. This may mean taking extreme measures. A family that lives in a community or sends its children to a school where drugs are prevalent and their use out of control may choose to move or change schools. Some parents decide that their child would do better living for a while with a relative or close family friend in another part of town or even in another city or state.

Counselors and psychologists have found that teenagers sometimes act out or get into trouble as a way to call attention to a family problem. If the parents are experiencing severe marital distress, that may be a source of a teenager's troubled behavior; or if a parent is seriously depressed or alcoholic, that may be a cause. In these cases, even if we are resistant to the idea, the whole family probably needs to get professional help in the form of family therapy. It's never easy to confront a problem that's been a family secret for a long time, but our child's welfare may make that necessary.

It's also possible that our teenager's depression or anger is related to some serious incompatibility with family norms. To break through we may have to say directly or through our actions, "It's okay if you're gay." "It's okay if academics are not your strong point." "It's okay if you have a handicap." "It's okay if you're in love with someone who's not the person we would choose for you." In other words, we may have to give up our expectations of who we want our child to be and learn to accept him or her for who he or she is. This can be so difficult that in many families the parents' inability to do so has caused permanent rifts between them and their children. We are likely to need help and support in the form of professional counseling as well as from friends and relatives to replace our goals and dreams for our child with a more realistic understanding of what our child wants for him- or herself.

None of this will be easy. And even if we try everything we can think of we may find that our children are still taking drugs or getting into trouble in school or hurting themselves. There are limits on what we can do, and limits on the time and energy we can expend. Though most of us feel we are never going to give up on our child, we may at some point reach a time of "cooling it" for a while, of sitting tight to see whether "this too may pass":

> Jeanie spent most of her high school years depressed, overweight, angry at me. We spent all our time trying to help. Then when she was seventeen, I just decided, that's enough. This is it. My husband and I have got to spend more time with the other kids. She's just going to have to manage on her own. Whether we could do this because Jeanie was getting better or whether doing it helped her get better, I don't know. I couldn't tell you to this day.

How do we live with it? How do we ourselves survive and at the same time help our kids with heavy emotional problems like these? We have all sorts of reactions: our children make us angry; we are scared that they will get hurt; we feel guilty:

> When my son got into trouble with the police, I was scared and worried but I also felt, for the first time in my life, like I was a welfare client. I'm usually competent and efficient and happy, and here I was in a situation I could not take care of.

> When Beth was heavily into drugs, I lay in bed thinking to myself, "What kind of mother am I? I really hate this child. She's always making trouble for us."

> A lot of my son's problem was my fault. I used to be too wishy-washy with him. I was trying to make up for his father after our divorce.

Treat Yourself Well

The worst thing a parent can do is to react to a child's trouble by going crazy ourselves. This kind of reaction is very hard on ourselves but it also really keeps us from helping our teenagers. This is one of those statements that sound like it's easier said than done: these problems disrupt our lives as almost nothing else ever does. Understand that and try to be good to yourself. If you can get away, even for part of a day, take a little trip, jog, play tennis, go to the movies. Cover yourself at home but give yourself a little space to take a breath, a little distance from which to see the problem afresh.

If you have any way of doing it, spend a little money to make family life easier. Try to get a little household help, buy a treat for the children or for yourself, cut back on your working hours, hire people, even for an hour or two, to do chores. Get a massage. Join a gym.

You need to get help for your child but you also must get help for yourself. Here are some kinds of support systems that have worked for other people:

Parent Support Groups

Many parents have found it extremely helpful simply to be in a group of other adults who are going through the same troubles they are. Not only do you then realize that it's not solely your problem—or your fault—but also you see how other people are dealing with the situation.

These groups take several different forms. They can arise informally out of a school or neighborhood situation. They can be formal organizations like Families Anonymous, Alanon or Tough Love. They can have a professional group leader, a leader from among the parents, or they can be leaderless. Such groups exist within most communities and you should make contact with the one that seems most compatible to your own situation and your own ideas.

Help From Our Friends

Illness, death *and* these kinds of serious emotional problems with our children are the occasions for friends and families to support each other. It is all too easy to let our feelings of pride or shame keep us from getting the help we need from those who are closest to us.

Our own parents can help us—and, often, at least in the end—will be glad you gave them the chance:

When Peggy had to go to the hospital for intensive psychiatric therapy, we had no money left. I finally had to call my parents in California and they gave us the money. Since then they've been really supportive.

Friends can be helpful not only in aiding *us* to cope, they can often act as a friendly buffer between us and our troubled adolescents. Sharing these problems can be a way of cementing friendships not, as many of us fear, a divisive force:

When Esther got pregnant, her father was out of the picture. I called a friend of ours who's ten years younger than me and used to baby-sit for us. She came over and she was really wonderful. She was so good with my daughter because she was younger and had had a similar experience herself.

Perhaps the most important support we can get is from the other parent of the child. A very dramatic demonstration to the child that we are concerned and determined takes place when he or she sees both parents united in reaction as well as in support (even though they may not get along in other circumstances or not even live together or find it hard to communicate at all). Talk the situation over out of the child's presence. If possible, try to come up with a plan of action that you both feel comfortable with and that looks like it might be effective.

For divorced or separated parents, working together on anything can feel extremely threatening. It can reopen old wounds and reintroduce irreconcilable differences. We may not be able to overcome the anger and hurt we feel toward our ex-partner. But again, if we *can* find a way to come together in just this situation, it may make a difference for our child.

Sometimes the best help a parent can give is to stand back, to give up control and to let the other parent take over. Teenagers can focus on one parent as the source of their problems—whether they are right or wrong. Obviously, that parent is not the one who can help.

The important point here is that the "excluded" parent needs to understand that the other person may be, in the child's eye, more appropriate. Though it may be hard to back out, we may find that the best way to help is to do just that:

When Cindy was eleven or twelve we used to fight all the time. I'd say red, she'd say blue. She was failing in school and she seemed real unhappy. She decided she'd go live with her father in Arizona. It was the hardest thing I'd ever done, letting her go, but I can see now it was best for both of us.

Asking Your Child to Help You

Though some problems are so heavy they drive a wide wedge between teenagers and their parents, one of the best ways to heal ourselves as well as our family is to share the pain and confusion we are all feeling. Not every troubled teenager, and especially not those who are severely depressed, can handle this, but there is nothing that better illustrates our respect for our children than to tell them that we need their help:

Our daughter was only fourteen and she used to go up on Broadway and pick up men. The police would call, or some neighbor would see her, and we'd have to go and find her. You can imagine how scared and upset we were. One time she was in a car with a man and someone saw her. When I went and brought her home my wife was trembling and hysterical. I said to Ruthie, "Look, this can't go on anymore. What can we do about it? One more incident like this and—you can see for yourself—your mother's going to end up in an institution." And you know what? She just stopped. Never did that again. Maybe she was just looking for something to make her stop.

When John was drinking during those worst years, I felt like I was coming apart at the seams. I remember one day sitting down and telling him how scared I felt. I think that helped but, anyway, he isn't into that scene so heavily anymore.

Family Therapy

This is a psychological tool that works from the premise that if any one member of the family has a problem, the whole family should participate in finding a solution. You will be asked to go with the teenager while the problem is being diagnosed. Then, as the therapy proceeds, various family members will be asked to take part. This can be a healing place for you as well as your child when the system works well.

Group Therapy

Therapists of various schools of thought lead groups of clients in sessions designed to deal with emotional problems. For example, one group we saw consists of parents of teenagers who are food abusers. These parents meet regularly both to deal with their own as well as their children's problems. Other groups focus on women's issues, on assertiveness, on divorce and single parenting. Still others are more psychiatric in their approach and are based on Freudian, Jungian, Adlerian, Gestalt or other theories.

Individual Therapy

In order to get through your child's crisis and, perhaps, to work out your own problems, you may want to consider getting individual psychiatric or psychological help for yourself. The caution here is to try to make sure that the therapy you choose does, in fact, address and improve the problem at home. It may be that a combination of family and individual therapy is the most effective approach when a teenager's behavior affects us all.

LENI WILDFLOWER

BOOKS AND RESOURCES

Recommended Reading

Brenton, Myron. *How to Survive Your Child's Rebellious Teens*. New York: Bantam Books, Harper & Row, 1980.
Self-help program for parents, offering suggestions to give parents more insight into adolescent behavior.

Fine, Louis L. *"After All We've Done for Them": Understanding Adolescent Behavior*. Englewood Cliffs, N.J.: Prentice-Hall, 1977.
Written to help parents understand the characteristics of adolescent development so they will be able to respond appropriately to the needs of their teenage children.

Gardner, James E. *The Turbulent Teens*. San Diego, Calif.: Oak Tree Publications, Inc., 1982.
Well-written, practical guide for parents on teenage behavior.

Giffin, Mary, and Carol Felsenthal. *A Cry for Help*. Garden City, N.Y.: Doubleday & Company, Inc., 1983.
A guide for parents of adolescents exploring and exploding the myths about teenage suicide. Alerts parents to warning signals and describes appropriate intervention.

Hooper, Judith O. *Living with Your Teenager* (1979). Available from the University of Wisconsin, Extension, 1535 Observatory Dr., Madison, Wis. 53706.
This series of pamphlets presents practical, easy-to-read information on the emotional and physical development of adolescents. Titles include: "Understanding Physical Changes," "Understanding Emotional Changes," "Understanding Changes in Thinking," and "The Changing Parent-Child Relationship."

Lauton, Barry, and Arthur S. Freese. *The Healthy Adolescent: A Parent's Manual*. New York: Scribner, 1981.

A book written for parents that describes in detail what adolescence is all about and addresses issues concerned parents might have about their teenage child.

McCoy, Kathleen. *Coping with Teenage Depression: A Parent's Guide*. New York: New American Library, 1982.
Very good book for understanding the emotional health issues of teenagers. Excellent resource lists.

Pogrebin, Letty Cottin. *Growing Up Free: Raising Your Kids in the 80s*. New York: McGraw Hill, 1980 (hardcover); New York: Bantam Books, 1981 (paper).
Pogrebin, parent and feminist, advocates nonsexist child-rearing and provides guidance on how to do so.

Shanks, Ann Zane. *Busted Lives: Dialogues with Kids in Jail*. New York: Delacorte Press, 1982.
Takes a close look at the lives of juvenile offenders, in and out of jail. Useful bibliography and appendixes of national resources and agencies.

Thornburg, Hershel D. *The Bubblegum Years: Sticking with Kids from 9–13*. Tuscon, Ariz.: H-E-L-P Books, Inc., 1970.
Practical, easy-to-read book to help parents improve their understanding of nine- to thirteen-year-olds.

York, Phyliss, and David York and Ted Wachtel. *Toughlove*. Garden City, N.Y.: Doubleday, 1982.
Presents an approach to child-rearing and discipline during the teenage years. Considered *conservative* on this subject.

For Teenagers

Blume, Judy. *It's Not the End of the World*. New York: Bantam Books, Bradbury Press, 1973.
A twelve-year-old girl copes with the fact that her parents are going to get a divorce. Believable, but not depressing.

Childress, Alice. *Rainbow Jordan*. New York: Avon, 1982.
Beautifully written story about a black teenage girl being raised by her aunt.

Eagan, Andrea Boroff. *Why Am I So Miserable If These Are the Best Years of My Life?* New York: Avon Books, 1979. Spanish edition available from Lippincott and Crowell, 521 First Ave., New York, N.Y. 10017.
A readable guide for teenage girls presenting factual information and dealing with various psychological concerns of adolescence.

Gilbert, Sara. *How to Live With a Single Parent*. New York: Morrow, 1982.
Very good for younger adolescents.

Green, Hannah. *I Never Promised You a Rose Garden*. New York: New American Library, 1977.
Classic novel of a psychotic teenage girl's struggle toward sanity.

Guy, David. *Football Dreams*. New York: Seaview, 1980.
Deals with a teenage boy's need to succeed as a high school football player—mostly to prove himself to his father.

Hinton, S. E. *The Outsiders*. New York: Dell, 1980
Popular teenage story about three orphan boys raising each other in a small Southern town.

Hunter, Evan. *Me and Mr. Stenner*. New York: Dell, 1978.
First-person narrative by an eleven-year-old girl who's parents are getting divorced and who's mother is remarrying immediately.

Klein, Norma. *Mom, the Wolf Man & Me*. New York: Avon, 1977.
Popular novel about a teenage girl's reactions to her mother's romance.

McCoy, Kathy. *The Teenage Survival Guide*. New York: Simon and Schuster, 1981.
Helpful in answering lots of questions about problems in everyday life—everything from dealing with siblings and parents to coping with school.

Petersen, P. J. *Would You Settle for Improbable?* New York: Delacorte, 1981.
Story about a ninth-grade boy's adjustment to public school after being released from juvenile hall.

Richards, Arlene. *How to Get It Together When Your Parents Are Coming Apart*. New York: Bantam, 1977.
Guide to help adolescents deal with their parents' marital problems and divorce.

Rofes, Eric, ed. *Kids' Book of Divorce: By, For and About Kids*. New York: Random House, 1982.
Addresses divorce specifically from a child's point of view.

Simon, Nissa. *Don't Worry, You're Normal: A Teenager's Guide to Self-Health*. New York: Crowell Junior Books, 1982.
Helpful for young people dealing with a broad range of emotional and physical changes during adolescence.

Books dealing with suicide and death (for teenagers)

Arrick, Fran. *Tunnel Vision*. New York: Holt, 1980.
Story about how family and friends attempt to come to grips with the suicide of a fifteen-year-old boy.

Krementz, Jill. *How It Feels When a Parent Dies*. New York: Knopf, 1981.
Teenagers talk about the continuation of their lives after losing a parent.

Suicide Prevention:

HOTLINE: most areas have suicide prevention hotlines. Look in the telephone book under Suicide or Samaritans or call Information (411).

Booklet for parents:
"Suicide in Young People" by Nancy H. Allen, M.P.H. and Michael L. Peck, Ph.D.
Write to: Merck Sharp & Dohme
West Point, Penna. 19486

For information and/or help: Look in the white pages of the telephone book for local Suicide Prevention Centers. Or contact one of the organizations below:

Samaritans
802 Boylston St.
Boston, Mass. 02199
(617) 247-0220 (24-hour hotline)

Suicide Prevention Center
1041 So. Menlo Ave.
Los Angeles, Calif. 90006
(213) 381-5111 (24-hour crisis counseling)
Also has Bereavement Group for those who have lost a loved one to suicide.

Runaways:

HOTLINE: Most hotlines are set up for the runaway, not for the parents of the runaway.

If your child is missing, call your local police department or call
Child Find
(914) 255-1848
New Paltz, N.Y.

Child Abuse:

HOTLINE: 1 (800) 352-0386 (toll free)

Parents Anonymous—self help
22330 Hawthorne Blvd., Suite 208
Torrance, Calif. 90506
1 (800) 421-0353—outside California
1 (800) 352-0386—California

Parents United (Child Sexual Abuse)
P.O. Box 952
San Jose, Calif. 95108
(408) 280-5055

National Center for Prevention of Child Abuse and Neglect
Denver, Col.
(303) 321-3963

National Committee for Prevention of Child Abuse and Neglect
Chicago, Ill.
(312) 565-1100

Sexual Assault and Abuse:

Recommended Reading:

Booher, Dianna Daniels. *Rape: What Would You Do If. . . ?* New York: Messner, 1981.
Gives guidelines on how to judge a potential rape situation and what to do if a rape should occur.

Griffin, Susan. *The Power of Consciousness.* New York: Harper and Row, 1979.
Excellent overview of rape including cultural and social attitudes.

Grossman, Rochel, and Joan Sutherland. Edited for Los Angeles Commission on Assaults Against Women and L.A. Section of National Council of Jewish Women. *Surviving Sexual Assault.* New York, Congdon and Weed, 1983.
Excellent resource for people who have been sexually assaulted, their families and friends.

Miklowitz, Gloria D. *Did You Hear What Happened to Andrea?* New York: Delacorte, 1979.
Fiction for teenagers. Story of a teenage girl who is raped and how she and her family react.

Rush, Florence. *The Best Kept Secret.* Englewood Cliffs, N.J.: Prentice Hall, 1980.
Written for adults about child sexual abuse. Excellent.

Tegner, B., and A. McGrath. *Self Defense and Assault Prevention for Girls and Women.* Ventura, Calif.: Thor Publishing, 1977.
A practical guide including photos.

Tschart, Linda Sanford. *The Silent Children.* New York: Doubleday, 1980.
Another excellent book on child sexual abuse.

Several good booklets are available:

"Top Secret: Sexual Assault Information for Teenagers Only" ($4.00; bulk rates available)

"He Told Me Not to Tell"
For parents of younger children to help them discuss sexual assault with their children ($2.00; bulk rates available).

Both of the above are produced by and available through:
King County Rape Relief
305 So. 43rd
Renton, Wash. 98055

"Taking Action: What to Do If You Are Raped" (free)
Write to:
Rape Treatment Center
Santa Monica Hospital Medical Center
1225 Fifteenth St.
Santa Monica, Calif. 90404
(213) 451-1511

Resources:

Rape HOTLINE: Most communities have 24-hour crisis numbers to call in case of rape or sexual abuse. Look in the white pages of the telephone book under Rape or Rape Crisis Center. Or call your local hospital.
Information about local services is available through
National Center for the Prevention and Control of Rape
National Institute of Mental Health
Room 15-99 Parklawn Building
5600 Fishers Lane
Rockville, Md. 20857
(301) 443-1910

For victims of incest, through
VOICE, Inc. (Victims of Incest Concerned Efforts)
P.O. Box 3724
Grand Junction, Colo. 81502
(303) 243-3552

VI

SEXUALITY

During these years it's very likely that our adolescents will be experimenting with sex and most of them will have some form of sexual activity with another person—anything from kissing, to making out, to petting, to intercourse. That's the way it's always been to varying degrees in individual teenagers. However, when we were kids there were strict sanctions against premarital intercourse, especially for girls, and for many of us as a result, sexual activity went only "so far."

Now society's attitude toward premarital sex has changed considerably and the timetable for experimentation has accelerted. It's not unusual these days to hear about fourteen- and fifteen-year-olds having intercourse. According to the best research data available, 65 percent of all boys and 55 percent of all girls have sexual intercourse before they turn eighteen.

For us as parents this brings up the issue of how to help our kids make wise decisions about sex, how to encourage them to wait before becoming too sexually active. Those of us with strong religious sanctions against sex outside marriage have a very concrete statement to make: it's wrong and goes against our religious precepts. However, lots of people don't have such definite beliefs. Before the days of readily available birth control, pregnancy was a good enough reason for most people to stop before things went too far, but what are the reasons now?

At one parent's home we had a discussion of just that question, and a father of three said:

"When you really think about it, outside of pregnancy, why is it so wrong for teenagers to have intercourse?" And the mother sitting next to him said, "Because we weren't allowed, that's why."

There may be a little jealousy involved, but there's much more than that. It's simply hard to accept that our children are doing things we thought were wrong or dangerous when we were their age. From our adult perspective we understand that intercourse can be an emotionally charged activity. Casual or premature sexual involvement is risky—emotional scars, unhappy commitments, sexually transmitted diseases or pregnancy can result. We know how much energy goes into making a relationship work; we know how hurtful a broken love affair can be. Most of us think our teenagers and certainly our preteens are too young to be able to or to have to handle those things.

Yet adolescents aren't getting enough support in our society for being cautious about sex. They hear very few messages from the media or from their friends that say it's okay to take your time.

Sexual development brings a complicated mix of strong emotions and physical longings. Our kids respond to those feelings in a variety of ways. Most adolescents masturbate—not as children touch themselves unconsciously, but with conscious attention to the pleasure masturbation can bring. They have all kinds of romantic fantasies—from the mundane to the melodramatic—and some that may seem bizarre and scary to them. They may imagine themselves in wild sexual situations or with partners of the same sex or with older people like teachers, relatives, even us. They might have fantasies about sexual violence. All of this is absolutely normal, but they don't know that. Lots of adolescents fear that they may be abnormal or perverted for having such drives and ideas.

Adolescents and preadolescents are extremely interested in bodies—their own, ours, their friends—and can become very shy about body development and sexual parts and/or overly eager to catch glimpses of whatever they can. *Playboy* magazine may no longer suffice as our teenagers surreptitiously seek out hard-core pornography, both for its pictures and for its descriptions of what people do and how they do it. They wonder uneasily if, when the time comes, they'll be able to perform in the required mode or whether they'll make fools of themselves by not knowing what to do.

Competence is an important issue for adolescents and sexual competence is a vital concern. Will I know how to kiss? What do I do when a boy or girl wants to touch me? How am I going to know what I'm supposed to know—what everybody else seems to know? Many of these questions occur to our children way before situations arise in which they would be relevant. It's a kind of preparation, an initiation ritual that all of us have gone through and probably a part of what makes adolescent sexuality so exciting and passionate. It's unknown territory about which they fantasize and dream—so much so that just holding hands with the person you like can be thrilling.

AMERICAN STOCK PHOTOS

Love is intense during adolescence and lovesickness is authentic. It can be quite serious, causing moodiness, changes in behavior, appetite swings and depression. Our children may fall deeply in love, completely unself-consciously, with people who don't even know they exist much less return their attention. Movie stars, singers, TV personalities, teachers, are all potential love objects, and although this may seem ridiculous to us, it's real to many teenagers. We met one bright eighth grader who was carrying on a correspondence with a rock and roll singer, and she was absolutely convinced that as soon as she met this man, he would fall as in love with her as she was with him. It was no joke. She meant to save her money to go meet him in New York.

Many adolescents feel strong emotions toward people of their own sex. Infrequently this is a precursor to future homosexuality; more often it is a natural expression of the passion of adolescence, which calls forth deep feelings of attraction whenever affection is felt. Yet these feelings of love toward same-sex friends may startle our kids and fill them with apprehension about their sexuality. (Needless to say, it is likely to have the same effect on us.)

Adolescent sexuality is powerful precisely because it creates feelings of pleasure and pain not experienced before. It forces our kids to confront a variety of pressures that come out of their new sexual consciousness: friends teasing about how your body looks or how sexually experienced you are; dirty jokes and locker room talk and the need to be part of them; media images of the ideal man and woman.

The media, in particular, has profound influence. Our teenagers see young models their own age acting sexy and selling sexy clothes; they see adolescent sex promoted in the movies and on television. They are put on the defensive, feeling that they are inadequate if they don't fit the image.

Other pressures haunt them as well. Their own unfamiliarity with sex is worrisome—what's okay to do? What isn't? Will they know when they're nearing the edge of their own limits? They may have fears about getting pregnant or getting their girl pregnant. Or perhaps they worry about picking up a sexually transmitted disease. How do you catch a disease anyway? Rape and sexual violence are discussed openly on television and in the newspapers, revealing to our children the dark underside of sexuality, placing sex in a context broader than as part of a loving relationship.

Our adolescents have internalized many "shoulds" about sex they learned from us, from their religious training, from school, from their friends. They find themselves having to sort through these beliefs to discover what makes sense to them and what doesn't. Their values give shape to their developing sexuality, but sometimes what they experience negates or calls into question those previously untested ideals.

Going against or even feeling like you might want to go against parental teaching or religious tenets is frightening. It can leave an adolescent feeling alone and guilty. Yet sexual drives and feelings can be powerful enough to make our kids break the rules. They experience guilt about masturbating or about loving people of the same sex or of a different religion or color. Many adolescents feel guilty about sexuality in general, worrying that there's something wrong with them for having feelings they can't control.

Sometimes, to cover their confusion about these matters, they put on an air of indifference, superiority or cool sophistication. At other times they revert to more childish behavior, wanting us to comfort them and take care of them as we used to. They may still sleep with the light on or with their arm around a favorite stuffed animal, but at the same time they are becoming aware of a grown-up side of themselves, not experienced before.

OUR ROLE

Few of us feel completely open and honest about our own sexuality. Yet, in order to help our kids, a certain level of openness and honesty is required. In the end, our willingness to be direct and even allow our children to see us as vulnerable in this area will do more to help them feel comfortable about their sexual feelings and experiences than any "expert" position on the subject:

Have you ever watched TV with your kids? It's amazing how much sex there is. It seems like every other program has people jumping into bed together. So I said to my fourteen-year-old the other day when we were watching some trashy show, ''Well I know sex is something on everybody's mind, but don't you think this is going a little too far?'' And he laughed. But then he said, ''Do you really think sex is on everybody's mind?'' And I said, ''Yeah, I think everybody thinks about sex at least sometimes.'' And we went on to have this really neat conversation about him thinking he was strange for thinking about sex so much.

I went with Jason to see *An Officer and a Gentleman* and there was a very explicit sex scene in it which made me very uncomfortable—especially sitting next to my fifteen-year-old son. So I reached over and whispered to him, ''This is making me embarrassed,'' and he patted me on the shoulder and said, ''Yeah. Me too.'' I felt good about that because it cleared the air and let each of us know that the other knew what was going on.

Our honesty and availability are critical, but so is providing accurate information—facts about sex, pregnancy, birth control, sexually transmitted disease . . . Adolescents need information about sexual responsibility and relationships. They want definitions for the words they've heard—like sixty-nine, Trojans, blue balls. Those things may feel too intimate and embarrassing for some of us to talk about, especially with our children:

When my boys were little sex was a cinch. They wanted to know where babies came from; I told them where babies came from. They wanted to know why some people had penises and others had vaginas; I told them without blinking an eye. But now that they're teenagers I freeze whenever the subject comes up because it's so awkward now. I feel like a woman sharing the intimate details of her life with two young men when we talk about sex now.

There's something funny—incestuous really—in parents talking to their teenagers about sex. You can't help but feel weird. It's so intrusive.

But that in itself can feel like a heavy load. A recent survey found that only about 12 percent of all parents have ever discussed basic sexuality with their children. It is our feeling from talking to parents and from looking at this issue in our own lives that, finally, none of us can be anything more than who we are with this subject. We can try to be available, we can try to communicate openly, but we can't be any wiser than we are. We can't be any more relaxed about sex than we are. We can't be any more certain about what's right and wrong or more comfortable talking about it than we are.

Yet we don't have to become experts in the field to be able to give them the facts they need. Our teenagers don't expect or want us to be an encyclopedia of sexual knowledge or a sex guide for them. Books can help us with the necessary information. The only thing we have to do is to make sure the information they need is available to them.

The truth is, regardless of what we say or choose not to say, we wind up communicating our values about sex to our children. It's part of the furniture. By being in our home they know a lot about how we feel about touching, about privacy, about nudity, about relationships, about open expressions of love. From the way we talk, from jokes that are made, from our silences on the subject, they know many of our attitudes about sex. Our task during their adolescence is to acknowledge those attitudes openly in order to provide clarity and substance to what may only have been implicit up till now:

Sex is not a recreation as far as I'm concerned. It's an expression of love—of a mature kind of love—and my kids know that's how I feel.

You know, whenever I have the opportunity I try to say something about my attitudes about sex, like that the boy is responsible, too, in sex and that sex is to be enjoyed by both people in the relationship.

I don't want my son to be one of those ''love 'em and leave 'em'' kinds of men so I try to let him know that the relationship is an important part of lovemaking.

I hope my children won't be afraid of sex the way I was. I want them to be able to experience it joyfully without guilt so I try to reinforce their positive feelings whenever I can.

It's reassuring to realize that we don't have to try to be something we're not when it comes to communicating with our adolescents about sex. That same point is reassuring to them too. They want to know that they're okay, that they're normal. By letting them know that everyone has questions, feelings and concerns about sex and that all of us feel uncertain about our sexuality, we can relieve a lot of their anxiety. High self-esteem is the most crucial component in responsible sexual behavior. For that reason our teenagers need strong emotional support for their sexual development.

WHY IT'S HARD TO TALK TO OUR KIDS ABOUT SEX

Embarrassment aside, the most powerful deterrent to communicating about sex is our own confusion about it. It's an ambivalence that comes straight from our culture, which in spite of its preoccupation with sexiness remains deeply conflicted about sexual morality. In the face of our children's developing sexuality all our own mixed feelings come to the surface.

It's almost impossible not to project those feelings onto them. Our adolescents sometimes make us feel competitive, jealous, impotent, angry, frustrated, pleased and even turned on—and that last one can make us all the more confused. So, although we may want our children to feel good and comfortable with their sexuality, we would probably feel a lot safer if our teenagers kept sex out of our lives and theirs—at least until they were older:

When my daughter was sixteen she announced to us that she'd finally met *the guy*. From the very moment she told us about him I developed an instinctive dislike for the kid and by the time he showed up at our house for the first time, I was ready to jump down his throat. I just knew he was out for one thing only and I had all sorts of fantasies about throwing him out of the house. In fact, he seemed like a nice enough kid, but when they left together I worked myself into a frenzy. I kept having these images of wild, passionate lovemaking in the back seat of his car. And when my daughter came home early with this crushed look on her face that told me things hadn't gone the way she'd hoped they would, I felt enormously relieved, like jumping for joy. Instead, I commiserated and played the understanding father. I still feel pretty shitty about the whole incident.

Many of us also have a purely pragmatic hesitation: we fear that talking to our adolescents about sex will in effect put pressure on them or give them license to be more sexually adventurous than they might be if we left the subject alone:

I think there's a fine line between giving your kids the information they need and pushing them into sex. I mean if you say something to your kids when they're thirteen or fourteen, isn't that like saying, "Well, I know you're going to be doing this, so here's what you need to know." Like giving your approval.

My daughter knows the facts of life and I would hope that if she were sexually active she would use birth control. But I haven't said anything like that to her because the situation hasn't arisen and I don't want to imply that at age sixteen I think she should be considering a sexual relationship. I think she's too young.

Communicating about sex *does* provide more space for children to make choices, but it *doesn't* promote sexual activity. On the contrary, we know from having interviewed hundreds of teenagers across the country and from having reviewed the recent studies* that adolescents who feel they can discuss sex with their parents are generally the most careful about their sexual activity. They get support from their parents to wait before getting involved in sexual relations; when they do become sexually active, they know about birth control and VD protection.

Conversely, teenagers who feel they can't discuss sex with their parents without being lectured or grounded are more likely to sneak sex anyway and less likely to seek their parents' help if problems arise:

I was having sex with my boyfriend from the time I was fourteen and my parents would never have found out except I got pregnant. The clinic sent the bill for my abortion to my house and my mom found it.

It's confusing to try to decide how much to say to our kids and when to say it? Does a twelve-year-old need specific facts about birth control? Should we tell our fifteen-year-old

about premature ejaculation or mutual satisfaction? Unfortunately there are no simple answers. We're on our own to assess our own situation based on the maturity and sexual development of our child. The only constant is our availability, the growing need to let our kids know that we are there for them as a resource and an ally.

If it were only our own resistance to talking about sex that were the problem, we could work on getting over it. However, even if we do muster enough determination to try to discuss it with our teenagers, *their* reluctance may hold us back. They're usually running out the door or engrossed in a heavy conversation on the phone just when we decide it's time to talk. And if and when we finally do connect with them, they're likely to appear preoccupied, bored, embarrassed or disdainful:

I've only tried talking about sex with my kids four or five times and I've failed four or five times because they'll take one look at me and say, "Oh Mom, you've got that look on your face again."

Rebecca will mention something about sex and I'll start in explaining and she'll say, "Daddy, give me a break."

Our son works in a teen clinic and even was on national TV discussing teenage sexuality. The commentator asked the kids how many had parents who never talked to them about sex. Well everybody's hand went up, including Tim's. I was sitting there with him watching the show and I said, "Damn it Tim. Every time I ever said anything to you about sex you'd say, 'Oh Mom that's gross,' and you'd walk away." He wouldn't listen, and then he tells the whole country that his parents never talked to him about sex.

We can't let their attitude put us off. Even though our kids may seem disinterested or embarrassed on the surface, they all do have questions and concerns about sex. They're coming face to face with a lot of the same myths and misinformation we heard in our youth, and they need to know that girls *can* get pregnant: the first time they have sex; or if they have sex during their period; or if they do it standing up. They need reassurance that masturbating won't make them blind or impotent and that sexual fantasies don't mean they're perverted.

Here's a sampling of questions asked by middle-class ninth graders in a course on human sexuality:

- Will I know how to have sex the right way?
- How far can you go with a guy without losing your virginity?
- What is masturbation and is it okay?
- When a person has oral sex, do they get hair in their mouth?
- Can a girl get pregnant from swallowing sperm?
- Can you have an orgasm without having intercourse?
- Does intercourse feel good for women?
- Can you tell if someone is still a virgin?
- What is a hand job?

*Kantor & Zelnick, etc.

It's easy to see how little most adolescents know about sex—and how important it is to help them get information.

HOW TO OPEN UP COMMUNICATION ABOUT SEX

As we've said before, more than anything else we have to be as reassuring as we can:

I knew my son was masturbating because I'd seen him doing it a few months ago. I wanted to talk to him about it because I didn't want him to feel guilty. A couple of days ago, we were sitting together talking about massage, I think, and I said, "You know it took me a long time to realize that there's nothing wrong with satisfying yourself, even sexually." And Andy said, "Yeah, I know what you mean." That was it. All I really cared about was him knowing that I knew and that it was okay. I made it real short, but I think he was reassured.

I was talking to my daughter and her friends about how when I was younger we would spend long hours necking on the front porch and I think they really appreciated hearing that I liked sex, too, when I was their age.

Although it works pretty well for some people, the sit-down-and-have-a-talk-with-them format seems intimidating to a lot of parents and adolescents. Most of us have stories from our own adolescence about our parents' attempts to do that with us:

My husband tells everyone about when he was fifteen his mom said, "Lou, it's time for us to have a talk." So she sat him down and said, "Now I know you know about the facts of life, and I know you know what not to do. So don't do it."

From the time I turned eleven my dad kept hinting that pretty soon we'd have to have a talk. I'm thirty-eight now and I'm still waiting.

Many parents have discovered that one way to open up the conversation is to use what's around. We're literally surrounded by opportunities to discuss sex with our kids. Billboards showing half-clad men and women selling products; teenagers modeling sexy jeans on TV; people necking in the street; vivid love scenes in the movies; advertisements for products to make us look sexier and more attractive; magazine and newspaper articles about sexual violence and exploitation; television programs; books; poetry; art; all these can be used to inspire conversation with our children about sex:

I just couldn't have one of those sit-down sessions about sex with my kids. It was too embarrassing for both of us, but when we go to the movies I always manage to say something like, "I wonder why they didn't use birth control?" Or, "They never show how awkward you can feel when you go out with someone for the first time." Little messages here and there. Sometimes they lead into a discussion, sometimes they don't. We play it by ear.

Driving through the red-light section of our town got us started on a long conversation about prostitution and sexual exploitation.

My daughter and her friends were talking about "General Hospital" and how Luke raped Laura and then she fell in love with him. They were romanticizing it so much that I just had to put my two cents in about how rape is violence, never love. We ended up talking for an hour about it.

We can, and probably should, start talking about whatever is easiest for us to talk about. Many parents say that for them a good opening is a discussion of the superficial and self-destructive role models pushed at us through the media—how women continue to be portrayed as sex objects and men as "macho" types who always have it all together. Lots of us have spent years with feelings of inadequacy created in part by that media "hype." The chances are that our children are also contending with a sense of not being pretty enough or macho enough or thin enough or sexy enough because they are absorbing the same messages. By simply mentioning to them how shallow and destructive the media image is, we help our adolescents develop a much needed perspective:

I was watching TV with the boys the other night and I couldn't help saying, "You know it's funny how nobody ever has to burp or go to the bathroom in a TV love scene." Everybody laughed, but I think they got the point.

My daughter's always comparing herself to TV stars and complaining, so I'm always saying to her, "You're not fat, you're not ugly—you're gorgeous." And then she says, "Well you're supposed to say that, you're my mother." But if I didn't tell her, what would she think then?

Some parents find that talking to their kids about their own adolescent experiences and feelings is both easy and enjoyable. When something reminds us of our past, it can be very appropriate to share that with our kids:

I told my son how I think kids these days miss so much by rushing into intercourse. We used to have passionate make-out sessions that lasted for hours because we knew that intercourse was a no-no.

My daughter asked me how old I was when I first had intercourse and I told her I was twenty, which I was. She was shocked that I'd been so "old."

I told my daughter that she should be grateful because when I was her age my parents started shoving articles about unwed pregnant girls under my bedroom door. There'd be at least one a week and I remember thinking, Okay, I get it already.

As we've already said, books about sexuality and physiology are useful to have around too. When your kids have questions to which you don't have answers you can look up the answers together, or if that isn't workable, at least the books are around for your kids to find:

I bought my seventh grader this book on sex and I thought he was going to die of embarrassment on the spot. He wouldn't touch it. So I left it on the living room table and one day, about three or four weeks later, I noticed the book was gone. Sure enough, when I was straightening up his room I found the book next to his bed.

My kids didn't want a sit-down facts of life talk. Suzanne wanted books, so she got books, and Lois wasn't even interested in books because I'm sure she's read her sister's. I don't feel shut out. I think they know they can come to us if they have to.

When my fourteen-year-old finally went off to summer camp I invaded his room to try to do some cleaning up and there was our copy of *Human Sexuality* under his bed.

A number of parents we talked with said that they try to set aside special time to be with each child individually, and that's when important subjects get discussed:

Once a month I take each of my teenagers to dinner. Just the two of us and they pick the restaurant so they're operating on their best level. It's neutral territory and we both feel freer talking about stuff. That's when all our heavy sex conversations have happened.

We started taking family walks after dinner—basically to walk the dogs, but they became as important to us as to the dogs. Sometimes when Bill is out of town on business, just Richie and I go. And we've talked about everything on those walks.

And even a formal discussion about sex can work very well when it's set up without too much fanfare:

I said to my twelve-year-old, ''You know, I think we'd better talk about some of the things you'll need to know about sex. You may not need them right away, but you will someday.'' Then we talked about pregnancy and birth control and VD. It was okay.

I remember my dad took me on a drive one day and said, ''I don't know if you're involved with anyone yet, but it's important to know about birth control and VD *before* you get involved.'' That felt good to me and I'm going to do the same thing with my son.

The traditional approach has always been mother-daughter and father-son talks, with single parent families having to improvise. Actually, it's to our teenager's advantage to be able to talk about sex with the parent or a family friend of the opposite sex too. A father said:

You don't want your kids to be afraid of talking about sex with their sex partners, so we can start them off on the right track by making it a point for fathers to talk to the girls and mothers to talk to their sons as well as the other way around.

Close family friends and relatives are a good resource, especially if they are between the two generations. Our adolescents may be more willing to confide in or listen to a person they like who's just a half-step older than they are:

My daughter and I are very close, and I told her that if the time comes when she needs birth control, she should come to me. But she said she wouldn't be able to. She would be too embarrassed; she wouldn't want me to know. We decided that if that happened she should go to my friend Jenny. Jenny's ten years younger than me and Susan feels very close to her. And Jenny promised that it would just be between the two of them and that's how Susie wanted it.

There are other suggestions too. Nearly everyone we spoke with agrees that it doesn't work to put your kids on the spot by asking them personal questions like: ''Did you have fun with Terry?'' or ''How was your date?'' Most teenagers clam up when the finger is pointing at them. Instead, parents suggest being indirect. Start off asking about their friends or something objective, like the movie they saw or what they ate at the restaurant. One thing leads to another and if they have something bothering them, it may eventually come out.

Another approach is to talk with their friends around. If they let you, stay around long enough to chat with them. Or if it feels right, you can introduce a subject yourself:

My sixteen-year-old and her two girlfriends were sitting in the kitchen while I was fixing dinner and I asked them if they'd seen the article in the paper about herpes. One of them had and she asked me if it was true that there was no cure for it. We had a long conversation about it and although my daughter didn't say much, at least she was there.

Adolescents sometimes feel comfortable enough or curious enough to start the conversation, and their comments or questions can be outrageously blunt:

We were driving to the market and the girls were in the back seat giggling and nudging each other, so I turned around and asked what was going on. At that, the twelve-year-old shouted out, ''Did it hurt?'' and I said, ''Did what hurt?'' and she said, ''You know, when you and Daddy did it, did it hurt?'' And that was the way we got into a discussion of intercourse—not exactly the way I'd had it planned in my head.

There's this one main street near us where a lot of teenage male prostitutes hang out. Well, we were driving there one day when John (who was twelve or thirteen at the time) asked, ''How can a guy do it with another guy?'' I gulped and started as matter-of-factly as I could about anal sex, and Johnny stopped me in the middle and said, ''Oh, you mean butt-fucking? I thought so.''

Last night we were watching a show on TV and a man said he was impotent, and my thirteen-year-old asked me what that meant. So I started off mildly—saying something about him not being able to have sex, but she kept looking at me funny, and I was so tired, so I finally just said, ''Lynnie, it means he can't get a hard-on.'' And she said, ''Oh, okay.''

Although teenagers want answers to their questions, they want even more to know that it's all right with us if they ask. So, while we may find ourselves stammering through an explanation or turning bright red with embarrassment, it's still better to try to respond than to get angry or ignore them.

As difficult as it may be to initiate, most of us find that once we open up communication about sex the process gets easier and easier over time. What initially felt hard and anxiety-ridden can become an arena of closeness and mutual trust. Furthermore, since sex is such an important issue in our teenagers' lives, if they can talk to us about that, they're likely to feel they can talk to us about other very personal subjects too.

RON FINE

READING THEIR SIGNS

For communication to work, though, it has to be a two-way process. We can become so preoccupied with what we want to say to our kids about sex that we miss some of the things they are communicating to us. Much of their communication is indirect, in a kind of code. They aren't sure how we're going to react to their sexuality, and they assume it will be with a good deal of ambivalence at best. So to protect themselves against our judgments and possible anger, they may send out trial balloons to test our response. They may tell us about their friend—who is pregnant or in love or doing something they think we won't like. How we react to their gossip gives them a clue as to how we'd respond if they themselves were in the subject under discussion:

Polly came in yesterday and said, "Angie told me she has oral sex with her boyfriend. Isn't that disgusting?" Now Angie is this sweet, Little Miss Perfect kind of kid, so you can imagine how surprised I was, but I didn't feel like touching that one with a ten-foot pole, so I just said, "I didn't know Angie had a boyfriend."

Instead of talking, they may leave evidence of their sexuality around, and what we do when we discover it indicates how approachable we are:

A father: When I was about twelve or thirteen, my mom found my stash of *Playboy*s and when I got home from school she let me know how disgusting "those dirty magazines" were and that she never wanted to find me reading anything like that again. Her reaction was pretty consistent with what I expected and I just figured I'd have to find a better hiding place.

Sixteen-year-old girl: My mom found some birth control in my purse and I was amazed that instead of yelling at me she told me I should have come to her to talk about having sex. She wanted to make sure I knew what I was doing, but I didn't go to her because I was sure she'd kill me.

If we're open to watching for clues, we'll realize that our teenagers are constantly letting us know about their involvement and interest in sex. From the changes in the way they dress and groom themselves as preteens and young teenagers, to the way they respond to sexual topics on TV or in the movies, to what they talk about with their friends, they're indirectly giving us messages about what's going on with them:

Nancy would never comb her hair because she was emulating her brother who I don't think has combed his hair in two years. Now suddenly she's in the seventh grade and every hair has to be in place. Until she gets ready for school in the morning we all have to hold our breath.

We heard our son telling our daughter, "There are nice girls and there are sluts. Don't be a slut."

My son and his friends, boys and girls, go out in groups instead of on one-to-one dates. I think that these days dates mean that you're expected to have sex and they don't want to get into that yet.

There was a friend over the other day who told a dirty joke to me while my fifteen-year-old was in the room and I was very embarrassed. I couldn't even look at Jimmy, but he was really comfortable with it. He was laughing away.

SETTING LIMITS

At some point it's almost inevitable that our adolescents will become involved in a sexual relationship, and whether or not they're ready for this experience, it may happen before *we're* ready for it. While we may not want to give them our approval for their behavior, our teenagers need to know that we aren't going to reject them for it either.

That's difficult. We walk in and see our thirteen-year-old sprawled out on the couch with some boy. Our fifteen-year-old comes home with "hickies" all over his neck. Our daughter, sixteen, is out every night and she gets phone calls from men we don't know but she won't tell us anything about them. We notice how close our son is to his best friend: they sleep on the floor together, wrestle and touch all the time. In these situations parents wonder what's going on. Should we do something? We know we don't want our children getting into situations that will be hard for them to handle, but we also can't help asking ourselves if we aren't making a mountain out of a molehill.

The initial discovery of our teenagers' sexual activity usually has the most jarring impact on us:

> We were at the beach the summer Joanie turned fifteen and one night I went to her room to say good night and she wasn't there. Well, I'd seen her during the day with this older guy from the Coast Guard so I went storming over to the station house and barged into the house and right into the bedroom and there she was making out in bed with this twenty-two-year-old guy. I pulled her away and screamed at the guy and at Joanie. She was crying. Everybody was embarrassed. But I sure as hell made my point.

> I walked in on my thirteen-year-old boy passionately kissing some girl I'd never met. In my bedroom in front of the TV. And when they heard me they moved apart from each other. But I was furious and I said to my son, "Young man, this is *my* bedroom! It's *not* a motel."

> It's not unusual for Paula, our sixteen-year-old, to come home after midnight and we sometimes fall asleep waiting for her to come in. But one morning we woke up and she wasn't in her bed. I was frantic. I went to the police. I called the hospitals. My wife drove around to her friends' houses. Then around eleven that morning Paula showed up and I totally broke down. I was enraged and crying, really beside myself. I couldn't stop screaming at her and shaking her. When I finally calmed down enough to listen to her story, it turned out she fell asleep at the apartment of this guy she'd been dating. So there was another crisis—not just that she didn't call to let us know she was okay, but that she was sleeping with some guy too.

To a large degree our response is colored by expectations of what kids their age "should" be doing. If they're acting in ways that feel familiar or seem appropriate to us, then we may not be too concerned. If, however, they're behaving very differently from what we expect or want, that's much harder to handle.

There's no prescription for what to do, of course. It can be tempting to try to curtail all their sexual activity on threat of punishment, but that usually doesn't work. Teenagers who are forbidden by their parents from any sexual contact or who have been allowed only the most restricted dating privileges often rebel completely. Many of them choose dishonesty and subterfuge to keep their parents from finding out that they're still having sexual relationships:

> My mother was much too strict with me. She tried to stop me from going out on dates and she never let me have my boyfriends over to the house. So I would just tell her I was going out with a girlfriend and then I'd meet a guy instead. Or we'd pick up some guys on the street and go to their houses. I didn't even really feel bad about it because I thought she was being unreasonable.

> My parents won't let me see my boyfriend because they think I'm too young—I'm thirteen—so we have to meet secretly. Like last week we met in the park near my school and went for a long walk and we made out. But I didn't realize that if you kissed for a lot your lips would turn red, so when I got home with grass stains on my pants and red lips I never lied so much in my life. I couldn't believe how fast I made up excuses.

Not wanting to put a total ban on sex, many parents feel stumped by the whole issue. How can we encourage restraint without setting the stage for deception?

> I'm really confused about what to tell my kids. I mean, if your kid knows what she or he's doing and they're taking care of themselves and not exploiting the other person, then it's not a simple "No, you can't do it." Why can't they do it? I don't have a good answer.

> Danny and two of his friends want to go away with their girlfriends for a weekend. One boy's parents will be in the cabin with them and everybody seems to think it's a fine idea. They expect me and Bill to say, "Why sure, go right ahead." But I don't know. Danny's only fifteen and that to me sounds like something grown-ups do. Not fifteen-year-olds.

Some basic rules are in order for young teenagers especially. Limits about where boyfriends and girlfriends are allowed to be and where they aren't; curfew times; expectations about being respectful and cognizant of the other members of the family—these standards are necessary and appropriate to keep order at home if nothing more:

> It makes me upset to be in the living room watching TV while Tony and his girlfriend are smooching in the next room. I finally had to say something to him because I was getting so tense. Now the rule is that when we're in the main part of the apartment, they can be there too, but no making out.

> My seventeen-year-old knows that as long as he lives here no girls spend the night. And he knows if he comes in too late the dogs are going to start barking and wake everybody up, so he can't be coming in at three or four in the morning. Once in a while if it's planned and we're expecting it. But not every weekend.

Along with "house" rules, though, many of us would like to set limits on the extent of our childrens' sexual experiences. This is a lot more difficult to do effectively.

Sexual experimentation is perfectly normal during adolescence and always has been. What worries many of us is that ideas about sex have changed. The time between a first kiss and intercourse seems to have diminished radically for many adolescents, taking only hours or weeks rather than the years of dating, making out, petting . . . which were normal in our youth. For that reason some of us become concerned at even the first sign of sexual interest.

It helps to remember that teenagers themselves are fearful about sex: it's new to them; they wonder what is expected of them; they are concerned about pregnancy, VD, broken hearts and bad reputations too. Our voice urging them to slow down can be helpful to them, offering them some reasonable guidelines for their sexual behavior. Yet in order to be meaningful our message has to be realistic and geared to an understanding of who our child is. A thirteen-year-old girl told us:

> If only my parents were just a little more trusting of me. Like if they said, ''Just don't have intercourse. You can make out; we know that's normal.'' I don't want them to think I'm a slut just because I kiss a boy for more than two seconds.

> I told my daughter that in my experience intercourse changes a relationship. It intensifies it. I also told her she may not feel very good about herself if she does it too casually.

Most of us still have a double standard in matters of sex. We tend to be far more careful about setting limits with our girls than we do with our boys. Obviously there are reasons for that. Girls do bear the major burden of pregnancy, childbirth, child-rearing and even reputation. But both boys and girls can catch sexually transmitted diseases and both boys and girls can suffer the emotional scarring of painful relationships.

There's so much pressure on boys to ''get as much as they can as fast as they can.'' We must emphasize to our sons that sex for the sake of scoring is not okay with us, that boys have a responsibility to care for and protect a partner (by using, for example, birth control), that sex is best when it occurs in a trusting, intimate relationship, that having had intercourse doesn't make a man out of him:

> My oldest is sixteen and he has his first girlfriend and he's been getting a lot of pressure from his friends to have intercourse. My husband's sister, who's not all that much older than Bill, actually came right out and told him that he was certainly old enough to have done it by now. So one night a couple of months ago he came in to me and told me about it and asked what did I think. I just knew he really wanted me to say that he should wait until he and his girlfriend felt they wanted to have intercourse. I told him that in sex it's always better to wait if you're not sure. And he really seemed relieved to hear that.

A number of teenagers use their sexuality to act out in self-destructive ways or in ways that hurt others. Excessive flirting and seductive behavior with us or our friends; promiscuity; repeated pregnancies or infections with sexually transmitted diseases; rape; soliciting sexual favors from strangers; continually and openly disobeying our rules about sexual activity. Any of these conditions indicate a need for our increased involvement in their lives in order to help them change their behavior. We discuss this issue more thoroughly in the chapter ''Emotional Health Care'' on p. 54.

As parents we'd like to be *sure* that our teenagers won't hurt themselves or get into trouble through their sexual activity. To that end we set curfews or regulate their dating habits or tell them we don't want them going to certain parties. Our hope is that by so doing we'll limit the potential for problems. But their retort to our rules and limits almost invariably is: ''What's the matter, don't you trust me?''

The answer can only be that no matter how much we trust them, we know that everyone makes mistakes. It's important for us to share our concerns with our teenagers and to give them all the information they need. But, from there on, especially with older teenagers, it's up to them:

> I confronted my seventeen-year-old the other day about her relationship with her boyfriend. And she said, ''Look, Daddy, what is it you're really worried about? If I'm going to do something there's really no way you can stop me. But you have to realize that I don't want to get pregnant. I don't want to get raped or mugged. I'm more worried about that than you. After all, it's *me*. What do you think I am, stupid?'' That was an enormous relief to me and I had to sit down and really think, ''What were my objections to her having sex?'' It was the opening of a terrific conversation that brought us a lot closer together.

> My daughter had an abortion when she was fifteen. It was a tremendous shock and very traumatic for her and me both. So you can imagine how angry I was to find this boy's phone number showing up on our bill a few months later. I asked her if she'd been calling him and she said she was lonely. She asked me what I'd do if she saw him again. I said, ''Listen. I dislike that kid intensely. I don't have to like him and I don't have to see him in my house. But if you want to see him there's no way I can stop you. That's your decision.''

The reality is that if our teenagers want to have a sexual relationship with someone, they'll find a way to do it. We can only hope they'll be careful and that our communication with them is such that they'll feel free to come to us if they need to.

Some teenagers want their parents to know that they are having sex. They may not exactly be asking for our approval; they'd just prefer not being underhanded about something so important. In a funny way, although some of us find it embarrassing, their choice to tell us may be a real compliment, a statement that they feel close to us and open to our opinion:

> I got a phone call from my eldest daughter who was seventeen at the time, and she said, ''Howie and I have decided to sleep together. Is it okay if I bring him home?'' My feeling was, well, if you're going to have a committed relationship with someone and you're going to have sex, I'd rather have it happen in a secure, nice place than in the back of some car or some seedy motel. So that's what I told her, not without trepidation. I felt good that she'd called, even if I wasn't delighted that it was happening.

> My son hung around for a long time after dinner the other night. Basically he wanted to talk about what was going

on with his girlfriend. That they were getting very close and that maybe they'd have intercourse. He wanted to know what I thought about it. Did birth control always work? What would he do if she got pregnant? It was wonderful talk. He sounded so mature, but at the same time so frightened.

When our daughter was fifteen she came to us and said, ''I think by the time I'm sixteen I'd like to get birth control. I don't have anybody in mind, but I feel like by then I might be ready to have sex and I want to give you guys time to get used to the idea.'' How can I say this? We were shocked, of course, but at the same time we really respected her openness and responsibility.

However, no matter what their reasons for telling us about their sexual activity, no matter how open the communication is between us, it's not appropriate for parents to become overly involved in their teenagers' sex lives. For example, some parents rearrange their homes and their schedules to accommodate a child's boyfriend or girlfriend. That's not our role. Similarly, it's not our place to promote their sexual activity:

> We had a whole summer of my seventeen-year-old wanting to go camping with her boyfriend and my husband saying, ''No, I won't give you my permission to go.'' It was a real scene and it was going on and on for weeks so I said to him, ''Well you know how much time she spends over at Eric's apartment anyway.'' And Mel said, ''Fine. But I'm not going to encourage a more intense relationship by giving them my consent to go away together.''

> I happened to be in the store the other day and I remembered Heidi said that she needed more Ortho—and I don't mean the bug spray—and I was about to pick some up for her but I stopped myself. That's their private business. There's a difference between a mother buying Tampax for her daughters and buying them birth control.

> When my son came home from his freshman year at col-

lege he brought his girlfriend with him and I just couldn't allow them to sleep together in the same room. In a way I knew it was stupid because they probably live together up there, but I still couldn't do it.

The rest of this chapter covers four specific areas of sexuality about which teenagers need information: birth control, pregnancy, homosexuality and sexually transmitted disease. We hope you will be able to use these summaries as a basis for your own discussion with your son or daughter about sex. (See Books and Resources for other books on the subject.)

Birth Control

When I was growing up my parents never told me about birth control. I just knew that if I had intercourse I'd probably get pregnant, and as far as I was concerned, that was a fate worse than death. So I didn't have intercourse. Period.

Twenty-five years ago birth control wasn't a big issue for parents because the pill was experimental and most other forms weren't available to teenagers. Condoms could be purchased, so fathers would warn their sons to ''be careful'' and that was pretty much the extent of it. Abortions, of course, were out of the question, since even if they could be obtained, the hazards of illegal abortions were well known. Consequently, parents could tell their adolescents, with justification, that since intercourse would undoubtedly lead to pregnancy, the best advice was to avoid intercourse.

Now birth control is very easy to obtain. Most teenagers know it exists even if they don't know the details of how it works or where you can get it. And abortion, compared to a generation ago, is safe and available. Those facts, along with other social changes, have altered sexual mores. As we have pointed out, recent studies report that over two-thirds of all boys and one-half of all girls have had sexual intercourse by the time they are eighteen.

The statistics also show, however, that over 1.2 million teenage girls get pregnant every year. These are girls from every sort of family. Why? To be sure, some simply don't know about contraception. Yet, most don't use it even though they do know about it. In place of birth control, millions of teenagers substitute massive denial of the fact that they can get pregnant from having unprotected intercourse. One fifteen-year-old told us:

> My friend got pregnant three times and when I asked her why she didn't use birth control she said, ''Because I didn't think I'd get pregnant.''

Adolescents also say they don't use birth control because it's embarrassing to get, difficult and embarrassing to use, and it takes a certain amount of forethought—something teenagers, especially teenage girls, feel shy about. Unconsciously they reason that if they get ''carried away'' with passion that's one thing, but if they actually plan to have intercourse and prove it by being prepared with birth control, that's something else again. So the overwhelming majority of teens do not use contraception, at least the first few times they have sex. Many of them get pregnant as a result.

As parents we're caught in a double bind. We may not want our kids having sex, but even more, most of us don't want them getting pregnant or getting someone else pregnant. We're ambivalent. If we believe in using contraception, we want our kids to know about it and to be prepared to use it, even the first time they have intercourse; at the same time, we don't want to appear to be promoting their sexual activity by informing them of the details of birth control.

The truth is that information about birth control does not increase the likelihood that our children will have sex.* On the contrary. Clear knowledge about the consequences of unprotected intercourse tends to encourage teenagers to delay having sex until they feel able to deal with the complexities of contraception or possible pregnancy. This is particularly true if birth control information is delivered in the context of our values. We can make it clear to our teenagers that we want them to be informed and that we have feelings about when and under what circumstances sexual activity should be initiated:

I talked to my daughters about what they want for their lives. Like what are their plans for the future and how would a baby fit into those plans. I told them about contraception, but I also let them know that no contraceptive works 100 percent of the time.

I want my kids to think of sex as part of a loving relationship, not as something you do like shaking hands. Just because you can keep from getting pregnant doesn't mean you should have sex anytime it strikes your fancy.

The subject of birth control isn't necessarily easy for us to talk about. It can be embarrassing because it's so personal. Particularly when we have grown up with moral or religious sanctions against birth control, we may feel guilty or hypocritical discussing it with our children. Nonetheless, it is important to make the effort to communicate. And it's all right to let our children know that we feel confused or ambivalent or guilty about the subject. Chances are that our kids share some of those feelings too, and our ability to articulate how we feel will help our children do the same. Even parents who are totally opposed to contraception on moral or religious grounds need to share that opposition with their kids by explaining *why* they feel the way they do. Knowing where we stand makes it easier for our adolescents to make conscious and intelligent decisions for themselves.

There's no way we can talk about everything, but most of the parents we interviewed agreed that these are some of the most significant points to consider:

*Kantor & Zelnick study.

—Teenagers need to be told that pregnancy is not an accident. Many teenagers who are experimenting with sex approach the possibility armed only with wishful thinking and denial. They see pregnancy as an accident that happens only sometimes: if they're lucky, they think, it won't happen to them.

In fact, four out of five teenagers who have intercourse without protection will eventually start a pregnancy. Many teens get pregnant the very first time they have sex. And in our interviews we met two girls who got pregnant before they even had their first period (see p. 39). Pregnancy is not an accident; it's exactly what's supposed to happen when people have unprotected intercourse.

—Our input encourages our kids to be responsible. The interviewing we have done strongly suggests that adolescents who have discussed birth control with their parents are the ones most likely to use it when the time comes. By talking with them about contraception we give our kids both accurate information, which they need, and also a sense that we care about them and want them to protect themselves.

—Most teenagers believe, correctly or not, that we're opposed to them having sexual intercourse and would be very angry if we found out. It's probably a rationalization, but that fact actually discourages them from using contraceptives. They fear that we'll discover their pill packets or foam containers or condoms or diaphragms, so they don't use those methods for protection.

Regardless of what we feel about our children having sex, we can help them understand that if they don't feel strong enough to take responsibility for their actions by getting and using birth control, if they feel unsure and guilty about what they're doing, then they're probably not ready to have intercourse. People who have sex have to be ready to prevent pregnancy or be ready to have a baby.

At this point virtually all clinics that provide birth control to teenagers do so without requiring parental consent. Groups are lobbying to have that changed, but as of now teenagers who are motivated to get birth control should have no trouble getting it. It is often available to them free or at minimal cost.

—The teenagers who are most likely to use birth control are the ones who have a strong enough sense of self to be able to take on that responsibility. They are the ones who feel there are things they want to do and experiences they want to have *before* having a baby. Their own sense of direction and personal goals become their motivation for using birth control.

As parents we have a responsibility to try to help our teenagers feel good about themselves and to prepare our girls as well as our boys for jobs and careers. Even teenagers whose specific goal is marriage and child-rearing can understand the importance of postponing pregnancy until they are ready for it.

Teenagers who are uncertain and confused about their future altogether are the least likely to use birth control. Consciously or not, these kids may feel that a baby would provide fulfillment and love and represent a kind of success, something that may have been missing from their lives up until then.

—Most of us are more careful to discuss birth control with our daughters than with our sons because biologically and socially teenage girls still bear the major burden of an unplanned pregnancy:

> My son used to bring girlfriends home to his room and we became pretty convinced that there was sex going on. We let it go on for a while before we said anything. But I think if my daughter had been bringing boys home my first words to her would have been, ''Do you know about birth control and are you using it?'' I did eventually ask Jonathan the same thing, but not with quite the same fear and trembling.

Social sanctions against female assertiveness and female sexuality are changing, but many teenage girls still feel extremely timid about introducing the subject of contraception with a boy. They also feel embarrassed being prepared with birth control themselves, since that means they've been thinking about sex. It's very important that we speak to our boys about sharing the responsibility for contraception, either by supporting the girl in her decision to use protection or by using condoms himself.

—Saying no is a perfectly legitimate method of birth control. It's one way people have always dealt with the issue.

Some adolescents think saying no will be taken as a sign that they're scared of sex or a tease or that they're immature. Many of them are embarrassed to say no. We want to let them know that it's fine to stop at any point during sex if you don't want to or aren't ready to go further.

Facts About Birth Control: Birth control (contraception) is anything that interferes with the process of conception. Obviously there are many methods that fit into that category, but only some are consistently effective in preventing pregnancy. Also, when we talk about effectiveness with teenagers, it doesn't make sense to discuss ideal effectiveness. What matters is whether they will use the method and use it properly. If they don't, it won't be effective no matter what the books say.

The five methods of contraception most commonly used by teenagers that *are* effective in preventing pregnancy are: condoms, foam, diaphragm with spermicide, the pill, and the IUD. We recommend the combination of condoms and foam for teenagers who have intercourse only occasionally, since they are relatively cheap, easy to use, safe, and tempo-

rary. We don't recommend the IUD for teenage girls—or any woman who may want to get pregnant someday—because it has been associated with promoting pelvic infection, which can cause permanent sterility.

Condoms: Latex or animal membrane sheaths, which are worn by the boy to cover his penis during intercourse.

Condoms fit over the erect penis and keep sperm from reaching the vagina during intercourse; they also protect against the transfer of gonorrhea. Teenagers can buy condoms without prescription at drugstores, in some markets, and from wall dispensers in some public toilets. Family planning clinics and public health facilities also distribute condoms, free or at minimal cost.

Other names for condoms are rubbers, prophylactics, safes, protection, sheaths, shields. They come in one size that fits everyone.

Condoms must be placed over the erect penis *before* intercourse and a new condom has to be used for each successive act. When used alone, condoms are about 85 percent to 90 percent effective as protection against pregnancy. When used together with contraceptive foam they are 98 percent effective.

Condoms cost anywhere from $.45–$1.50 apiece.

They can be bought in packages of three or boxes of twelve.

> Condoms, especially when used together with foam, are an excellent method of birth control for teenagers. They are highly effective, have no serious side effects or health hazards, and also protect against the spread of gonorrhea. Teenagers can buy them without adult consent and without a doctor's prescription. Best of all, they only have to be used during intercourse. To be successful they have to be used *every* time you have intercourse. Most so-called failures are due to lack of use.

Foam: Aerated, spermicidal cream that coats the cervix to block and kill sperm.

Foam comes in both pressurized containers or individual applicators. Teenagers can buy it in drugstores, markets, or family planning facilities. Instructions come with the foam. An applicator must be used with the pressurized container. The girl fills the applicator with foam and inserts it into her vagina no more than half an hour before intercourse. She shouldn't dance or walk around too much after inserting the foam, since it can leak away from the cervix and leave her vulnerable to impregnation.

When used alone foam is only about 80 percent effective. When two applications are used together it is more effective, but when foam and condoms are used together they are 98 percent effective against conception.

On occasion someone will have an allergic reaction to a

particular brand of foam. This can cause a rash or a burning sensation especially during urination. Using another brand usually eliminates the problem.

Foam costs approximately $3–$5 for a large container and $3–$5 for a box of six individually wrapped applications.

Diaphragm and Spermicidal Jelly or Cream: A flexible rubber disc that holds contraceptive jelly or cream against the cervix.

Most sperm are blocked by the diaphragm and the ones that aren't are killed by the spermicide.

A diaphragm has to be fitted, so for teenagers this means a gynecological checkup, including an internal examination. For many girls this will be their first internal exam.* The health practitioner will demonstrate how to use the diaphragm and will teach your teenager how to insert it herself. That's important because it takes a certain amount of practice to be able to do it properly.

To use, the diaphragm is coated with about a tablespoon of cream or jelly and inserted into the vagina to cover the cervix. This must be done no more than two hours before intercourse. (New evidence suggests that insertion up to six hours before may be acceptable.)

Spermicidal jelly and cream can be bought at drug stores and some markets. It costs anywhere from $6 to $10, depending on the store, for a large size tube with enough for about twenty applications.

The diaphragm is 98 percent effective against conception when used properly and every time a couple has intercourse. It is safe, free from health hazards, and relatively easy to use. The diaphragm itself lasts about two years and should be checked for cracks or holes before use.

To use the diaphragm properly requires a certain amount of planning and discipline. Teenagers have to be willing to interrupt lovemaking, if necessary, to insert the diaphragm. After intercourse the diaphragm has to be left in place for at least eight hours.

The Sponge: This is a new product, so long-range statistics on its effectiveness are not yet available. However, it has recently been approved for marketing by the FDA and will be sold as an over-the-counter, nonprescription contraceptive by the time this book goes to press. The sponge is said to be as effective as the diaphragm if used properly, although tests have indicated its effectiveness to be lower, between 75 and 85 percent effective.

Each sponge contains a spermicidal agent, so no extra spermicide need be applied. It can be inserted (like a tampon) up to twenty-four hours before intercourse. In order to work properly, the sponge must be dampened before insertion.

*See Bell, Ruth, et al. *Changing Bodies, Changing Lives*. New York: Random House, 1980, pp. 156–7, for a description of an internal examination.

At this writing, the sponge is projected to cost approximately $1. A new sponge is needed after the initial twenty-four hour use.

The Birth Control Pill: The pill contains synthetic female hormones that inhibit the development and release of eggs. A girl on the pill doesn't ovulate, so she can't conceive.

Birth control pills have to be prescribed by a doctor and require a full gynecological checkup. The health practitioner will take a complete medical history from each girl, since there are health conditions that prohibit pill use. Some of these are: blood clotting disorders, heart trouble, liver trouble, migraine headaches, varicose veins, heavy smoking, and pregnancy. Once prescribed, the pill can be bought at pharmacies or family planning clinics or women's health centers. Each packet contains enough pills for one month's use. A girl takes one pill every day at approximately the same time, since each pill has a twenty-four-hour potency. No hormones are taken for seven days each month during which time a menstrual-like bleeding occurs. It is 99 percent effective protection against pregnancy.

Although millions of women use the pill successfully for contraception, it has serious drawbacks. It can cause heart disease, strokes, vitamin deficiencies, blood clotting disorders, depression, weight gain, headaches, and permanently impaired ovulation. The longer it's used, the more serious the potential complications. Some effects are cumulative.

> No one should use the pill without first reading about it more thoroughly in one or more of the books mentioned in the bibliography.

The IUD: *We do not recommend the IUD for teenagers.* The intrauterine device (IUD) is a small, plastic implement that sits in the uterus.

No one knows for certain how the IUD works but the most widely accepted theory is that it causes a continual, low-grade irritation in the lining of the uterus, which keeps it from building up properly. Without a thick healthy lining the products of conception can't implant and the pregnancy can't proceed normally.

Some IUD's contain copper; some contain synthetic progesterone. IUD's with copper are thought to be less easy to expel than the others, especially in women who haven't had babies.

A girl needs a complete gynecological checkup with an internal exam before an IUD can be inserted. The insertion itself is done by the doctor. It can hurt since the cervix has to be dilated before the IUD can be put in place. Once inserted the IUD can stay for two or three years before having to be replaced.

When the girl wants to stop using the IUD, she has it removed by a doctor. Removal usually doesn't hurt.

IUD's can be expelled spontaneously. They can also migrate from the uterus to another part of the abdominal cavity, which, although very rare, is extremely serious and requires surgery to locate and remove it.

A string attached to the IUD dangles through the cervical opening so placement can be checked. If the string feels longer, the IUD may be coming out. If the string feels short, it may have embedded itself in the uterus. If the string is gone, the IUD either fell out or worked its way into the abdomen.

The health practitioner should be called right away in these cases. Women who feel uncomfortable touching their vaginas shouldn't use the IUD because they may not want to feel for the string to check placement.

The IUD is 98 percent effective protection against pregnancy.

Some dangers associated with IUD use are perforation of the uterus, embedding of the IUD in the uterine wall, ectopic pregnancy, heavy menstrual bleeding, heavy cramping, more frequent, longer lasting periods.

Most serious is the increased danger of widespread pelvic infection due to IUD use. Germs from the vagina (gonorrhea, for example) travel up the IUD string and enter the uterus, creating infections that are often not discovered until they have done permanent damage—in many cases indirectly causing scar tissue to block the fallopian tubes. This is a major cause of sterility in women, and the reason we don't recommend the IUD for anyone who hopes to bear children eventually.

> Don't use the IUD until you have read more about it in one or more of the books listed in the Books and Resources.

Natural Family Planning—The Mucus-Temperature Method: This is a method of detecting fertile days so intercourse can be avoided then.

Each day the girl takes her temperature reading on a special basal body thermometer and checks the mucus inside her vagina. With proper training she can learn to interpret vaginal secretions as indications of fertility.

This is a sophisticated method that requires commitment and discipline. It's recommended only for responsible teenagers who are willing to do the required reading and take the required course. Training classes are available in most cities (see Resources, p. 91) and there are several books that describe the method in detail.

When used accurately, this method is 100 percent effective against pregnancy, since it lets you know exactly when you're about to ovulate and you can abstain from intercourse then.

Some very popular, widely used methods of birth control

are *not* effective. We list them here because teenagers should be warned against relying on them as contraception.

Withdrawal: The boy withdraws his penis before ejaculating.

Most teenagers who use any method of birth control use withdrawal because they don't have to think about it beforehand. It's spontaneous. The problem is that you can't control sperm; it can leak out of the penis at any time during intercourse and usually some does even before ejaculation. Only one sperm is needed to start a pregnancy if the girl is fertile. Also, teenage boys aren't always in control of their climax, so miscalculation is a real risk.

Withdrawal is better than nothing, but it's only about 70 percent effective.

Douching: The girl washes out her vagina after intercourse.

Douching doesn't work. Sperm can reach the uterus in seconds, and the force of the douching solution can help push the sperm up.

Contraceptive Suppositories: Tablets of spermicide that liquify inside the vagina to coat the cervix and block sperm.

These can be bought in drugstores and markets. They have to be inserted at least and no more than ten to fifteen minutes before intercourse to give the foaming action a chance to work. The suppository doesn't always cover the cervix adequately so it provides only partial protection. Suppositories are better than nothing, but they are not as effective as foam or a diaphragm with spermicide.

Rhythm—The Calendar Method: Based on the fact that a girl is only fertile during part of the month.

The teenager charts her periods on a calendar for several months and tries to see a pattern. Ovulation occurs two weeks before menstruation, so if she has regular periods, she can pretty much judge when she'll be ovulating. If she avoids intercourse for about eight days around ovulation, she probably won't get pregnant.

The major flaw in the calendar method is that almost no one is always regular. Sickness, anxiety, travel, and more can interrupt the cycle and cause ovulation to come on sooner or be delayed. Teenagers in particular are likely to have irregular cycles, so it's impossible to know exactly when two weeks before your period is. *It's a very unreliable method.* (See Natural Family Planning for a more effective rhythm-type method.)

Pregnancy

Literally millions of American teenagers are having sexual intercourse without using any contraception. Whatever we think of premarital sex, the fact remains that each year over two million of those adolescent boys and girls start unplanned pregnancies. Teenage mothers face severe financial and emotional stress. Teenage marriages generally end after only a few years, and children of teenage parents statistically develop more physical and emotional problems than other children.* The real tragedy is that while our society does little to support teenagers who are unlucky enough to get pregnant, it makes it hard for adolescents to get the information and protection they need to keep themselves from becoming pregnant in the first place.

EARLY SIGNS OF PREGNANCY

Some girls have many of these symptoms, others have few or none.

A missed or unusually light period
Enlarged, sore breasts
Sleepiness
Nausea and/or vomiting
Changes in appetite
Lethargy
Irritability

An unplanned pregnancy is undeniably serious even for adults or married couples, but for teenagers it can be devastating: their choices are so much more stark. It is much, much harder to handle the physical, emotional, psychological, and financial burdens of parenthood at that age.

Something *has* to be done, because even not doing anything is a choice to have a baby. When you're fifteen and suddenly faced with the prospect of having to make a decision about such a monumental event in your life, it can be overwhelming. Almost every teenage girl who finds herself pregnant feels terrified, alone, and vulnerable. Some girls feel desperate enough to attempt suicide or go to foolish and dangerous extremes to cause a spontaneous abortion:

A mother: My friend's daughter threw herself down a flight of stairs because she was so scared about being pregnant. She almost killed herself.

A sixteen-year-old: When I was pregnant I kept banging into the sharp corner of my desk over and over. I lost the baby, but I also wrecked my insides.

A fourteen-year-old: I jumped off a bus to give myself a miscarriage.

For us as parents, no matter how many times we've gone over the scenario in our nightmares, there's no way to anticipate its emotional impact. After the initial shock, many parents are flooded with rage:

The first thing that came to me when Sharon told me she was pregnant was this incredible anger at Bob. How could he have done this to her, to my baby. I was so furious I couldn't look at him or hear his name.

*McGee, Elizabeth. *Too Little, Too Late: Services for Teenage Parents.* Ford Foundation, 1982.

Jenny told me she was pregnant and the floor dropped out. I felt myself filling with rage at her for being so stupid, so irresponsible. She knew about birth control—I told her about it myself. I couldn't believe she could have let this happen to her.

If, before the pregnancy, we didn't know they were having sex, we may feel foolish for not having noticed any signs, but even more, we may feel betrayed by them for having abused our trust. Then too, we may feel very afraid for our daughter, knowing the physical and psychological trauma she's facing. If we have strong moral or religious feelings against premarital sex, we may not be able to feel anything but revulsion at the thought of our child's act.

Parents of girls feel the effects of the pregnancy most severely, of course, but parents of boys are affected too, to the extent that the boy is involved. Once your son learns about the pregnancy it is likely he will also be required to make some serious decisions—about marriage, child support, abortion, adoption—and he will be experiencing his own share of remorse and regret whatever happens.

Everyone concerned will need time to sort through the mixed emotions they feel before being able to decide how best to proceed. Time is short, though. If your child wants a choice about how to deal with the pregnancy, she must act quickly because a simple abortion can be performed no later than twelve weeks *after her last menstrual period.* (If your daughter has completely irregular periods, she will have to be examined by a gynecologist, who can determine the approximate length of gestation. However, twelve weeks is still the limit for a simple abortion.) Unfortunately, teenage girls can be so frightened by the thought of pregnancy that they'll deny it even to themselves until it's too late for abortion to be possible.

For us, too, denial can interfere with our ability to see what's going on:

When my daughter finally came to me and told me she thought she was pregnant I thought to myself, "You stupid ass. You're so aware of these things and here your own daughter is pregnant right under your nose and you didn't see it."

I felt totally dumb when I realized that my daughter was probably pregnant. I'd thought she had the flu, and I let those symptoms go on for weeks without realizing that this flu was hanging on much too long. The thought had passed through my mind that something wasn't right, but I ignored it. Until one morning I was getting ready for work and it was like horror struck me. I felt like throwing up.

What Can We Do?   In spite of all our feelings and reservations, it is critical that we come through for our children at this time. Above all, they need our support. And there are concrete ways to help them:

—Encourage your daughter or your son's girlfriend to have a pregnancy test if she hasn't already. As soon as there's a suspicion of pregnancy a urine or blood test should be performed before anything else:

> My daughter had been throwing up for about a week, so one morning I went into her room and said, "I want to ask you something. If I'm way off base, don't be insulted, but do you think you could be pregnant?" She looked down and started crying and I just felt sick inside. She was only fourteen, I stayed home from work that day and took her to our doctor for a pregnancy test. I hated to think of her having to go alone.

FACTS ABOUT PREGNANCY

Early and thorough prenatal care is necessary, especially for teenagers, who are more likely to have premature babies than older women.

Any drug, alcohol, nicotine, or caffeine the girl ingests during her pregnancy will cross the placenta and affect the fetus.

Prenatal vitamins are recommended for teenagers.

Childbirth classes are available for teenagers in most communities. Check with your hospital or clinic.

A blood test can be accurate ten days after conception; a urine test gives accurate results about two weeks after the first missed period. The first urine of the morning should be used for the test. These tests are offered at labs, clinics, and doctor's offices. The results are available within hours. Home pregnancy test kits are also available, but they're not as accurate. Even a test at the doctor's office can give a false negative reading, so if your teenager's symptoms persist, another test should be taken.

—Help them make a decision. A decision has to be made about what to do, and this is when we can be the most supportive. There are several choices available. Your teenager can elect to have an abortion; she can have the baby and put it up for adoption or foster care; she can have the baby and raise it either by herself or with support from the father. It's important for us to go over these choices with our children because they are likely to be so scared and so confused that they won't be thinking clearly:

> When her test results came back positive, Mary and I discussed what she wanted to do. It was very, very difficult because we're very active in our church and we have strong religious beliefs. And although I've never condemned abortion, I certainly don't think of it casually and neither does she. I know I wanted her to have the abortion and not be burdened with a child at her age (fifteen). I wanted her to, yet I wanted to let her know I would be sup-

portive of her no matter what decision she made . . . I was glad when she finally decided to have the abortion.

Our teenagers need a realistic description about what parenthood involves. Many young people have a romanticized view of parenthood and child-rearing. They imagine the soft, cuddly baby smiling at them from the crib and overlook the sleepless nights, dirty diapers, endless hours of supervision and general emotional, physical and financial drain of having a baby. As much as we can, we should let them know what it's like being a parent—the joys *and* the hardships.

—Be clear about what you can and can't do for them in this crisis. Many young teenagers assume that we will take over their child-rearing responsibilities for them. It's important for us to be direct with them about what's possible for us, because how much we are willing and able to support our children—financially and with our time and energy—can influence their decision:

> At first Toni said she wanted to have an abortion and then two days before it was going to happen she changed her mind. I thought I was going to kill myself because I couldn't imagine her having a baby at age sixteen and I knew I couldn't help much, working full-time and all. It would have been horrendous. So I had a long talk with her and she also talked to my friend's boss, who's a counselor, and finally she changed her mind back again.

> For our daughter adoption was never a possibility and we wouldn't even consider abortion. She wanted to keep the baby and we couldn't have stood it if she had chosen to give the baby away. I don't see how people can go through that. We told her we'd help her out in whatever way we could. She and the baby are living with us and so far it's worked out pretty well.

> We're helping our son and daughter-in-law financially as much as we can. They're so young and they still have to finish high school. We help them pay their rent and I baby-sit for Laura while they're at school.

—Abortion. If we're not personally opposed to abortion, we should discuss it as an option. Many adolescents have heard stories about throwing live fetuses in garbage cans or other such horrors and they have no understanding of what a simple abortion is. (See box: Facts About Abortion.) We can let them know that at three months the fetus is only about three inches long and couldn't possibly survive outside the mother. Also, it helps them deal with their own ambivalences about abortion if we discuss our feelings with them— the pros and the cons:

> My daughter has always taken a very definite stand against abortion; she thinks it's murder and people who have abortions are murderers. So when she first realized she was pregnant she completely broke down, since she knew she couldn't have the baby and she also knew she wouldn't be able to give it up for adoption. There was just

no other alternative but abortion, and she needed a lot of love and support from me and her dad to feel okay about herself afterward.

An early abortion is easier, safer, less physically traumatic, and in many instances less emotionally stressful than having a baby. However, many girls experience mild to severe psychological strain after having an abortion. Some become depressed or angry with themselves for having done it. We can help by giving them the opportunity to talk about their feelings whenever they want to. If they don't talk, we can watch for signs of unhappiness. (For a full discussion of teenage abortion, see *Changing Bodies, Changing Lives,* pp. 189–206.)

Bonnie had a real bad time about two months after her abortion. She made it through the whole thing, but then went into a deep depression where she was staying in her room almost all the time and she was putting on weight. I was worried about her, I even thought she might need a shrink or something, but just my spending time with her talking about her feelings pulled her out of it.

—Adoption. In some ways adoption is the forgotten alternative these days, since the social sanctions against unwed motherhood have weakened. If your daughter is opposed to abortion and if it is unrealistic for her to consider raising the baby herself, adoption is a viable choice. You can help her find the appropriate agencies to handle the necessary details (see Facts About Adoption, p. 80). Adoption is an alternative that can be chosen at any point, but it's much better for both the mother and the baby if adoption is decided on before the baby's birth. Newborns are more likely to be adopted than are older children, and the mother has less time to become attached to the baby.

A girl who gives her baby up for adoption is also likely to have varying degrees of regret and sadness. These emotions need to be talked about openly, within the family if that's feasible, but at least with a trained counselor or family friend. Talking to other girls who gave babies up can be helpful.

—Birth Control. It's important for us to discuss birth control with our teenagers as a way to keep an unwanted pregnancy from happening again. Although many teens who go through a pregnancy or a pregnancy scare think they'll never have sex again, it's unrealistic to count on that. Instead, they need a thorough understanding of contraception and encouragement to find a type of birth control that will work for them:

After the abortion the counselors talked to Ginny about birth control, but she said she didn't want any because she said, "I'll never do that again." But when we got home I talked to her about how you can think you'll never do something again, but then it happens anyway. I said, "I hope in the future you'll come to me so I can help you get what you need for protection."

FACTS ABOUT ABORTION

—Abortion is legal, although there are some medical restrictions.

—In many states a teenage girl does not need parental consent for a first trimester or other simple abortion.

—Having a medical abortion does not, except in rare instances with serious complications, interfere with a girl's ability to get pregnant or deliver a baby in the future.

—No one can force a girl to have an abortion against her will. Only she can sign the consent form allowing an abortion to be performed.

Types of Abortion:
An early abortion is a relatively uncomplicated procedure that takes only a few minutes and can be performed at a clinic, doctor's office, or hospital. It can be done with no anesthesia at all, or a choice of local or general anesthesia.

Vacuum Suction (Vacuum Aspiration): This is the easiest and the least traumatic physically and psychologically. It's done within the first twelve weeks since the last menstrual period (LMP). The cervix is dilated and a suction tube is introduced into the uterus. Gentle suction is created to remove the products of conception from the uterus.

Dilatation of the cervix can be painful, so some girls choose local or general anesthesia.

Dilatation and Curettage Abortion: This procedure can be performed between twelve and fourteen weeks LMP. The cervix is dilated and the doctor uses a curette (sharp instrument) to scrape out the fetal tissue and excess lining of the uterus. This method involves slightly more risk than the suction abortion, since scraping can in rare instances injure the uterus. It can be done in a clinic, doctor's office or hospital.

Dilatation and Evacuation Abortion: This newer form of abortion combines the suction and the D and C methods. It can be performed between twelve and eighteen weeks of pregnancy LMP.

Induced Abortion: This type of abortion is used if a woman is over sixteen weeks pregnant. It is a medically induced delivery, involving a hospital stay, a period of labor, and a regular delivery. We do not recommend it for teenagers except in emergency situations, if the mother's life is at stake.

—Sometimes what we want them to do about the pregnancy is not what our teenagers want to do. Even if we're opposed to abortion, they may decide that's the best choice for them; or if we don't want them to get married, they may decide that's the only alternative they can live with. In most states, teenage girls don't need parental consent for an abortion within the first three months of pregnancy, and many girls do have abortions without telling their parents. On the other hand, children under eighteen are generally not allowed to marry without parental consent, so we will have to reach some agreement with our kids about that.

This can be an agonizing time, since the stake—our children's future—is so high, but in the end it's their decision because it's their life. Even if we try to force them to make the decision we think is right for them, we probably won't succeed and, in so doing, may create a permanent rift between us.

The best thing we can do is help our teenagers see the alternatives clearly and give them the strength and confidence to make a decision that works well for them. Naturally, how we respond to that decision will play a critical role in their ability to live with the choice they've made. By supporting them, we help them to go on with their lives.

FACTS ABOUT FOSTER CARE

Foster care is meant to be a temporary arrangement. It is *not* a baby-sitting service. The child is placed in a foster home until one or both parents can care for it.

The biological parents are responsible for visiting the child regularly and helping out financially if possible.

Foster homes can be arranged through the state Department of Child Welfare or one of the agencies listed under Adoption.

Both parents, whether married or not, must consent to the foster care arrangements, unless one parent is unfit or cannot be found. If the parents disagree, a judge will decide what's best for the child.

Private foster care arrangements can be made informally through family or friends.

If the conditions of placement are not met by the biological parents, the child can legally be taken from the parent for permanent placement.

On the face of it, foster care appeals to many teenagers because they think it's a way to have their child cared for while they're still finishing school or starting a career. However, foster care is very hard on the child. A child needs to form bonds with his or her parents and can suffer severe psychological damage from being placed temporarily. Some children are put in two or three or more homes before their parents take them or before they are permanently adopted.

FACTS ABOUT ADOPTION

A legal adoption must be arranged through a government-authorized adoption agency or private lawyer or state judge. The final approval for adoption is always by a state judge.

Some of the agencies that can arrange adoptions are:
   United Community Services
   Catholic Charities
   The Federation of Protestant Welfare Agencies
   The United Federation of Jewish Philanthropies
   The Department (or Bureau) of Child Welfare in
      each state
   Authorized adoption agencies

No one can make a girl give her baby up for adoption unless the court decides that she is an unfit parent.

Legal adoption means that the birth parents legally give over to another party their rights to their child.

Both biological parents must consent to the adoption even if they are not married. Only when the father or mother is legally declared unfit or cannot be located does he or she lose that right.

If the biological parents disagree about adoption, the court will decide what to do in the child's best interests.

Homosexuality

Note: Gay parents who read this section may not experience the same negative feelings about a child's homosexuality as "straight" parents. We are writing this with "straight" parents in mind, since this issue may be harder for them to deal with.

For many of us, the discovery that our child is gay is one of the most complicated and difficult experiences of our life. It's nearly impossible not to feel pain and disappointment, as well as, perhaps, embarrassment, fear, guilt, sadness, or, in some cases, even disgust about it. There are a variety of reasons for these strong emotions—some based on our fears about homosexuality; some based on the myths and misconceptions we and our society have about it; and some based simply on the fact that we had certain expectations and dreams about who our children would be. Their homosexuality forces us to change some of those dreams:

A mother said: These days I can ask my son about his lover. I know Gary is a very important part of Joe's life. But I will always be disappointed that he isn't part of a "normal" family; that he isn't going to be a father. I have to give that up and to tell you the truth, I'm happy that he has so many other things in his life that are important and full. He has his own kind of family.

A father: I want to see my grandchildren. I want to have the family go on. It tears my heart to think none of that will be.

The act of declaring to yourself and others that you are gay is hard enough when you're an adult living on your own. For a teenager, when you're dealing with transition on every front and your identity is shaky anyway, coping with the fact of being gay can be enormously frightening. Many gay adults report that they felt "different" as young teenagers but didn't "come out" (openly acknowledge their homosexuality) then because it would have been too overwhelming. As an adolescent, when you're still so dependent on your family for physical and emotional support, it's devastating to think that something about you, beyond your control, may cause your parents, siblings, relatives and friends to stop loving you:

For me it was such a lonely experience. I couldn't show the real me to anyone because I was afraid that would mean no one would want to be with me. I was sure that if I told them about my homosexual feelings no one would care about me anymore.

Several other adolescents told us how they tried to keep their homosexual feelings to themselves:

A boy: I knew from about the time I was eleven or twelve that my fantasies were about men, not women. But I would say to myself, "Not me, man. I'm not one of those gays. That's the last thing I'll ever be." So for about four years I squashed those feelings whenever they came to me. I spent four years pretending.

A girl: In junior high I would look at girls' bodies and they'd be aware of it, so I'd look down at the floor and try to control it. I did everything I could to cover up my impulses. One time a friend asked me to zip up her dress and I remember my hand shaking.

Gay teenagers have their own expectations. If they've grown up in a family with love and support, where they've been encouraged to be themselves, chances are they will expect us to give them that same love and support now. Like all children, gay teenagers want their parents' acceptance:

It made me really mad that people—and especially my parents—had to get used to the kind of person I was, that they had to learn to accept me, as if I was a freak or something.

The day my mother told me to invite Bill for Thanksgiving I felt I had her blessing. And it was a wonderful feeling.

In this society it takes a lot of courage to come out and say you are homosexual. It takes equal courage for parents to accept their child's homosexuality. We are all familiar with the stigma and prejudice against gay people. Undoubtedly we have or have had in the past some of those prejudices ourselves. We're told that homosexuals are sick, perverse, dangerous, sinful. Those aren't easy ideas to overcome. Consequently, our first response when learning of our child's homosexuality may often come from anger, pain, and disappointment:

A gay man: When I came out to my parents, one of the first things my mother said to me, "It's a good thing your grandmother is dead." My grandmother had just died and she and I were very close. Basically what my mother was saying was that this would have killed my grandmother.

A gay woman: When I first came out to my father he said some pretty vicious things to me. I realize now that he was only expressing his pain, but I don't think I'll ever forget those first words he said. They hurt me too much.

There are a lot of myths about homosexuality that need to be dispelled before we can come to terms with it. The most damaging is that homosexuality is unnatural. Actually homosexual behavior occurs in all mammals. It has always existed among humans, and today it is estimated that as much as one tenth of our population is gay.

Children don't become homosexual to spite their family or to rebel against society. Certainly a lifestyle so different from the mainstream of society can be extremely stressful. But not all gay men and women live hard lives. On the contrary, many homosexuals are part of loving, caring, communities and have long-term relationships. Most homosexuals feel happier being gay than trying to pretend they aren't.

There is no predictable pattern to determine who will be gay and who won't. Homosexuals come from every ethnic group, every educational level, every economic class, every religion, from domineering mothers or fathers or from those who are easygoing, from absent mothers or fathers or from those who are always present. In families with many children, only one may be gay, or sometimes more than one will be. Some homosexuals come from big cities; others were raised in small country towns. No one has yet come up with a definitive or convincing answer to why some people are heterosexual and others are homosexual.

A misconception many of us have is that homosexual experiences will make a child gay. People don't "catch" homosexuality. Same-sex experiences don't make someone gay any more than opposite sex experiences make someone straight. About one in every three men and one in every five women has had at least one homosexual experience during their lives. Particularly as adolescents, people are likely to experiment with homosexual encounters. That doesn't necessarily mean much about their future sexual orientation.

However, as parents, our fear of homosexuality (homophobia) may cause us to discourage our child from having close same-sex friendships. We may make sarcastic remarks or jokes about gays and we may try to steer our children into opposite-sex romances:

My dad is always saying, ''What's the matter, you gay or something?'' Just kidding, right? But he doesn't realize how much that gets me.

My folks put heavy pressure on me to call girls and go out with girls. I mean they don't leave me alone. Every time the phone rings they want to know if it was a girl.

A lot of the time such pressure only creates a wall between us and our children. They feel we're forcing them into something they can't do, and such feelings may cause them to rebel. Many homosexual kids who run away say they couldn't get along at home, that no one understood them at home, that they were under pressure there.

It's common for us to think we're molding our children—that what we do or don't do has a major effect on how our child turns out. In part this is true, of course. But children come into this world with some traits and talents over which we have very little influence, and their sexual orientation may be one of those traits. A 1981 study by the Kinsey Institute for Sex Research concluded that homosexuality seems to be innate. These scientists believe that some children are apparently born with a strong ''gender nonformity.'' On the other hand, the Masters and Johnson report on homosexuality states a different conclusion: that homosexuality is in many instances a learned behavior. As we said before, no one really knows.

Another theory is that homosexuality is a psychological problem that can be corrected with the proper therapy. As a result many of us, and many of our gay children, seek help to encourage more heterosexually oriented behavior. This kind of treatment almost never ''works'' and may cause a child to withdraw and try to suppress his or her feelings:

My son told us he was gay by leaving a note and running away when he was eighteen. It was a terrible thing. It was traumatic for us because the word homosexual was frightening to us. We found Greg after a few days and asked our doctor what he advised and he directed us to a psychiatrist. Greg went for five years. We didn't talk about it for all those years. We just assumed he was being cured. Finally he said to us, ''Look. I can't change. If we're going to have any kind of relationship, you're going to have to change. You're going to have to accept me for who I am. You're going to have to love me in spite of my sexuality.''

My friend suspected that her son was gay from the time he was really little. He seemed effeminate to her so she took him to a child psychologist and he went for years. When he was fifteen he had a nervous breakdown from all that hassling.

Therapy or counseling can help a teenager or adult deal with some of his or her feelings about being homosexual and help a person come to terms with it. Therapy can also help parents accept their child's homosexuality. However, many parents of gays say that what helped them more than anything was talking to other parents in the same situation:

When my daughter told me she was gay, she introduced me to the mother of a friend of hers who was gay also. She herself was struggling with her own feelings, but she was very helpful to me. She was supportive because she had been dealing with it for longer than I.

The thing that saved me was the rap group we started attending. At first my husband was very reluctant to go so I went without him. I came home glowing so the next time he went too. I can't tell you how wonderful it made us feel to hear everybody talking about the same things we were feeling.

Even if it feels like you're the only one going through this problem, you're not. Gay people live everywhere and so do their parents. However, a lot of us want to keep the fact of our child's gayness a secret. We want to cover it up to avoid embarrassment and shame, so we hesitate to tell anyone about it. Unfortunately, that usually leads to other problems. We're left to ourselves to wonder why this is happening to our family. What did we do to cause this?

My husband and I have been married over thirty years and we feel we've had a good marriage. Yet when this came up, we started questioning each other. Paul worried that maybe he hadn't spent enough time with our son. I thought, well maybe I did yell at him too much. You think all these things. You even blame each other. After all, we thought it was so terrible and all the authorities told us it was so terrible, so what alternative do you have but to blame someone? And they always tell you parents cause it, so how are you supposed to feel?

What was the worst was how guilty we felt when we found out that Peter was gay. Here, because of something terrible we must've done to him in raising him, our kid was doomed to a life of difficulty and suffering. Later on, when we understood more, those feelings changed, but I cried for hours and hours about that.

Blaming ourselves or our children for their homosexuality is destructive for everyone, and it doesn't help us deal with the real issue, which is trying to work through our feelings enough to accept our child as he or she is. A father told us:

You have to accept it. If your child is gay, there are only two alternatives. Cut off your child completely or accept it. And you can accept it. It takes time and it takes learning; it takes working at it because we've spent our lives being brainwashed, so we have to unlearn all our conceptions about homosexuals. But once you do that, it can become a nonproblem. I know that from my own experience. It can be put out of the way and you can get on with the rest of your life.

A young woman said: What I decided to tell my parents I was gay, I was very scared. But I finally told them I was in this relationship with another woman and we were deeply in love. It was the first time I was really happy and I wanted them to know. At first they were shocked. But then they both came over and hugged me. We talked a long time. They really do accept me and trust that what I'm doing is right for me.

A parent of a grown son puts it this way: Right after we found out that our son was gay, I happened to be at a dinner party where he also was a guest. I could see how well he got along with all the people there (and they were these high-powered Establishment types), how funny he was and respected for his professional accomplishments. I said to myself, For God's sake, he's the same great kid he was two weeks ago, before I knew he was gay, and anyhow, I don't tell him what I do in bed—what's that got to do with anything?

Gay teenagers need the most understanding. There's no support system for gay adolescents, since our whole social structure is geared toward heterosexual dating and mating. Everything's set up for heterosexual encounters so it's very difficult for gay teenagers to make social contact with each other. For that reason, when gay teenagers finally do come out, they may become wild. They've been holding in so much tension and apprehension that when they release it, they may want to grab all the experiences they can right away. If they live in a place with little or no apparent homosexual culture, they may feel compelled to leave home for a larger city where they think homosexuals may be.

There are dangers in a gay lifestyle, and we have to help our teenagers become aware of them and learn how to avoid them. Cruising and picking up strangers is dangerous for anyone, gay or straight. However, since homosexuals have so few other ways of meeting each other, cruising can become a way of life for young gays. They need to understand that picking up strangers is extremely hazardous. Hitchhiking and accepting rides from strangers is full of risk. It doesn't help to scare our kids with gruesome stories about rape and murder, but it is very important to let them know that those things happen all too frequently.

Moreover, there are laws against homosexuality in many states, and as a result, homosexuals can get into trouble with the law for soliciting or allowing themselves to be solicited. (The same is true for heterosexual prostitution.) Sometimes policemen pose as homosexuals to try to entrap gays and arrest them. Young people may not be aware of that, or even if they are aware of it, they may have enough youthful bravado to think it could never happen to them:

When David was nineteen he was visiting friends of ours on the West Coast. We got a call that he'd been picked up for "lewd behavior" and was being held in the police station. You can imagine the terror we felt—a policeman had made some move on him and then when he responded, arrested him. After a lot of suffering—and a lot of money—the thing was resolved, but I was furious: at the police for entrapping people, and at my son for being so stupid. Also, I couldn't understand—I still can't—what makes somebody who's attractive and bright and can safely get all the lovers he wants, get into that kind of brutalizing, cruising scene.

> **FACTS ABOUT HOMOSEXUALITY**
>
> About 10 percent of the world population is homosexual.
>
> Some gay people appear stereotypically gay; most look and act like everyone else. Physical appearance and mannerisms have nothing to do with a person's homosexuality.
>
> Homosexuality usually is not a choice; it is a deep-seated sexual orientation.
>
> Experimenting with homosexuality will not make a person homosexual.
>
> One family in four has a gay member.
>
> Homosexuals are rarely child molesters. Ninety percent of all sexual child abuse is committed by heterosexual men on minor females.

Sexually transmitted disease is a problem for every sexually active person who is not in a monogamous relationship. There are some STDs which are particularly common in the male gay population and particularly lethal. (See p. 85 for details about these.) Some people think mistakenly that STDs are not a problem for homosexuals. Make sure your child, especially your son, is aware of the risks and understands how to protect against sexually transmitted diseases. This can be very difficult to bring up but it also can be very important.

What Can We Do? Regardless of our background, regardless of our attitudes about homosexuality, if we learn that our child is gay, our task becomes to learn how best to accept the situation and give our child the love and support he or she needs. It's not easy, but it is necessary and possible. As we said, the most important thing to do is seek out the support of other parents going through this experience. Attend a support meeting. Try to air your feelings and get out your anger and disappointment in a setting that is sympathetic. It's nothing to be ashamed of. See the Resource section of this chapter for names of organizations to contact.

—Read some of the books listed in the Resource section.

—Try to remain open and available to your child during this time. He or she will need your love now more than ever.

When your family can be a haven, then at least you have a source of strength and support. Otherwise it's terrible. You have to deal with ridicule and discrimination everywhere, and if you can't get any support at home you're really alone.

I remember thinking to myself, Paula is the same wonderful person I thought she was yesterday, why should this change everything?

It's very easy to be a fair-weather parent, but to be a parent when our children really need us—whether it's pregnancy, an abortion, some trouble with the law, homosexuality, or what—that's when the real test comes.

—Your gay child needs facts about sex the same way a ''straight'' child does. In particular, he or she needs to know about STDs.

—Parents of gay teenagers report that there's often no way to tell that your child is homosexual. However, it's important to watch for signs of loneliness, withdrawal, and depression. Many gay teenagers don't know how to handle their feelings and run away or even commit suicide rather than tell anyone about themselves.

Sexually Transmitted Diseases (STDs)

Note: STDs used to be referred to as VD (veneral disease), but VD came to be associated most frequently with gonorrhea and syphilis. Since there are twenty or more diseases that are contracted and passed mainly through sexual contact, the whole category is now called sexually transmitted disease.

The problem of sexually transmitted disease is widespread. NGU, gonorrhea, genital herpes, trichomoniasis, and hepatitis (all of which will be explained in detail in the pages that follow) are so common as to be considered epidemic, with millions of cases being reported each year. The highest rate of gonorrhea in women is among eighteen-year-old girls.*

It's essential for teenagers to know about STDs—what they are and how they are passed—before they ever have sexual contacts, since STDs can be caught the first time a person has sex. Teenagers don't even have to be having intercourse to get some STDs; gonorrhea, syphilis, hepatitis, and others can be passed through oral sex and possibly through French kissing too.

It's up to us as their parents to tell our teenagers about sexually transmitted diseases. And even though the topic lends itself to horror stories and scare tactics, it helps if we can make our discussion as matter-of-fact as possible. Many teenagers stop paying attention when the information sounds too frightening or represents something they feel is out of their control. As one sixteen-year-old told us:

You know they tell you you're going to get brain damage or something from having sex and you know they're just saying that to keep you from having sex, so you don't listen. I mean there are plenty of folks walking around out there who are having sex and they don't look brain-damaged to me.

Yet how can we be expected to be matter-of-fact about sexually transmitted disease? Most of us have mixed feelings at best about our adolescents' sexual activity anyway. To think about them catching a disease from sex, and a serious disease at that, is much harder to deal with. The descriptions alone of how STDs are passed are enough to keep most of us away from the subject:

How do you say to your daughter, ''Now remember dear, if you have oral sex with Tommy you can catch gonorrhea in your throat if he has it.'' I can't say that.

Unfortunately, there's no alternative. STDs are very serious. They can cause severe bodily injury, create major health problems, and most important, they don't go away by themselves. They have be treated to be cured, which means recognizing the symptoms and knowing how and where to get treatment. Most teenagers don't know those things. And as with everything else about sex, the best, most accurate and sensitive information can come from us, because we care the most about our kids.

Many STDs are actually very common, easy-to-catch diseases, as ordinary as the common cold or the flu or strep throat. However, since they are mostly caught through sexual activity, society tends to label them dirty or sleazy or a punishment for immoral acts. ''Nice people don't catch VD'' has been the unarticulated slogan for a long time, and that seems to be behind a lot of the discussion of STDs in school sex education courses. But nice people do get VD, and they always have. These days more and more people are getting it, since more and more people are having sex outside of monogamous relationships.

Teenagers don't pick up an STD simply because they are having sex. Sexual activity in and of itself doesn't cause disease. The only way you can catch an STD is if your partner has one, and it stands to reason that the more partners you have, the higher your risk of catching an STD. That's a very straightforward argument against promiscuous sexual behavior, and we can say that to our kids. However, promiscuity, especially among teenagers, is usually a sign of other problems and if our kids are involved in cruising and having lots of sex partners, we need to help them deal with the problems causing that behavior (see p. 54).

While some people have many sexual partners and never catch an STD, others get something the first time they have sex, or the first time they have sex outside an exclusive relationship. A college sophomore told us:

I got herpes the first time I ever slept with anyone. He was this terrifically sweet law student who was a friend of my brother's and we made love once and that one time I got herpes. He didn't even know he was contagious.

*As reported in ''Adolescent Sexual Behavior'' by Jerome T. Y. Shen, M.D., *Postgraduate Medicine*, Vol. 71, No. 4, April 1982, p. 51.

A number of people are asymptomatic carriers of certain STDs. They don't know they have the disease but they can and do pass it on during sex. Other people seem to have a natural immunity to at least some forms of STD, because even though they've been exposed, they haven't contracted the disease themselves.

For the most part, STD germs can only stay alive in warm, moist, dark body openings—in mucus membranes—like vaginas, urethras (the male's urethra is in his penis), anuses, throats, mouths, eyes, open cuts and sores. The germs are not airborne so you don't catch an STD because somebody with one sneezes near you. Most STD germs are passed from person to person as contact is made between one body opening and another. In other words, if someone has gonorrhea in his penis and you kiss him on the mouth you won't catch it, but if you have oral sex (fellatio) you may get gonorrhea in your throat, and if you have intercourse you may get it in your vagina. The symptoms appear—when they appear—at the site of contact.

Sexually transmitted diseases pose a special problem for teenagers. Most adolescents have sex secretly—or at least without our knowledge—so they often don't seek treatment for fear of having their sexual activity discovered by us. Actually, most clinics that treat STDs do so without informing the teenager's parents, but many kids don't realize that. By hesitating to go for treatment, they give the disease a chance to spread to internal body organs and cause more serious, secondary infections.

This is another one of those issues, like pregnancy, that really has to be discussed between us and our adolescents. We have to let them know that we are willing to put aside our feelings about their sexual activity enough to help them seek treatment for an STD.

If our society were more open about STDs, they would be much less widespread than they are now. With massive advertising campaigns aimed at teaching teenagers and all of us how to recognize STD symptoms and how to protect against catching STDs, we could begin to eliminate the problem. And making the effort public would remove some of the stigma now associated with STDs, so those of us who become infected would probably feel less timid about revealing that fact to our sex partners.

People who find out they are infected *must* inform their sex partners because not everyone has symptoms. Some people discover they have an STD, like gonorrhea or NGU, only when they are told by a partner of the partner's infection. Otherwise a person may not realize the problem until he or she goes for a routine medical checkup or until the disease gets so bad it causes secondary symptoms. This is what we heard from a sixteen-year-old who is afraid she might now be infertile due to gonorrhea-caused PID (pelvic inflammatory disease—see p. 47):

I had these real bad pains in my stomach so I went to the clinic and they said I had PID and that my tubes were in-

fected. They said it was because of gonorrhea, but I told them I didn't have gonorrhea. They did a test and found out I did have it and they told me to call my old boyfriend so he could get checked too. So I called him and he said, "Oh yeah, I had the clap a couple of months ago but I got it taken care of." He never even told me. I probably could have died before he would have told me.

What Can We Do? —Above all, we have to make sure our adolescents know about the various sexually transmitted diseases and how to protect against them. (Specific information follows this section.)

—It's important for us to reassure our teenagers that STDs aren't punishment for having sex. Anyone can get an STD if their partner has one, and lots of people do get them—lots of perfectly nice, respectable people.

—If we suspect our teenagers are having sex with more than one person, or if their partner is having sex with other people, we should let them know they are at risk. They should have a medical checkup at least once and preferably twice a year, during which they should receive tests for gonorrhea and syphilis.

We need to encourage our adolescents to take their health care seriously because teenagers tend to think of themselves as invulnerable—at least when it comes to health.

—Teenage boys who are having homosexual experiences must be warned about diseases particularly rampant in male homosexual populations. Hepatitis B may become a chronic liver disorder for which there is currently no treatment. There is no cure for it at present. Another disease, which has only recently been recognized, is called AIDS, Acquired Immune Deficiency Syndrome. This can lead to severe, even fatal illnesses. Both these diseases are discussed in more detail on the following pages. NGU, gonorrhea, and syphilis are also very common among homosexual men, and having many partners creates a greater risk of catching these diseases.

—Our adolescents may feel embarrassed or frightened to go to an STD clinic by themselves for treatment. We have to make our own choice about how involved we want to be. We can tell them what to expect and how to go for treatment even before there's any problem. And if we and they feel comfortable with it, we can accompany them to the treatment center, as this father said he would do:

When my son first started dating I told him about birth control and VD—and I told him where the clinic near us is so he could go himself. But I also let him know that I'd be willing to take him if he ever needed to go.

Other parents feel that their teenagers should be responsible for taking care of themselves when it comes to sex. A mother said:

When my daughter went to Planned Parenthood to get her birth control, they really scared her about VD and I was actually glad they gave her such a heavy rap. But when it came time for her to go for a VD checkup she wanted me to take her. I told her no; in fact we had a fight about it because I said, ''I think if you're big enough to get involved sexually then you're big enough to get yourself down to the clinic on your own.''

WAYS TO PREVENT OR LIMIT
THE SPREAD OF STDS

—Use **condoms** with **foam** for protection. Together these are very effective in preventing many STD germs from being transmitted.

—**Look carefully.** Examine yourself and your partner for sores, discharge, rashes, itchiness, redness, bugs. Don't have sex if any of those signs are apparent. If you do have sex anyway, you are taking a chance. Have a checkup soon afterward.

—**Urinate** before and after sex. That may wash some of the STD germs away, though this is not a very effective way to avoid illness.

—**Gargle** with hot salt water after oral sex. If done right away this may remove some STD germs. Again, this is not effective prevention.

—**Have regular checkups.** As soon as you begin to have sexual contact with other people you should have medical checkups at least once or twice a year. If you are having oral sex or intercourse you should be tested for gonorrhea, syphilis, and NGU routinely.

—If you know you are in a completely exclusive relationship, and if neither you nor your partner came to the relationship with an STD, then you probably don't have to worry about STDs.

—**Watch for symptoms.** Beginning on this page we describe the most common STDs and list the symptoms of each. If you notice any of those symptoms, have them checked by a health practitioner right away.

Where to Go for Treatment of STDs The best place for teenagers to go to be checked for an STD is to a clinic that specializes in treating sexually transmitted diseases. These clinics are able to perform most of the diagnostic tests and they have the most reliable treatments on hand. If your teenager prefers going to a private doctor, you should make sure that that person is well equipped and knowledgeable in this field. If you have any doubts, the teenager should ask about whether a referral to an STD clinic would be helpful.

Most family planning clinics provide services for patients with STDs. Look in the phone book to find such clinics and call to find out if they have STD service. Also, cities and large communities provide state-run Board of Health facilities that offer free STD tests and treatment. These will be listed in the phone book under the name of your city, county, or state.

Many areas have local VD or STD hot lines listed in the phone book under VD or STD. There is also a National VD hot line: from every state but California call 1(800)227-8922. From California call 1(800)982-5883. This is a free call. The people who answer the hot line call will be able to help you find a place in your area to go for treatment. They will also provide general information about STDs if you desire it.

Facts on the Most Common Sexually Transmitted Diseases As we said earlier, there are many diseases that can be transmitted through sexual contact. Here we will list eight of the most common STDs, with information about their symptoms and treatment.

AIDS (ACQUIRED IMMUNE DEFICIENCY SYNDROME)*

What Is It? AIDS is a breakdown in a person's normal immune system, which leaves that person vulnerable to a variety of diseases not usually contracted by the general population. Such diseases include a severe form of cancer; a potentially fatal type of pneumonia; other forms of pneumonia; meningitis; and other less well-known diseases.

It has mainly been seen in homosexual or bisexual men and less frequently in drug abusers who take drugs intravenously and in some hemophiliacs as well as certain Haitian immigrants. Between June 1, 1981, and November 12, 1982, the Center for Disease Control in Atlanta received reports of 732 cases of AIDS; 284 (more than one-third) of those cases resulted in death. Seventy-three percent of the reported cases were gay or bisexual men.

How Is It Passed? AIDS is such a new disease syndrome that very little is known about it. Researchers think it is passed through semen during sexual contact or through contact with an infected person's blood. So far, reports of AIDS have come mainly from Los Angeles, San Francisco, and the East Coast. The incidence of this disease seems to be growing, but as yet it has appeared in only a very limited population.

Symptoms. The symptoms now associated with AIDS are recurrent fever, unexplained weight loss, enlarged lymph nodes.

Diagnosis. Only very sophisticated medical techniques are at present able to confirm the diagnosis, and these are available only at the largest, most specialized centers. Normally AIDS would be suspected if all other possible causes of a symptom were ruled out. In other words, a patient would be tested for hepatitis or mononucleosis and if the tests were negative, AIDS might be suspected.

*This information comes from the Center for Disease Control in Atlanta, Georgia.

Treatment. There is as yet no specific treatment for AIDS, although research is being done to find existing drugs that will have an effect on it. So far, treatment is usually limited to attempts to cure the diseases caused by the immune deficiency. Sexual abstinence is an important element in treatment to avoid reinfection.

Complications. As we said, AIDS leaves one vulnerable to many infections and diseases that are caused by defects in normal cellular immunity. Kaposi's sarcoma, a severe and a rare form of cancer, which is very difficult to treat, is one such disease. Another is *Pneumocystis carinii,* a pneumonia that is also extremely rare.

Prevention. A promiscuous sex life that includes frequent sex with many partners may create the conditions for AIDS. As of now it is limited mainly to a homosexual population, but some cases have been reported in heterosexuals as mentioned above.

Until more is known about this disease we can only advise our children as to the dangers of having sex with lots of different partners, and we should be especially careful to warn sons who have homosexual relationships. No one knows yet whether AIDS can be contracted from one sexual encounter or whether it is the result of repeated infections.

GENITAL HERPES (HERPES SIMPLEX II)

What Is It? Common cold sores or fever blisters which appear around the mouth are one form of herpes (herpes simplex I). Genital herpes are sores which appear on and in the penis, vagina, or anus. In some cases Type II sores also appear around the mouth.

Herpes is a virus and there is no cure for it yet. The virus causes painful reddish blisters to appear at the site of contact. When the blisters heal the virus goes into a latent stage inside the body. The blisters may recur at various times during one's life, usually during periods of stress, fatigue, or illness. Some people never have a second attack after the initial outbreak of blisters.

How Is It Passed? The virus is passed from one person to another as direct contact is made with the sores. Unfortunately, it can also be passed during the twenty-four hours before sores erupt, so the person with herpes may not realize he or she is contagious. The virus enters the body through cuts, openings in mucous membranes in the genitals, through mouth, eyes, and possibly even through pores. Using condoms may help prevent transmittal of the virus.

No one with herpes should have any sexual contact when the sores are present or if they have a suspicion that an outbreak is about to occur. (There is a slight possibility that the virus can be passed in some cases even when the sores are not present or about to erupt.*)

Modern Medicine (October 1982), p. 68.

Symptoms. At first there is likely to be itchiness or aching around the genitals and then possibly a general body achiness. There may be a slight fever, a headache, or swollen glands. After that the sores will appear, and they can be very painful. In a few days the sores may crack and become blistered, and they may bleed or ooze fluid.

During the first attack—which appears two to twenty days after contact usually—the sores may last for up to two weeks. Usually subsequent attacks are less severe.

Some people report that their symptoms appeared months or even a year after contact with an infected person.

Diagnosis. Sometimes herpes sores are mistaken for syphilis, but herpes sores are painful and the syphilitic chancre is not (see p. 89). Usually a doctor or health practitioner will be able to diagnose herpes just from seeing the sores. There is also a tissue culture test available for positive identification.

Treatment. There is no medication known to kill the herpes virus at present. Researchers are working on a possible vaccine, but so far that is still only a future hope.

Acyclovir ointment, 5 percent, can be applied topically to the affected area according to instructions, and this may reduce some of the pain, but it may not prevent recurrences of the disease.

Basically treatment is symptomatic:
Keep the sores clean and dry.
Numb the area with an ice bag.
Dry the area thoroughly after washing.
Try not to let your body get run-down.

Complications. Herpes can complicate pregnancies, sometimes causing miscarriages. It can infect the unborn baby and cause brain damage, birth defects, or even death, especially during the mother's first outbreak. If the mother has an active case of herpes during delivery, the baby should be removed through Caesarean section to avoid contact with the sores.

Medical researchers have suggested a possible relationship between genital herpes and cervical cancer, which is why women with herpes should have a Pap smear at least every year.

Men who get genital herpes are not subject to any complications other than pain and annoyance.

GONORRHEA

What Is It? Gonorrhea is an infection caused by gonococcus bacteria, which can live on mucus membranes within the body. Other names for gonorrhea are the clap, the drip, morning dew, gleet.

How Is It Passed? The disease is passed from person to person when contact is made with the infected site. The gonococci usually grow in the vagina, penis, mouth or throat, and anus. Eyes can also be affected if they come in contact with the bacteria.

Gonorrhea is not spread by toilet seats, door knobs, towels or clothes.

Symptoms. Symptoms appear very soon after contact, usually within a few days to two weeks.

In females:
    —vaginal discharge with unusual odor
    —painful, burning urination
    —sore throat or swollen glands (if throat is infected)
    —anal discharge (if anus is infected)
    —lower abdominal pain (if the disease has spread to the pelvic area)

80 percent of all females notice no symptoms until the disease has spread to the pelvic area.

In males:
    —discharge from penis—sometimes noticed as a drip appearing in the morning before urinating; sometimes it is a continual discharge throughout the day
    —burning, itching or pain during urination
    —pain during erection
    —sore throat or swollen glands
    —discharge from anus
    —pain in groin or lower abdomen (if reproductive organs have been infected)

10 to 20 percent of all males notice no symptoms until the disease spreads to reproductive organs.

Most girls find out they have gonorrhea when they are told by a sex partner who has the disease to go for a checkup. Otherwise they would not have known about it. That's why it's so important for boys to tell their partners (and vice versa) if they find out they have gonorrhea—or any other STD.

Diagnosis. In males with a discharge, a sample of the discharge can be examined under a microscope. This is called a Gram-stained smear and it is reliable for males but not for females. For females and males without discharge, a culture of tissue from the cervix or urethra is allowed to grow for eighteen to twenty-four hours, after which time it becomes apparent whether gonorrhea is present. A throat culture should be taken if there was oral sex.

Treatment. Gonorrhea is treated with penicillin, tetracycline, or ampicillin. Pregnant girls shouldn't take tetracycline as it can cause damage to the fetus' bones and teeth. Otherwise, tetracycline may be advised because it also kills the organisms that cause NGU (see p. 89).

Resistant strains may create the need for more than one attempt at treatment. Infected teenagers should return to the clinic for follow-up tests after the first round of treatment. They must not have any sexual contact until the gonorrhea is completely cured.

Complications. If untreated, gonorrhea may spread throughout the reproductive organs. As a result of these advanced infections, scar tissue may form in the fallopian tubes of girls or the epididymis of boys, creating the potential for permanent infertility. If gonorrhea infects the eye, blindness may result. In males, gonorrhea may cause a chronic inflammation of the urethra.

HEPATITIS

What Is It? Hepatitis is a disease caused by several different viruses. It is a generalized illness, but mainly affects the liver.

How Is It Passed? There are at least three different types of hepatitis, each passed somewhat differently.

Hepatitis A is transmitted primarily by fecal contamination, through direct contact with infected body wastes—through anal intercourse, through mouth-anus or finger-anus contact. It is not purely a sexually transmitted disease, since contaminated drinking water and undercooked seafood can also carry the disease.

Hepatitis B is found in all body fluids such as blood, saliva, vaginal secretions, semen, feces, urine, and even tears. It can be acquired through sexual contact and also through contact with contaminated objects such as toothbrushes, razors, needles used for tattooing, instruments for ear piercing, needles used for taking drugs, etc.

Non-A, Non-B Hepatitis is the least known of the various forms of hepatitis. Mainly it is contracted through blood transfusions, although it may also be passed sexually or through intravenous drug use.

Symptoms. There are generalized symptoms like nausea, vomiting, muscle achiness, excessive fatigue, fever, loss of appetite, weight loss, headaches, and dizziness. Many people with hepatitis don't recognize their disease immediately because the symptoms are so much like those of flu.

Only some people with hepatitis develop yellowing of eyes and skin (jaundice), darkening of urine, lightening of stool color, tenderness in the area of the liver (the right upper abdomen).

Sometimes the symptoms will appear within a month after contact; or they may not appear for up to six months.

Diagnosis. A blood test can identify the extent and nature of the infection.

Treatment. Since hepatitis is caused by a virus, there is no specific drug treatment available. Bed rest, drinking lots of fluids (nonalcoholic), and eating a light, healthy diet is the recommended treatment. Hepatitis A never becomes chronic, but Hepatitis B may become chronic in a small percentage of patients. Such people may become asymptomatic carriers of the virus. Carriers may transmit the disease through sexual contact or blood donations.

KNOWN HEPATITIS CARRIERS MUST NOT DONATE BLOOD.

Complications. Chronic liver problems are a possible complication. In extreme cases hepatitis may result in permanent liver damage and after some years even death due to cirrhosis and liver failure. Hepatitis in late pregnancy may be transmitted to the newborn.

NON-GONOCOCCAL URETHRITIS (NGU)

What Is It? NGU is an inflammation of the urethra in men and of the genital tract (cervix and vagina) in women. It is most commonly caused by the microorganism *chlamydia trachomatis*. Three million cases of *chlamydia*-caused genital tract infections are reported each year in the United States. It is more common than any other sexually transmitted disease.

How Is It Passed? NGU is passed through sexual contact with an infected genital tract—through oral, anal, and vaginal sex. People can pass the disease to their partners without showing symptoms themselves.

Symptoms. Symptoms of NGU usually appear gradually within ten to twenty days after contact. They are similar to the symptoms of gonorrhea: burning or pain during urination; a turbid discharge from penis, vagina, or anus; feeling that you have to urinate more often than usual; itchiness around the genital area. Secondary problems are cervicitis and urethritis in women (infections of the cervix or urethra) and epididymitis in men (infection of the epididymis). These are characterized by low abdominal pain or pain in the groin area.

Diagnosis. The culture test for *chlamydia* is very costly so few laboratories do it. Instead, NGU is diagnosed when gonorrhea is ruled out. If a person doesn't have a positive gonorrhea smear, but does have symptoms, NGU will be assumed in most cases.

Treatment. Tetracycline is the treatment of choice for NGU. Penicillin, which cures gonorrhea, does *not* cure NGU. People who are allergic to tetracycline, or pregnant women, will be offered a substitute medication.

All sexual contacts must be treated or they may continue to pass the disease back and forth to each other.

Complications. NGU can lead to infections in the reproductive organs, possibly resulting in impaired fertility. Some strains of non-gonococcal urethritis cause birth defects, eye damage and pneumonia in newborns born to mothers with the disease. NGU can also cause spontaneous abortions and stillbirths.

In both males and females, NGU can leave the urethra scarred, possibly causing problems with urination.

SYPHILIS

What Is It? Syphilis is a disease caused by spiral-shaped organisms called spirochetes. In its earliest stage syphilis causes painless sores to appear at the infected site.

How Is It Passed? The germs are passed when contact is made with the sores or with the rash, most often through genital or oral sexual contact. Syphilis is much less prevalent these days than it used to be. It is still seen fairly frequently in male homosexual populations, however.

Symptoms. There are three stages of syphilis. If it isn't cured in stage one, the disease will go underground for a while and then a rash will appear. If the syphilis isn't treated, the symptoms will disappear again and then months or even years later stage three complications may occur.

The disease is most contagious during stages one and two; it is most dangerous to the infected person during stage three. Stage one symptoms generally appear about a month after contact with an infected person.

Stage I: — Painless sores called chancres (pronounced *shankers*) appear at the site of infection. If the sores are inside the body, they may be unnoticeable.

Stage II: — Fever, achiness, sore throat, mouth sores, patchy hair loss, swollen glands, flulike syndrome.
— A rash may appear all over or just on the palms of the hands or soles of the feet.
— These symptoms will disappear after a few months, but the disease will still be active in the body if not treated.

Stage III: — The disease can affect vital organs, eventually causing heart disease; blindness; muscle incoordination; deafness; paralysis; insanity; death.

A fetus can contract syphilis from its infected mother.

Diagnosis. A special blood test, called VDRL, can be accurate about one week to ten days after the chancre appears. A VDRL will detect syphilis during any of the three stages.

Treatment. Long-acting shots of penicillin are curative for syphilis. Penicillin is the drug of choice, but for people who are allergic to penicillin another antibiotic such as tetracycline may be equally effective.

No one with syphilis should have sexual contact *until the disease is completely cured*—not until a doctor or health professional certifies that the syphilis is no longer active.

Blood tests are recommended every three months for one year to make sure that the disease has been cured.

Complications. See discussion under Stage III.

VAGINAL INFECTIONS

Vaginal infections are not necessarily caused by sexual activity, but they can be transmitted that way.

What Are They? There are two main types of vaginal infection, yeast infections (candida, monilia, and fungus) and trichomoniasis. Yeast lives normally in the vagina, but an infection occurs when an imbalance of organisms causes the yeast to overgrow. "Trich" (pronounced *trick*) is caused by a one-celled parasite.

How Are They Passed? Yeast infections can be passed from one body opening to another, usually in the genital area. Sometimes they are caused by contact with fecal matter from the anus, a reason why girls should learn to wipe themselves from front to back—not from back to front. Also, careless anal sex practices can cause yeast infections. But yeast infections can also be exacerbated by soap; toilet paper; tight pants and pantyhose that don't allow air to circulate; douching; birth control pills; and as a result of antibiotic treatment for other diseases. The antibiotics kill off the normal bacterial flora in the vagina or penis, allowing the yeast to multiply and cause an infection.

Trichomoniasis is not a yeast infection but has many of the same symptoms. It is passed through sexual activity: penis-genital or vagina-genital contact and also through finger-genital contact. By touching an infected partner's genitals and then touching your own penis or vagina you can spread the disease to your own body. Trich can be passed too by using someone else's washcloth or by wearing someone else's bathing suit or unclean underpants. The germ can stay alive long enough in air to be transmittable on a toilet seat as well.

Symptoms. Yeast infections cause genital itching; pain or redness around the opening of the vagina or penis; a yeast-like odor in the genital area; and a cottage-cheeselike discharge.

Trich creates intense itching in the vagina, pain during urination, and red, tender labia. There may also be a thin yellow-green or gray foamy discharge from the vagina, which will have a foul odor. Boys may have a discharge from the penis and perhaps a tickling sensation in the penis.

The problem is that about one half of vaginal trich infections and nearly all trich infections of the urethra are asymptomatic. Even infections without symptoms must be treated if they are discovered during a routine checkup, however, because they may show symptoms later on and they can be transmitted to sex partners at any time.

Diagnosis. A sample of the discharge or secretions from the vagina or penis are examined under a microscope. Yeast cells and trich organisms can be easily seen by the technician.

Treatment. The treatment for yeast infections is a medication called nystatin (one common brand name is Mycostatin). It is prescribed as either a cream, a vaginal suppository, or oral medication. Gentian violet may be used to paint the inside of the vagina. There are also some home remedies to cure yeast infections. See *Changing Bodies, Changing Lives* p. 231, or *Our Bodies, Ourselves*.

Yeast infections can be hard to get rid of, and many people have recurring infections. Don't wear tight pants. Don't use colored or scented toilet paper. Don't use genital deodorants. All those things can exacerbate the problem.

Trichomoniasis can only be cured effectively by the drug Flagyl. Both sex partners must take the treatment and abstain from sex until the trich is completely eliminated. Unfortunately, Flagyl can produce side effects such as dizziness, nausea, and headaches in some people, and more seriously, it has been associated with birth defects in animals and cancer in rats and mice. Pregnant girls must never take Flagyl or any product containing metronidazole.

The best treatment for trich is to prevent it in the first place by using foam and condoms during intercourse. They serve as protective barriers.

Complications. Trich can cause an inflamed cervix, urethritis, and abnormal Pap smears in girls. In boys it can cause an infected prostate gland, bladder infections, and infected testicles.

PARASITES: CRABS AND SCABIES

What Are They? Crabs (pubic lice) are tiny animals the size of a pinhead, yellowish-gray in color. They feed on human blood and live in moist, hairy spots on the body: in pubic hair, eyelashes, underarm hair, and chest hair. They look like tiny crabs.

Scabies are microscopic parasites that burrow under the skin and lay their eggs there.

How Are They Passed? Crabs are passed through close contact with a person who has them. They can also be passed by wearing an infected person's clothes, sleeping in the same bed, or even sitting on the same upholstered furniture. The crabs themselves can live for about twenty-four hours without a host; the eggs can live for up to a week without human contact.

Scabies are passed by direct contact with an infected site. For example, if the scabies are on someone's hands or arms, just shaking hands or embracing can pass the scabies to the other person. They are *highly* contagious.

Symptoms. Intense itching is a symptom of both crabs and scabies. On close examination, one can actually see the crabs or their eggs. Scabies appear as a red sore or a series of sores, or raised, reddish tracks along the skin, usually between the fingers.

Diagnosis. A health practitioner will be able to see the crabs or crab eggs without a microscope. Scabies can be seen under the microscope.

Treatment. Soap will not kill crabs or scabies. A cream treatment called Kwell is available in drug stores, by prescription. The directions for use are on the package.

All clothes and bed linens must be washed in very hot water or dry-cleaned.

Complications. It's difficult to let this problem go on too long because the itching is unbearable. The more a person scratches, however, the more the crabs or scabies will spread to other parts of the body. Scratching can also cause secondary infections.

BOOKS AND RESOURCES

Recommended Reading

Bell, Ruth, et al. *Changing Bodies, Changing Lives*. New York: Random House, 1980.
Facts and feelings about puberty, relationships, sexuality, birth control, STDs, etc. for teenagers. Written by some of the authors of *Our Bodies, Ourselves* with quotes from many teenagers.

Calderone, Mary, and Eric Johnson. *The Family Book About Sexuality*. New York: Harper & Row, 1981 (hardcover); New York: Bantam Books, 1983 (paper).
Comprehensive guide to sexuality for the entire family.

Calderone, Mary, and James Ramey. *Talking with Your Child About Sex*. New York: Random House, 1982.
Easy-to-read book to help parents talk about sex with their children from infancy to puberty.

Carrera, Michael. *Sex: The Facts, The Acts and Your Feelings*. New York: Crown Publishers, Inc., 1981.
A wonderful, readable encyclopedia on sexuality that every family would find useful to have in their library. Presented in a nonjudgmental manner.

Comfort, Alex, and Jane Comfort. *The Facts of Love: Living, Loving, and Growing Up*. New York: Crown Publishers, Inc., 1979.
Good book for young people and their parents. Beautiful illustrations.

Gitchel, Sam, and Lorri Foster. *Let's Talk About . . . Sex: A Read-and-Discuss Guide for People 9 to 12 and Their Parents*. Single copies are available for $4.80 from: Planned Parenthood of Fresno, Education Department, 633 North Van Ness Ave., Fresno, Calif. 93728.
This booklet has been very well received by parents and children. Helpful in opening up the lines of communication about sexual topics.

Johnson, Corinne, and Eric Johnson. *Love and Sex and Growing Up*. New York: Bantam Books, 1979.
Discusses a broad range of topics to prepare preadolescents for growing up.

Johnson, Eric W. *Love and Sex in Plain Language*. New York: Bantam Books, 1979.
Easy-to-read book on sexuality for early teens. Emphasizes the importance for responsible interpersonal relationships.

Johnson, Eric W. *Sex: Telling It Straight*. New York: Harper & Row, 1979.
Similar in content and style to the two other books listed by Johnson, but this one is written especially for teenage slow readers.

Kelly, Gary F. *Learning About Sex: The Contemporary Guide for Young Adults*. Woodbury, N.Y.: Barron's Educational Series, Inc., 1978.
Informative book for older teens. Focuses on values and the process of sexual decision-making in addition to presenting basic factual information. Covers controversial areas such as rape prevention and pornography.

Lewis, Howard, and Martha Lewis. *The Parent's Guide to Teenage Sex and Pregnancy*. New York: St. Martin's Press, 1980; Berkley Book, 1982.
Informative book on sexuality that devotes one chapter to the exploration of parents' feelings about their teenagers being sexual.

McCary, James L. *Human Sexuality*. New York: Van Nostrand Reinhold, 1978.
Excellent textbook on the subject.

McCoy, Kathy, and Charles Wibbelsman, M.D. *The Teenage Body Book*. New York: Simon & Schuster, Inc., 1979.
Readable and useful resource book for adolescents, dealing with various physiological and psychological aspects of growing up.

SIECUS Bibliography. Human Sexuality: Books for Everyone. Single copies are available on receipt of $1.00 and a stamped, self-addressed business-size envelope from SIECUS, 80 Fifth Ave., New York, N.Y. 10011.
The Sex Information and Education Council of the U.S. updates their comprehensive Human Sexuality bibliography every two years.

Fiction for teenagers

Blume, Judy. *Forever*. Scarsdale, N.Y.: Bradbury Press, 1975; New York: Simon and Schuster (paper).
Widely read story of first love with explicit passages about adolescent sexual experiences.

Klein, Norma. *It's OK If You Don't Love Me*. New York: Fawcett Crest Books, 1982.
Story of first love and the confusion created by today's sexual standards.

Mazer, Harry. *I Love You, Stupid*. New York: Crowell, 1981.
Story about a first love, written from a teenage boy's point of view.

General Resources

Sex Information HOTLINE: Many areas now have this service available. Trained counselors answer the phone and give information, answer questions, and make general referrals. Look in the white pages of your telephone book under Sex Information.

To find family planning clinics in your area look in the Yellow Pages under Family Planning, Health Clinics, Women's Health, Pregnancy, or in the white pages under Planned Parenthood.

or contact:

National Family Planning Office
Office of Population Affairs
725 Hubert H. Humphrey Building
Washington, D.C. 20201
(202)472-5588

Planned Parenthood Federation of America
810 7th Ave.
New York, N.Y. 10019
(212)541-7800

Pregnancy

McGuire, Paula. *It Won't Happen to Me: Teenagers Talk About Pregnancy*. New York: Delta, Delacorte Press, 1983.
Teenagers, parents, and pregnancy counselors talk about their experiences.

Oettinger, Katherine B., with Elizabeth Monney. *Not My Daughter: Facing Up to Adolescent Pregnancy*. Englewood Cliffs, N.J.: Prentice-Hall, 1979.
Helpful discussion for parents about the problem of unplanned pregnancy in young people and ways to prevent it.

Witt, Reni L., and Michael Witt and Jeannine Masterson. *Mom, I'm Pregnant*. Briarcliff Manor, N.Y.: Stein and Day, Scarborough House, 1982.
This book concentrates on the emotional and practical considerations of the problem for teenagers who are faced with the possibility of pregnancy and for parents who care.

Pregnancy Resources

Information and Counseling:

Planned Parenthood Federation of America
Main Office
810 7th Ave.
New York, N.Y. 10019
(212)541-7800

Most local areas have their own Planned Parenthood clinics. Counselors there will help you explore all alternatives including abortion and adoption.

Florence Crittenton Association
Main Office
67 Irving Pl.
New York, N.Y. 10011
(212)254-7410

This association also exists in many states. Look in the telephone book. Its focus is on alternatives to abortion.

Services for pregnant and parenting teenagers:

An excellent booklet is available, entitled "Too Little, Too Late: Services for Teenage Parents," by Elizabeth A. McGee. Write to:

Office of Reports
The Ford Foundation
320 East 43rd St.
New York, N.Y. 10017

For general information contact:

National Organization on Adolescent Pregnancy and Parenting, Inc.
512 West 4th St.
Fort Worth, Tex. 76102

Homosexuality

Fairchild, Betty and Nancy Hayward. *Now That You Know: What Every Parent Should Know About Homosexuality*. New York: Harcourt Brace Jovanovich, 1981 (paper).
An informative and thoughtfully written book for parents of homosexuals.

Fricke, Aaron. *Reflections of a Rock Lobster: A Story About Growing Up Gay*. Boston: Alyson Publications, 1981.

For a copy write P.O. Box 2783, Dept. B2, Boston, Mass. 02208.
Moving autobiographical account of a young man coming to terms with his homosexuality and his family's and friends' feelings about it.

Hanckel, Frances, and John Cunningham. *A Way of Love, A Way of Life: A Young Person's Introduction to What It Means to Be Gay*. New York: Lee and Shepard, 1979.
A sensitively written book to help young people understand their feelings of homosexuality.

Scoppetone, Sandra. *Happy Endings Are All Alike*. New York: Harper & Row, 1978.
Fiction. Story about two teenage girls who are lesbians and their relationship.

Scoppetone, Sandra. *Trying Hard to Hear You*. New York: Harper & Row, 1974.
Fiction. Story about a girl who falls in love with a boy only to discover he is gay.

Silverstein, Dr. Charles. *A Family Matter: A Parents' Guide to Homosexuality*. New York: McGraw-Hill, 1977.
Provides a very good overview for parents with a homosexual child and suggests ways of making this a positive experience for parents and children.

Homosexuality Resources

A booklet for parents entitled "About Our Children" is available by writing to:

Parents FLAG
P.O. Box 24565
Los Angeles, Calif. 90024

This organization, Parents and Friends of Lesbians and Gays, has support groups and HOTLINES in many communities throughout the country. Look in the white pages of the telephone book or contact them at the above address. The Los Angeles phone number is (213) 472-8952. Call for local referrals.

Other organizations to contact:

National Federation of Parents and Friends of Gays
5715 16th St. N.W.
Washington, D.C. 20011
(202)726-3223

National Gay Task Force
80 Fifth Ave.
New York, N.Y. 10010
(212)741-5815

GAY Yellow Pages
Renaissance House
Box 292 Village Station
New York, N.Y. 10014
(212)929-7720

Sexual Assault (also see pp. 58–59)

Rape HOTLINE: Most communities have 24-four-hour crisis numbers to call in case of rape or sexual abuse. Look in the white pages of the telephone book under Rape or Rape Crisis Center. Or call your local hospital.

Information about local services is available through

National Center for the Prevention and Control of Rape
National Institute of Mental Health
Room 15–99 Parklawn Building
5600 Fishers Lane
Rockville, Md. 20857
(301)443-1910

For victims of incest, through

VOICE, Inc. (Victims of Incest Concerned Efforts)
P.O. Box 3724
Grand Junction, Colo. 81502
(303)243-3552

Several goood booklets are available:

"Top Secret: Sexual Assault Information for Teenagers Only" ($4.00; book rates available)

"He Told Me Not to Tell"
For parents of younger children, to help them discuss sexual assault with their children ($2.00; bulk rates available)

Both of the above are produced by and available through:
King County Rape Relief
305 So. 43rd
Renton, Wash. 98055

"Taking Action: What to Do If You Are Raped" (free)
Write to:
Rape Treatment Center
Santa Monica Hospital Medical Center
1225 Fifteenth St.
Santa Monica, Calif. 90404
(213)451-1511

Sexually Transmitted Diseases (Also known as Venereal Disease)

National Hotline:
1(800)227-8922 (outside California)
1(800)982-5883 (inside California)

Look in the white pages of the telephone book under VD for a local listing.

VD services are generally available at most hospitals and health clinics as well as through the local Departments of Public Health.

VII

SUBSTANCE ABUSE: DRUGS, ALCOHOL, AND EATING DISORDERS

DRUGS AND ALCOHOL

People have always taken drugs. Ancient literature describes the use of marijuana and opium for intoxication as well as for medical and religious purposes; alcohol has been consumed by civilizations throughout recorded history; the Indians of the New World had long been smoking tobacco when Columbus discovered America. Within the last few generations, however, there has been an explosion in the variety of drugs used and in their availability. Drugs have invaded virtually every aspect of our society to a degree that makes the historical involvement pale by comparison.

Nowhere have the effects of this explosion been more profoundly felt than in the adolescent subculture. Not only is there widespread use of drugs and alcohol by teenagers, but children are confronted with the opportunity to use these substances at steadily younger ages. By eleven or twelve our children are likely to have been offered drugs, many of which may be unknown to us.

"Learning" to drink is one of the adolescent rites of passage in our culture. Given the importance of drinking to adults, it could hardly be any other way. Growing up has traditionally included either open, family-condoned opportunities to try it or secret experimentation with alcohol:

> I remember the first time I got drunk. A group of us went up to one of the family's summer cabins by a lake. We smuggled and stole booze from our parents, and proceeded to get rip-roaring drunk. It was a pretty hilarious experience, except that a couple of kids got pretty sick.

In the past, drug use and abuse and the presence of a drug subculture were most common in ghettoized low-income communities. This began to change in the mid-sixties with the appearance of a middle-class drug culture tied closely to the youth and social movements of that period. The "coun-terculture" of the sixties and seventies has pretty much disappeared, but the patterns of drug use and the plethora of substances introduced during that period have continued and expanded. For many of us, adolescence represented a ritual initiation into the experimental use of a few drugs; for our children it is a time of decision about whether and how to use a whole variety of substances. Many of our children are in contact with a drug- and alcohol-using community on a daily basis:

> A lot of people at school smoke marijuana, and they sell it to the other kids at school who want it. Even the guards at our school are selling pot.

> From the time we were fourteen on we were going to parties. Usually when you get to a party they almost always have liquor to drink. And drugs too.

Some of us are fearful of this phenomenon especially because we ourselves can recall the impact of these substances on us when we were teenagers:

> I am a recovered alcoholic and a mother of two teenage sons. I started drinking first when I was about fourteen or fifteen. I would drink before going out on a date or to a dance or a football game and I would drink at the event itself. I knew right from the beginning that drinking was very important to me. It gave me the courage to interact socially with boys . . . something I was scared to death of doing. It made me feel relaxed, confident.

> I started drinking as a teenager to relieve the pressures of school, sports, pressures with my family. Every Friday night, after the football game, my buddies and I would get completely plowed. It was a way to let off steam.

> I grew up in Chicago and I think I started smoking when I

was fourteen. Everyone smoked in those days. My parents smoked, my older brother smoked. I remember I started smoking to be more grown up.

We may have known kids who became heavily involved with alcohol or drugs, who became addicts, who broke down psychologically. These memories may make us fear for our children, and though later in this chapter we discuss some things that may help prevent these situations from arising, the fact remains that for most parents of teenagers, drug and alcohol abuse are constant fears—like the fear of polio used to be.

We live in a society that actively promotes the consumption of something—be it drugs, alcohol, food, or nicotine—as a way for all age groups to deal with life. We are told that the way to find relief from stress and worry is to take tranquilizers, smoke a cigarette, or have a glass of wine. We are also taught to associate some of our deepest needs and experiences with the consumption of drugs and alcohol.

The advertising industry does a brilliant job of playing these images back to us. Beer drinking is connected to manliness, with playing great basketball or watching Monday night football. It stands for friendship and family picnics, sailing the ocean or racing down mountain ski slopes. Wine means romance—candlelight dinners, snuggling by the fireplace, and passionate encounters. Cigarette smoking is forever linked in our minds with Marlboro country, with women's independence and sophistication ("You've come a long way, baby"), with the moment of closeness after making love.

The power of these images should not be underestimated. If they are at times irresistible to us, imagine the effect they have on our children! Teenagers are particularly vulnerable to suggestions of what is considered grown up or sophisticated.

Adolescents get the message from an early age that many experiences in life are potentially more pleasurable when accompanied by drugs or alcohol. In this way the substance, whatever it may be, can come to assume great importance in their lives, even though they may not use it frequently. Rather than a physical dependence, this is a form of psychological dependence. The association of happiness in life with the consumption of *something* is subtle, yet very powerful. The tragedy is that in the end it is also potentially damaging to the process of adolescence itself.

The Dangers of Drugs and Alcohol

Probably the most frightening aspect of teenagers using drugs or alcohol is that they are introduced to those substances at the very time when their adult skills and character are beginning to develop and just when they are beginning to accept adult responsibilities. Using drugs and alcohol can interfere with that process by providing a way to avoid experiencing negative feelings or struggling through difficult events. The lesson that life's painful moments can be survived without these substances never gets learned:

I know my son started drinking at first to cover his shyness. He was a terribly shy kid. He didn't have much self-esteem. He later told me he would drink to get up his courage and so he wouldn't feel so nervous around his friends.

Jane got into drugs just after we moved to a new neighborhood. She had a lot of problems with the new school. She had a big need to be popular and she couldn't seem to find a crowd where she fit in. I think she got into drugs partly because she just couldn't handle the move.

After my daughter stopped using drugs she told me that when she was getting stoned every day, she never had a fight with her boyfriend. Every time something would come up between them, like an argument, they would just smoke a joint.

Many teenagers are already aware of the fact that they use something as a way to cope. They will talk about getting "loaded" at school as a way to handle their boredom; going to the refrigerator to "pig out" when they feel frustrated with homework; or getting drunk at parties to cover up awkward, nervous feelings.

Drugs, food, and alcohol don't solve these problems, they merely medicate against painful feelings. And, as any frequent user will tell you, after a while they don't even do that. For a teenager who is dependent, getting high or drunk becomes necessary simply to feel normal.

Physical Dependence and Health Problems: While few drugs will cause great physical harm to the body if only taken once or twice, long-term or large-dose consumption can present serious, even fatal health problems. When this is made clear to kids who are interested in health and physical fitness, they are likely to respond. But many teenagers aren't persuaded by these health considerations, partly because they are so resilient and full of vitality that they don't believe their health will suffer. This feeling of "invulnerability" is very common in adolescence. Teenagers see lung cancer, alcoholism, heavy drug addiction, as things that happen to people who are older, not to them.

Adolescence *does* seem to be a time when you can do fairly destructive things to your body and get away with it without immediate bad results. However, there is really no such thing as a free ride when it comes to drug use. Sooner or later, in one form or another, heavy drug use catches up with everyone. Some drugs create a very strong physical dependency, which means that there is so powerful an alteration in body chemistry that the withdrawal of the drug produces physical problems. For some people, physical dependency seems almost instantaneous:

Almost as soon as I started smoking at age fifteen, I had this physical craving for cigarettes which continued well into my adult life. Even after I quit, for years I would still crave a cigarette.

For most people, physical dependency comes gradually and subtly:

As a teenager I drank rarely and I almost never took drugs. When I got married we used to drink socially, and for a while there we smoked pot pretty regularly. It wasn't until years after that, when my marriage began to fall apart, that I started using alcohol to make it through the day.

At a purely physical level, the opiates, barbiturates, and nicotine are the most addicting (see Facts About Specific Drugs, p. 105). But because of its widespread use and social acceptance, more people become addicted to alcohol than to any other substance. Other drugs that teenagers commonly consume, including marijuana, cocaine, the hallucinogens, and amphetamines, are highly addicting psychologically. Experts argue over the distinction between physical and psychological dependence, but at some point the difference becomes irrelevant. The symptoms of heavy dependence, the intense need for the drug, and the severe physical signs of withdrawal are the same:

Watching my son stop using marijuana after he had been smoking daily for almost five years was the hardest thing I've ever done. He couldn't sleep at night. He was shaky and irritable all the time. And when he wasn't irritable, he was depressed. He had no appetite and sometimes had trouble holding down food. He was a mess for several months.

Hazards of a Single Use: Dependency is not the only problem. Severe reactions can and do occur with a single drug dose if it is too much for the body to handle (overdose) or if the drug is laced or cut with other harmful substances. Cocaine is almost always diluted with a variety of substances including amphetamines, talcum powder (which may have a high asbestos content), and even kitchen cleanser. Marijuana may get sprayed with poisonous defoliants or laced with other stronger drugs such as PCP. Amphetamines or PCP can be mislabeled as mescaline and laced with strychnine (rat poison). Because so many of the drugs teenagers use are illegal there is virtually no way of regulating their purity.

I lost a cousin to LSD the first time she ever tried it. It was her first year of college. The dose was apparently mixed with strychnine. She died within a few hours.

Taking drugs in combination can also be dangerous. The most commonly combined hazardous pair is alcohol and a physical depressant such as barbiturates or Quaaludes. Both the alcohol and the drug act as physical depressants and, in large amounts, have resulted in the heart or breathing stopping.

A single drug experience can also cause severe psychological trauma, commonly referred to as a "bad trip." Users may have bizarre, terrifying, or even psychologically disconnecting experiences on a drug. These experiences are most likely to happen to people who consume any of the hallucinogens such as LSD, mescaline, or peyote, or when they take PCP. Although less common, these reactions also occur with marijuana or cocaine:

My daughter had a horrible experience on LSD, which I think still bothers her. She saw really frightening things, had this terrible paranoia that someone was out to get her. For hours she sat with her body rigid. Sometimes she screamed. She told me it was like having a nightmare. After that incident she was depressed and fearful for a long time. Her grades went down and she didn't want to go out with her friends.

How a teenager will respond to any drug depends on a variety of factors. The teenager who is under pressure or who has severe emotional problems is probably the most likely to suffer adverse effects from a single use. However, because we can never be completely sure about the quality of the drug, and because everyone responds differently under different circumstances, there is an element of risk in even one dose of any of these drugs.

Accidents: For teenagers, by far the most serious and possibly irreversible side effect of drug and alcohol use, even one-time use, is "driving under the influence." You don't have to be a steady user of any substance to wind up in a car accident because you were stoned or drunk. Statistics show that approximately 55 percent of all fatal car crashes involve an alcohol-impaired driver. In a study of 25,000 drunk-driving deaths, 35 percent were caused by sixteen- to twenty-four-year-olds.*

Teenagers are often unable to assess how drunk they actually are because their experience with drinking and their experience with driving are both relatively new. It is easy for them to think their driving is fine even though they're drunk. In fact, a person who is only slightly intoxicated will not be able to react as quickly as normal in an emergency situation.

Being stoned while driving is equally dangerous. The statistics for drug-related accidents are less dramatic, simply because alcohol is still the number one drug consumed by teenagers as well as adults. Also, until recently police hadn't developed methods for detecting marijuana intoxication. But being stoned does slow motor reaction time and alters depth perception enough so that it seriously threatens driving ability.

Kids who are "high" also drown, fall off mountain trails, set property (or themselves) on fire, walk through windows, and jump out of high buildings. The California Lifeguard Association estimates that over one-third of all the fatal drownings on California beaches involve a swimmer or surfer who is "under the influence." A majority of these people are teenagers.

It's Against the Law: When teenagers use drugs or alcohol they are breaking the law, and they run the risk of ar-

*Ellen Goodman, "New Kids–Parents Contract Has Promise," Los Angeles *Times* (January 18, 1983).

rest and entanglement with the juvenile or adult justice system. Of the drugs that teenagers consume, certain ones are illegal for the general population. These include cocaine, heroin, the hallucinogens and PCP, which come under the Federal Narcotics Act and carry felony charges for possession or sale. In the majority of states, marijuana also still falls under this category, though eleven states have made possession a lesser offense. These states define possession of a specific amount of marijuana as a misdemeanor or civil offense subject to fines rather than jail sentences.*

Drugs that are legal for the adult population or available by prescription are often obtained illegally by teenagers and used for recreational purposes. This is obviously true in the case of alcohol. It also applies to barbiturates, amphetamines, Quaaludes and other prescription drugs. A frightening problem is that while these drugs may be prescribed for adults in a limited dose, teenagers may take large or dangerous quantities to produce a high.

Because the use of drugs and alcohol is illegal very often teenagers are afraid to call the police when some emergency arises. The fear of getting caught also may prevent them from calling an ambulance or other emergency service for themselves or a friend. In the case of kids who are chronic users or abusers, the legal complications can create a situation with tragic consequences:

> There was an incident during the time Gwen was using drugs which I would like to forget. She was at a party and she was stoned and she got involved with a stranger there and he raped her. Her friends called me up to come get her. She was very upset, but we didn't press charges because we knew if we had there would be a trial and her drug use would come out, and there would be a whole other set of charges.

Some Teenagers Are More Likely to Become Dependent on Drugs or Alcohol: Depression, lack of direction, rebellion, low self-esteem, estrangement from family, and a feeling of being lost are characteristics that many, if not *all*, teenagers display at one time or another. It's when those feelings are chronic and when ties to family and community are weak, that teenagers are most susceptible to becoming dependent on drugs.

Not all teenagers who have these symptoms wind up abusing drugs. These patterns are simply warning signs. From our discussions with professionals in this field, as well as our interviews with parents and teenagers, we have compiled the following list:

Teenagers Most Likely to Become Dependent:

—come from families where one or both parents abuse them

—are having problems in other areas of their life, such as school, social relationships, family

—feel they don't measure up to family expectations

—don't feel connected to school or any other activities (sports, community, church)

—have trouble separating their desires and opinions from the opinions of their friends

—are depressed much of the time, feel anxious and pessimistic about life

—come from families where there is no clearly stated value system around drug use and where drugs aren't discussed (see What Can We Do . . . ? p. 101)

Despite all these signs, there are no strict formulas about who is likely to use or abuse. Drug use and abuse can cut across racial, economic, urban, and rural lines as well as confounding behavioral indicators. Although it is less likely, athletes, student body presidents, scholastic achievers, and outgoing kids with "regular" family ties can also have dependency and abuse problems. And some kids, for no apparent reason, seem to respond more sensitively to drugs or alcohol:

> When Dara's drug taking started, I was not aware that drugs would have the attraction they did for her . . . finally, the obsessive quality they had. She wanted to get high. She *enjoyed* being high. Drugs were very powerful for her.

> I would consider us a normal, average family. When Tim began smoking marijuana, he didn't seem to have too many problems. He never smoked at home, only at school. He performed at school. He wasn't doing great, but he's very charming and he could get by. The boys he smoked with are terrific kids, really nice. Two of them we took on family vacations with us. They participated in all of the family activities. It wasn't until later that I discovered that all of these kids were smoking every day.

How Can You Tell When Your Teenager Is Dependent on Drugs or Alcohol?: How can you tell if your teenagers have a drug or alcohol problem when they hide it from you? What are the signs and symptoms of drug abuse that parents can watch for?

In this the parents have to trust and rely on their intuition. Our children may not acknowledge having a drug or alcohol problem; there may be no "conclusive proof" that one exists, but as parents we may still feel very strongly that something is very wrong:

> All last summer, when Jeff first started getting into drugs, we knew something was wrong, but we just kept ignoring it. He would be gone a lot. Then when he came home he was always sleeping. My wife and I knew he was acting strange, but I think we didn't want to see it.

---

*The eleven states are: Alaska, California, Colorado, Maine, Minnesota, Mississippi, Nebraska, New York, North Carolina, Ohio, and Oregon.

When my daughter started drinking, she would go out to parties and get very drunk. When I asked her about it, she said that she just had a little too much to drink. That didn't sit right with me. My intuition told me this child is really unhappy. After the arrest it all came out in the open and she finally told us she did have a problem with alcohol and that she was pretty messed up emotionally.

On the other hand, though we may sense there is a problem, out of our own fear, or out of the desire not to have anything wrong, we don't act on our intuition. Many parents report that they never suspected their teenager was in trouble with drugs or alcohol until fairly late in the game when some crisis erupted.

There are several warning signs of a potential abuse problem (though not every teenager with these symptoms may be involved with drugs). The following is a list of behaviors that have been observed in teenagers who are dependent on drugs or alcohol:

—Losing interest in school. They often cut school and their grades drop.

—Being secretive and withdrawing from family activities.

—Being defensive about their behavior. They usually deny there is any problem with their drinking or drug taking.

—Finding a circle of friends who are also abusing.

—Frequently getting into anti-social problems. They can get in trouble at school or with the law. Many get caught stealing.

—Lying about their drug or alcohol consumption as well as frequently lying about other activities.

—Exhibiting specific signs of drug abuse (see p. 105).

What Can We Do . . . ?: Despite the well-publicized dangers, some adolescents and parents are blasé about drug use, write it off as merely a stage in adolescence to be largely ignored unless it gets out of hand. Many parents think, If the child's not in trouble with these substances, why talk about it?

Intervening early *can* help prevent problems. Parents of teenagers who do get into trouble with drugs or alcohol often report that prior to their child's involvement, the issue wasn't discussed in their home:

When Matthew was smoking marijuana, we knew it, but we never really sat down and talked about it—how much he was smoking or where he was getting it or who was paying for it. We never really addressed it directly, I think, because I had no idea how big of a problem it was. I figured he smoked a joint once in a while, but not that it was something he was doing every day.

As this subject opens up for our kids it is crucial that we be candid with them about our feelings on their using drugs and alcohol. To set up effective rules that will be respected involves absolute honesty on our part about our own behavior. How we act, and the part drugs and alcohol play in our own lives, is our children's strongest teacher. If we overuse drugs or alcohol, it is important that we acknowledge that fact to ourselves and to our teenager. But, unfortunately, simply admitting our weakness will not necessarily prevent our teenager from doing as we do:

I am a recovered alcoholic. My daughter usually never drinks. The other night she went to this party and had three beers. She said it was really fantastic. She got the giggles, and really let down her inhibitions, asked all these guys to dance. She said it was fabulous. She understands now why I drank for all those years.

I am a compulsive eater. I know I run to the refrigerator when I'm angry or nervous. The other day my son and I had a fight. And I watched him storm into the kitchen and grab a handful of cookies.

Many parents have found that the strongest statement they can make to their children at this time is to modify their own use of these substances. Efforts at cutting down on coffee or alcohol, giving up cigarettes or marijuana, dieting, or doing without tranquilizers at stressful moments will be observed by our teenagers:

When I found my daughter was smoking pot regularly I was very upset, and I realized I had to stop smoking marijuana myself. Actually, that made it easy for me to stop.

Some parents have found that they develop a really strong bond with their kids if they both work together to quit:

My daughter and I have been on a program together to quit. I am stopping smoking and she is giving up sugar. She hates the fact that I smoke, and I can't stand to see what she is doing to her complexion and her teeth by eating all those candy bars. We've been on our program now for three weeks and so far we're doing great.

Like this mother and daughter, our children can actually help us to change behaviors in ourselves that we don't like. But in the end, our kids cannot *make* us stop smoking any more than we can *make* them stop eating sugar (or smoking marijuana). What we can do, however, is create an environment where family members' efforts to change are acknowledged and encouraged.

In some families where their teenagers' substance abuse has been a big problem, parents have chosen to stop drinking and not have any liquor in the house while their children are still living at home. Even where the parents' own drinking has been moderate, if their teenagers have been abusing drugs or alcohol, they have decided that what their child needed most at that point was a drug- and alcohol-free environment.

Another thing we can do is sort out our own values and

attitudes: what do we feel about drugs and alcohol in our home? Is it acceptable to us if our child has drugs in his or her room? Is it acceptable to us if they drink or take drugs in our presence? Do we drink or take drugs in front of our kids? With our kids? What is our stand when our child is going to a party or rock concert where alcohol or drugs are likely to be available? Do we want them to tell us if they *are* planning to drink or use drugs?

There are no "correct" answers to these questions. We spoke with lots of parents and all of them deal with these issues differently. Here is what some parents say they've done:

- Now that our kids are teenagers, even though we sometimes drink, we don't have a cocktail every afternoon at six anymore to unwind.
- We do social drinking at home, and I will allow my daughters a glass of wine on special occasions or holidays, but no one drinks to get drunk.
- When we have a party with our friends, even if our kids are home, we don't let them drink with us because we think it's inappropriate.
- I don't allow my children to be "involved" in my vices. I don't want them to light my cigarettes for me or get me a drink or help out at parties with the cocktails. I've told them that I think it's very unhealthy.
- In our house, if someone's taking a pill, you figure they have to be seriously ill. That's our attitude, and the kids see that.
- My kids are now in their late twenties and we still don't smoke marijuana together because I don't think that's appropriate.
- We were driving on 125th Street the other day and my kids were making nasty cracks about the winos and addicts. I pointed out that some of those people started out just like them—that anybody who drinks or gets into drugs can wind up in the same place.
- I found that my older daughters were my best resource in persuading my son not to smoke marijuana. They'd seen what happened to some of their friends who had gotten involved with pot and they were much more effective with their younger brother than I could have been.
- Until our kids were sixteen, they couldn't go to parties without chaperones, or where we didn't know the parents.
- We feel like it has helped to tell our kids that you never know what's in the drugs you buy off the street. Once or twice a month there's a horror story in the paper about some kid getting poisoned from street drugs.
- We're a Christian family and we brought our children up in the Christian tradition. We feel their religion gives them the strength they need to resist the temptation to take drugs.
- My son and daughter are both big athletes. They are really concerned with keeping in good shape and competing, and I think that's what has kept them from getting heavily into drugs.
- I'm a fanatic about keeping my kids informed about drugs. I clip articles from the newspaper, and last week I brought home some pamphlets from work. If there's a program on TV about drugs we usually watch it together.
- We allowed some pot smoking on occasion when our kids were teenagers. We never said, "Thou shalt not experiment!" to our kids, but we've also never had a problem with it getting out of hand.
- I think the thing that kept my teenagers from getting involved with drinking or drugs is that they were always too busy in after-school activities and sports and religious school.

We're also going to have to inform ourselves about what the "drug scene" is like in our children's lives. The best way to do that is to ask them—without saying, "What do *you* do?" We don't want to scare off our kids. We need to remember that any discussion of this kind can work only at times when we feel able to listen openly—without overreacting or judging. Here are some questions that may be helpful:

Are kids you know getting drunk or stoned at school?

How does the school deal with this?

What kinds of drugs do kids at your school take?

Are drugs available at parties? What kinds?

How are other parents dealing with drug abuse? Do they know?

Learning what is going on in our child's world with drugs and alcohol, understanding more about his or her feelings about this "scene," and opening up communication puts us in a better position to set realistic limits. As in other areas, it's best not to make too many rules and not to make any you can't follow through on. You may not be able to enforce some of the limits that you set or agree on. There may be no way to be absolutely sure that your child will not drink and drive, but this hardly diminishes the importance of making clear what you expect:

I have learned that I can't forbid something that I can't enforce. Like about drugs, I can say, "I don't want you smoking marijuana, but I can't patrol you." I just have to trust them. Unless you're going to confine them to the house twenty-four hours a day, you really have to trust them.

In the end, the effectiveness of the limits you set has more to do with the quality of the communication with your child in this area than it does with the enforceability of the limit. Openly talking about our feelings about drugs or about drinking and driving can be a very effective deterrent:

When Jeremy was a teenager there was a tremendous amount of drugs around—LSD, mescaline, pot. It was very scary. Years later he said to me, " You know in those days, one of the things that kept me from going out and trying a lot of drugs was that I saw how frightened you were." My telling him I was scared acted like a brake.

As parents we can back up the "no driving" rule by making it clear that we are willing to pick up our teenagers if they have been drinking, no matter where they are or what time it is. We can also give them other alternatives, like money for taxis or public transportation and phone numbers of other adult relatives or friends who would be willing to get them in case of an emergency. It should also be stressed that if they are drunk and can't find a way home, *they should stay put.*

Communities throughout the country have instituted agreements between teenagers and their parents that say that if the teenagers call with a request for a ride because they or their friends have had too much liquor or drugs, parents will go pick them up with no questions asked at the moment.

We can negotiate this type of agreement with our own children and with friends who have teenagers without condoning drinking or taking drugs. The agreement simply allows a way for our children to be safe. The same is true in any other emergency situation where our teenagers may need to contact us or other adults. We can reassure them that regardless of how drunk or stoned everyone is, in an emergency they must call us.

In an effort to cope with the problem of adolescent drug abuse, some parents have initiated community groups (sometimes called Parent Power Groups) to set community limits and standards for teenage drug and alcohol use; to provide mutual support; provide chaperones; and initiate prevention education.

If Your Child Is Abusing Drugs or Alcohol: There is nothing more frightening than the realization that our child is in trouble with drugs or alcohol. But we may have many other strong feelings—guilt, anger, rage, frustration, helplessness, even despair. Parents who have been through this say that at one point or another they have experienced all of these emotions:

> When I first found out about Cynthia's drug use and about the shoplifting, I was very angry. My first reaction was that I had been betrayed. I consider myself a very honest person and I have taught all of my children to be honest. So this was really shocking.

> When my daughter was out drinking and taking drugs I used to be home with this feeling of complete dread that the phone would ring or that there would come a knock on the door . . . that any moment of the day or night I could be told once again that she had overdosed. It was a horror. I felt completely helpless, in such alien territory. It wasn't anything I had been prepared for. I was ashamed, too. But the deepest, strongest feeling I had was this desperate fear that she would die.

> When Jonathan was into drugs I had a lot of mixed feelings. There certainly was the feeling of failure; the feeling of fury. There was tremendous confusion. "How could it happen?" I have six other children. We've got a Harvard graduate in our family; we've got a Swarthmore graduate. We've got a lawyer with degrees in three states. We've got a senior editor of a national magazine. How could we also have this? We never had a child like this!

Nothing is easy about this kind of situation. As parents we want to protect, to intervene, to help. On the other hand, when it comes to the issue of substance abuse, perhaps more than other times, it's essential for us to do *whatever is necessary to enable our teenager to take responsibility for his or her own behavior*. We cannot fix this situation for them once they become abusers. Neither all our love and caring nor all our discipline and parental authority can make our teenager stop taking drugs or alcohol. They have to do that for themselves:

> I don't know how or why Steve decided he wanted to stop fooling around with drugs. He came to us himself and asked about going to a different school. Before that we had tried to get him to stop. He knew how we felt and how concerned we were for his grades and that we didn't like the boys he was hanging around with. We did everything: therapies, grounding him, curfews, all sorts of restrictions, but nothing stuck for very long. It was pretty awful around our house during those years. Then it changed. I'm still not sure how, but I think Steve was scared. He wanted to go to college and he knew he wasn't headed for college the way things were going.

Your teenager who is abusing needs your support. Giving this support, however, does not mean continually covering up or bailing him out every time there's a problem. Almost every parent we talked to had stories to tell both of incidents where they had let go and allowed their child to experience consequences, and situations where they had rescued their child. Unfortunately, there seems to be no magic formula that works best. We react according to who we are as people, the kind of relationship we have with our teenager, and our own attitudes in the area of drugs and alcohol.

Keep communication open and let your teenager know how you feel.

As difficult as it is, hang in there with your son or daughter. If they will let you, talk about what is happening to them and what they are feeling. And tell them how you feel. When we feel scared or angry or vulnerable, we should let them know. When our child is in trouble, doing something extremely dangerous, the truth is we usually don't know what to do. There isn't any simple way that we can fix it.

Some parents we talked to asked a friend or relative to spend time with their son or daughter. Probably what your teenager needs most at this point is an advocate, someone who is older, supportive, and with whom he or she feels free to talk. It's hard for you to be this person because in all likelihood you are too close to the situation.

Get outside help for your teenager.

There are a variety of treatment programs and therapies that may help. Many teenagers get involved with peer self-help programs like the teenage groups in Alcoholics Anonymous. These programs seem to be a successful model, but there are also a variety of private and group therapies and residential treatment programs specifically designed for teenagers.

The kind of help you choose depends on several factors, including what is available in your community, cost,* and what you and your child feel most comfortable with. (See Resources section.) Shop as carefully for a treatment program or therapy as you would for a cancer surgeon! Get the opinion of other professionals working in this field, and if you do find a program you like, try to find other parents who have used it and ask them how it worked for their family.

The most important factor involved in the success of a program is your child's willingness to participate. No treatment will work if your child is not ready to stop abusing drugs and alcohol, or if he or she doesn't want to enter treatment. Even when your teenager wants and asks for some kind of help, it's important not to view any of these programs as cure-alls. While some kids make immediate changes in their behavior, *most* have slips. They will backslide for periods of time or go in and out of various programs.

The problem is stubborn and difficult: our teenagers started taking drugs or drinking because they really liked the way those things made them feel. Even in heavy dependence, when the substances no longer work the way they used to, it is still *enormously difficult* to change this behavior. When teenagers stop abusing drugs they have to find a whole new set of friends, develop interests and activities that don't center around getting high, and learn ways of coping with their problems without the aid of drugs or alcohol. Even when our teenagers manage to stay off drugs or alcohol, they are still going to have all the problems of growing up to contend with.

Measure their progress realistically.

Try to be realistic about your child's improvement and to help him or her set workable goals. As AA teaches, teenagers need to worry only about staying off drugs or liquor for one day at a time, or one moment, not forever. Some parents have found it helpful to give concrete incentives to their children for changes in their behavior, such as greater privileges, or even money, for every day their teenager stays sober. Without being naïve, it is important that we view this progress incrementally. If they manage not to drink or use drugs for several months, rather than several days, before they "blow it," acknowledge that they were able *not* to use for a longer period of time.

Get some help for yourself.

This is critical. When your teenager is abusing drugs or alcohol, the whole family is affected. You not only have to

*Programs and therapies vary in cost, and some can be quite expensive. Insurance covers some of these programs, and groups like AA ask for small donations.

help your child cope with his or her problem, but also to learn to handle your own feelings in this crisis. When a teenager is abusing, *parents need help as much as their children do*. They need to talk to other parents who are in similar situations and to know they are not alone.

There are groups, such as Alanon, which are self-help networks for family and friends of alcoholics. Parents can also get help through a variety of private therapies and support groups (see Resources section). Parents have also gotten help through community drug prevention networks.

Be creative about your resources.

Because your child's problem is likely to affect the entire family deeply, some people end up sending their teenager to live with a relative or family friend where everyone, including the teenager, may feel more able to deal with the problem. Even if your own family relations are not so strained, it is easier on everyone if you can take a break from parenting and let someone else do it for a while. Sometimes teenagers can more easily comply with rules and limits set down by an adult who is not their parent. Short of a new living situation, many parents we talked with said they helped their children change schools, or helped them change their circle of friends.

For some parents the situation gets to the point where they feel that the only way to handle things is to make a radical choice. In some cases, the entire family made the decision to move out of the area. In other cases parents worked fewer hours or quit their job. Obviously these decisions are very personal. Even in the most desperate situation there are usually choices. What you do will be guided by the available resources and by what works best for your teenager and for the rest of your family.

Try not to take their behavior personally.

This is probably the hardest task of all, because some of your child's behavior *is* directed at you. Unfortunately, it doesn't help you or your teenager to beat your breast—or to overreact to their hostility. Try to let up on yourself; keep the time you spend feeling guilty to a minimum. Over and over again parents in this situation tell us they have learned that you can't change your children. What you *can* do is support them to find the strength necessary to do that for themselves. One mother put it this way:

I don't really know if I have any advice to give to parents. We tried so many things during the time Josh was involved with drugs. When I look back on it, I'm not sure what worked. In the end, maybe all you can do is try to keep your child from harming himself and wait and hope that on his own he will change. A lot of the time that's all we *could* do. So I guess that had to be enough.

Facts About Specific Drugs*

Getting good factual information about drugs and alcohol is not always easy. Often, what comes from the media and drug experts can be contradictory and inconclusive. Our own teenagers don't help the situation because they can make us feel unsure of ourselves. It's their world, not ours, and because we may not know the latest jargon, it is easy to feel out of touch. When our kids assert that marijuana smoking is not more harmful than an evening cocktail (and a lot less calories), we can feel defensive and uncertain. In fact, teenagers' information on drugs is very likely to be unreliable. Many teenagers function on the theory that "doing" is "knowing." In other words, people who take drugs or sell drugs know about drugs, is what they are saying. Don't believe it. It is almost always up to us to get accurate information and—if necessary—to find some way of making our kids hear it.

Depressants:	Alcohol
	Barbiturates
	Inhalants
	Opiates and painkillers
	Quaaludes
	Tranquilizers
Stimulants:	Amphetamines
	Preludin
	Caffeine
	Cocaine
	Look-Alike Drugs
Hallucinogens:	LSD
	Mushrooms and Psilocybin
	Peyote and Mescaline
Marijuana	
Nicotine	
PCP	

DEPRESSANTS:

Depressants are drugs that slow down body functions such as breathing, heart rate, and blood pressure. The drugs that fall into this category include alcohol, barbiturates, inhalants, the opiates, Quaaludes (methaqualone), and tranquilizers.

Alcohol   Alcohol is one of the most powerful and potentially dangerous of all drugs for teenagers. According to the National Council on Alcoholism, 3.3 million teenagers between the ages of fourteen and seventeen have a problem with alcohol.†

*Special thanks to Craig Weisman for his research on drugs and alcohol.

†*Alcoholism Fact Sheet,* National Council on Alcoholism, Los Angeles County, Inc.

Slang Names: Brew, brewski, JD, booze, Southern Comfort, Red Eye, White Lightning, horney water, wine, etc.

How Do Teenagers Get Alcohol? Most teenagers initially experiment with their parents' alcohol. They also purchase it through older friends or siblings and many large towns have stores that will sell alcohol to minors. Some teenagers use false identification in order to buy liquor or drive to nearby states where age regulations may be looser.

Effects: Alcohol is a sedative or central nervous system depressant, which initially relaxes the user and later removes inhibitions. A 12-ounce can of beer, a 5-ounce glass of wine, and 1.5 ounces of whiskey all contain the same amount of alcohol. Increased amounts of alcohol result in loss of concentration, slurred speech, and lack of coordination. An overdose of alcohol can result in coma and death.

How alcohol affects a person depends on how fast it is consumed, how strong the alcoholic content of the drink is, whether or not the drinker eats before or during alcohol consumption, and the body weight of the individual. Sipping a drink slowly and eating before or during drinking will lessen drunkenness.

Contrary to popular belief, the only thing that sobers you up from alcohol is time. It takes about one and a half hours to sober up for each drink consumed. Remedies such as black coffee, exercise, cold showers, fresh air, have no effect on blood alcohol content; they only produce wide awake drunks.

Dangers: Drinking while driving is the most immediate danger for teenagers. Another danger associated with recreational use is that drinking makes it very difficult for teenagers to think clearly. Many teenagers report having had a sexual experience or a dangerous experience like stealing while drunk, which they later regretted.

Over time, alcohol is both psychologically and physically addicting. Tolerance to the drug builds up rapidly and even moderate drinkers will need to consume more alcohol to reach the same level of intoxication. Prolonged drinking causes a lot of physical damage and can affect the brain, liver, kidney, heart, pancreas, throat, stomach, and nervous system. People who are alcoholics often suffer from malnutrition, because the drug is high in calories but provides no nourishment, and alcoholics are less likely to consume nutritious food.

The psychological health of a heavy drinker is usually affected. Alcohol often contributes to problems of child abuse, wife beating, broken marriages, employment difficulties, suicides, and homicides.

Teenagers often use alcohol with other drugs. The combination of alcohol and sedatives may stop breathing and cause death.

Withdrawal from alcohol is far more serious than heroin withdrawal, since it can result in death. The alcoholic may experience tremors, cramps, convulsions, hallucinations, sweating, heart failure, and coma.

Who Is Likely to Become an Alcoholic? Alcoholism affects people of all ages, races, sexes, religions, and economic status. The vast majority of alcoholics don't live on Skid Row. They function in society—go to school or work, raise children, and take family vacations.

An alcoholic is a person who is not able to control the amount of liquor he or she drinks. Some people say they were alcoholic almost from the first time they took a drink. Others drink for a number of years before they become dependent. Though we are not yet sure whether the causes are physiological or environmental (they may be both), many alcoholics come from families where one or both parents are also alcoholics. You are also more likely to develop a dependency on alcohol if your parents totally abstain from alcohol and make moral judgments about drinking.

Many authorities feel that alcoholism is a disease that gets worse over the long run. It can be arrested by not drinking, but not cured. In the same way that diabetics must not eat certain foods, even alcoholics who are recovered cannot drink socially because sooner or later their addiction to alcohol will take over again.

How Can You Tell If a Teenager Is Drunk? A drunken teenager will smell of alcohol (or a combination of alcohol and breath freshener) and he or she may show any or all of the following signs: slurred speech, talking too loud, forgetfulness, poor physical coordination, droopy eyelids, and inappropriate reactions like belligerence, depression, silliness, or increased affection. If you find a teenager who is drunk, asleep, and cannot be awakened, roll him onto his side and call for medical help—especially if there has been vomiting. If you suspect a combination of pills and alcohol, have the child's stomach pumped.

How Can You Tell If a Teenager Might Be an Alcoholic? The following are behavior patterns that are signs that a person is dependent on alcohol. They include:

• Drinking in the morning
• Drinking alone regularly
• Problems with school or work due to drinking
• Needing a drink at a definite time daily
• Having a loss of memory while or after drinking
• Drinking to relieve shyness, fear, inadequacy
• Becoming more moody or irritable after drinking

Barbiturates This group of drugs includes Amytal, Nembutal, Seconal, phenobarbital, chloral hydrate, and Tuinal. Such drugs are prescribed by physicians to relieve anxiety and to help people sleep. Teenagers take them while awake in order to feel high.

Slang Names: Downers, reds, rainbows, neb's, yellows, barbs.

How Do Teenagers Get Barbiturates? They are either sto-len from pharmacies or they are manufactured illegally and then sold on the street. Some teenagers steal their parents' barbiturates.

Cost: About $1 for a single pill.

How Are Barbiturates Taken? They are swallowed in pill form. Teenagers who get high on barbiturates often take two to four times the prescribed dose.

Effects: Barbiturates produce a drunklike state, and the user experiences a release of inhibitions, a loss of coordination, and slurred speech. These drugs are physically addicting and the body builds up a tolerance for them so that more of the drug is needed to produce similar effects.

Dangers: Barbiturates are considered as addicting as heroin and withdrawal from them is more severe than heroin withdrawal. It is not uncommon for a steady barbiturate user to die from severe seizures while withdrawing from the drug.

The greatest danger associated with taking barbiturates is the danger of overdose. It is easy to become confused while sedated and to lose count of how many pills you have taken. Like too much alcohol, barbiturates in large quantities suppress the gag reflex, which can result in a person drowning in their own saliva or vomit. Taking too many barbiturates at one time can also result in respiratory arrest.

Because taking barbiturates causes loss of coordination, accidents (downing, car accidents, burns) are far more common. People taking barbiturates have also inflicted violence on others and on themselves.

One of the greatest dangers associated with this type of drug is the common adolescent practice of mixing barbiturates and alcohol. Drinking and taking any sedative (barbiturates, tranquilizers, or Quaaludes) increases the risk of a toxic or fatal overdose, even in experienced users. In fact, because tolerance does develop to this drug, the experienced user is more likely to end up taking too many pills and risking a possible fatal dose.

If you think someone has overdosed on barbiturates, call for medical help immediately. Walk the person up and down to keep him conscious. *Do not* give coffee. If you suspect alcohol and pills have been consumed, see that the stomach is pumped.

How Can You Tell If a Teenager Is on Barbiturates? Barbiturate users will behave as if they are drunk, but there will be no odor of alcohol on their breath. Other signs include: droopy eyelids, slurred speech, stumbling and lack of coordination, belligerence, inappropriate laughter.

Inhalants Inhalants are a group of products containing chemicals that depress the central nervous system and that teenagers sniff or inhale in order to get high. They include spray paint (particularly metallic colors), glue, gasoline, hair spray, spray Freon, Pam, nail polish remover, Liquid Paper, Magic Markers, and paint thinner. Because inhalants are easy to obtain and relatively inexpensive, kids who use them tend to be young (the average age is eleven or twelve).

Slang Names: Slang includes the brand names of various products and the colors of the paints used. Particular favorites are clear crystal, gold, silver, copper.

How Do Teenagers Get Inhalants? There are no paint pushers. Solvents and aerosols are available in practically every home, and most teenagers can find stores where they buy or steal what they need.

Cost: The average child passes through this stage without paying anything because they use products they find at home. Teenagers who continue to abuse inhalants will purchase one or two cans of spray paint daily at the cost of $120 per month. Some stores have refused to sell glue or spray paint to minors.

How Are Inhalants Taken? Teenagers put socks or handkerchiefs soaked with these products in plastic bags, which are then sniffed or inhaled.

Effects: Inhalants produce a drunkenlike high. If the user continues to inhale, he may also experience blurred vision and hallucinations. One teenager described paint sniffing as a cheap PCP high. The effects can last for one or more hours after inhalation is stopped. Typically, teenagers will sniff periodically to maintain the high.

Dangers: There are so many different chemicals involved with inhalants that all the dangers associated with their use are probably not known. Inhalants have been known to cause numbness, confusion, nausea, vomiting, tremor, memory loss, visual impairment, and coma. There have been various reports of death due to inhalation, either from suffocation from the plastic bag, or from pulmonary arrest due to the lungs freezing. (This can happen when the user inhales Freon or spray aerosols directly into the mouth.)

There is evidence that chronic sniffers become brain impaired. Paint can also clog the lungs and cause oxygen deprivation or heart problems. Damage to kidneys, nervous system, and bone marrow has also been documented. Because of impaired coordination and a distorted view of reality, a teenager using an inhalant is often the victim of accidents.

How Can You Tell If a Teenager Is Sniffing Inhalants? Their clothes will smell of gasoline or paint. They will appear to be drunk and they may be belligerent. Signs of chronic use are a rash around the mouth, paint on the teeth, and finding a sock stiff with paint or glue. The odor of many of these products will continue to come out in a user's perspiration and breath for at least a day after he or she has inhaled the substance.

Opiates and Painkillers This group of drugs includes codeine, morphine, and heroin, which are all derived from the opium poppy. Heroin is illegal in any form in this country, but codeine and morphine are prescribed for pain and as a cough suppressant. There are also a number of synthetic drugs (Demerol, Dilaudids, methadone) that have similar effects to opiates and are prescribed for pain, but also sold illegally on the street. Another opiatelike substance is "lodes,"

illegally manufactured pills containing codeine and Doriden, a nonbarbiturate hypnotic. Of all these drugs, heroin is the most common drug of abuse.

Slang Names: Big H, white stuff, horse, chiva, junk, dope, smack, H, hard stuff, and shit.

How Do Teenagers Get Opiates? Heroin and the painkillers are sold illegally through drug dealers.

Cost: Heroin costs $25 for a spoon or $100 for a gram. Dilaudids cost $25 to $30 a piece. A habit could cost $2,500 to $5,000 a month. Many heroin and opium users steal or turn to prostitution to support their habit.

How Are the Opiates Taken? Heroin is normally injected in the vein. It can also be applied just under the skin ("skin popping"), and it is also sniffed or smoked. Painkillers are usually swallowed in pill form. Raw opium is smoked in a pipe.

Effects: The initial effect of heroin is usually a "rush," which users describe as a very intense, pleasurable feeling. The drug is a central nervous system depressant, but unlike alcohol and barbiturates, heroin depresses feelings of aggression. It also inhibits the sex drive and hunger.

Dangers: All the opiates and synthetic painkillers are physically and psychologically addicting. Heroin is more addicting than most. Because the drug is so expensive, it is often mixed with substances resembling heroin, including sugar, soap powder, Epsom salts, or talcum powder. Although the drug is strong and lethal in high doses, many of the dangers of using heroin come from the substances that are mixed with the drug. Users are also vulnerable to hepatitis, collapsed veins, and a variety of other infections. The cost of the habit often causes the user to resort to crime and a dangerous lifestyle. Ten percent of heroin addicts commit suicide.

Quaaludes (Methaqualone) Quaaludes are hypnotic sedatives that are prescribed primarily for sleep, but that are chemically unlike barbiturates. These pills are prescribed legally in "stress centers" around the country, or manufactured illegally or stolen and then sold on the street.

Slang Names: Ludes, lemons, 714s, pillows, disco biscuits, vitamin Q.

How Do Teenagers Get Quaaludes? They are purchased through friends or drug dealers. Sometimes Quaaludes bought on the street are, in fact, nothing more than tranquilizers and some may be cut with additives.

Cost: Quaaludes cost about $10 each on the street. A weekend Quaalude user will spend at least $60 a month.

How Are Quaaludes Taken? They are usually taken in tablet or capsule form, but can also be crushed and smoked in a marijuana cigarette. When teenagers become used to taking them, one Quaalude is usually not enough, so they buy two or three for a high.

Effects: The effects of this drug are similar to barbiturates, including physical addiction and withdrawal symptoms.

Quaaludes are known as an aphrodisiac because like all sedatives they lower inhibitions, but a Quaalude is no more stimulating sexually than a barbiturate or a glass of wine. Though a person taking Quaaludes will only experience the "high" for a few hours, the drug remains in the body for several days.

Dangers: Like barbiturates, Quaaludes are physically addicting, and the biggest danger associated with both these drugs is overdose. A person overdosing on Quaaludes will have convulsions, tremors, and vomiting. There is a possibility of breathing stopping and even if the person's pulse is normal, it's important to get medical help and to keep him moving and awake.

Withdrawal from Quaalude addiction is severe and can result in seizures or even death.

Taking Quaaludes with alcohol is a common practice with teenagers and this combination dramatically increases the chance of overdose or respiratory failure. Also, there are a number of incidents of teenagers who took Quaaludes, went swimming, and drowned.

How Can You Tell If a Teenager Is on Quaaludes? Like barbiturates, Quaalude users will appear drunk, but without the accompanying smell of alcohol. Their coordination will be off, their speech slurred, and they may appear drowsy.

Tranquilizers These drugs are not as powerful as barbiturates or Quaaludes, but like barbiturates they also depress the nervous system and relax muscles. Commonly prescribed tranquilizers include Librium, Miltown, Dalmane, and Valium. Tranquilizers are the third most consumed drug in this country and are outsold only by alcohol and nicotine. Contrary to popular belief, tranquilizers are physically as well as psychologically addicting and withdrawal from them can cause seizures or even death.

Of all the tranquilizers, Valium is by far the most commonly prescribed and it is also the one that teenagers get hold of and take to get high. If a tranquilizer overdose occurs, get medical help and walk the user until such help arrives.

STIMULANTS:

Stimulants are a group of drugs that accelerate body functions including breathing, heart rate, and blood pressure. The most commonly known drugs that act as stimulants are amphetamines, cocaine, caffeine, the look-alike drugs, and nicotine.

Amphetamines These are powerful drugs prescribed by physicians to decrease appetite, maintain alertness, or to counteract the sedative properties of other drugs. They usually come in pill form, but many are available in a white powder. Most commonly, amphetamines are available in white tablets with crosses on top. They also come in pink, heart-shaped pills and green, orange, or black capsules. Amphetamine brand names include Dexedrine, Biphetamine, Dexamyl, Appedrine, and Desoxyn. Another closely related substance is Methamphetamine, or "crystal," which is sold illegally in powder form.

Amphetamines are consumed most commonly by people who have to stay awake long hours, such as truck drivers and students, as well as by people trying to lose weight. Teenagers take amphetamines recreationally because they say the drug gives them a sense of increased alertness and euphoria. They report that thoughts rush into their minds, they become more talkative, and they feel like they can solve the world's problems.

Slang Names: Whites, uppers, meth, bennies, Black Beauties, beauties, Christmas trees, hearts, Methedrine, Benzedrine, Dexedrine, crank, speed, mini-whites, white crosses, Robins' Eggs.

How Do Teenagers Get Amphetamines? They buy them from each other. The pills are either stolen from medicine chests or pharmacies, or chemically manufactured in illegal labs.

Cost: Black Beauties cost from $1 to $1.50. Robins' eggs cost $2 to $4. A typical teenage abuse pattern is taking amphetamines on Friday and Saturday night and recovering on Sunday. Weekend use of this type will cost $15 to $30 a month. Some teenagers, particularly girls, will take small amounts of amphetamines daily to help control their weight. This could cost up to $65 a month.

How Is It Taken? Most commonly, orally, in pill form. In powder form ("crystal") the drug is either snorted like cocaine or injected (slammed) into the vein.

Effects: Amphetamines stimulate the central nervous system, increasing heart rate, respiration, blood pressure. They cause the eyes to dilate, they decrease peripheral circulation, stimulate the adrenal gland, suppress the appetite, and cause nervous twitching and talkativeness. There is a sense of increased energy, clear thinking, and confidence in one's abilities. Depending on the dose, the effect of amphetamines will last from four to twenty-four hours.

Dangers: Though death or overdose are unlikely with amphetamines, over a period of time the drug is extremely debilitating to the body. It causes insomnia and exhaustion, as well as depression and stomach problems after it has worn off.

Either a high dose of amphetamines or chronic use of the drug can result in destruction of teeth enamel, nervousness, emotional instability, irritability, and, in some cases, paranoia, delusions, and hallucinations. When people stop taking amphetamines after consuming them for a period of time, they often become quite depressed.

Although amphetamines are not physically addicting, people develop strong psychological dependency on the drug, and those who have abused amphetamines for a long period of time cannot seem to return to moderate use. People who take amphetamines build up tolerance to the drug, and after a while larger doses are needed to get the same effect. There is also evidence that chronic use of amphetamines can contribute to heart disease.

How Can You Tell If a Teenager Is on Amphetamines? He

or she will have dilated pupils, complain of a dry mouth, and may be very excited and talkative. If the dosage is high, he or she may be frightened, nervous, or paranoid.

Preludin This is a stimulant commonly prescribed for weight control. It is not classified as an amphetamine, but it produces similar effects. Like amphetamines, Preludin is illegally obtained and then sold on the street for a profit. The drug is either taken in pill form or crushed and injected into the vein.

Caffeine This legal, nonprescription drug is most commonly found in coffee, but it also appears in tea, cola drinks, and, to a lesser degree, in chocolate. It is also available in pills. Caffeine is a stimulant, similar to amphetamines and cocaine, but it does not affect the central nervous system and generally produces only moderate reactions. New evidence suggests that caffeine may be physically addicting, and people often become psychologically dependent on coffee or colas. Like amphetamines, tolerance builds up to caffeine, and withdrawal from the drug may cause headaches, irritability, jittery feelings, and sleepiness.

Recently, with the growing concern about caffeine in the diet, cola and coffee manufacturers have begun marketing caffeine-free beverages. Here is a list of the amount of caffeine in foods and medications:

Coffee (5 oz. cup)	64–150 mg.
Tea	30–38 mg.
Cocoa	5–40 mg.
Chocolate (1 oz.)	20 mg.
Coke (12 oz.)	65 mg.
Tab	50 mg.
Pepsi	43 mg.
Mountain Dew	55 mg.
Diet Rite	32 mg.
Dr Pepper	61 mg.
Diet Dr Pepper	54 mg.
Excedrin (1 tablet)	65 mg.
Anacin	32 mg.
Empirin	32 mg.
No-Doz	100 mg.
Caffedrine	200 mg.
Vivarin	100 mg.
Drisdan	16 mg.
Midol	32 mg.
Prenens Forte	100 mg.

Dangers: Although the evidence is not yet conclusive, most medical authorities feel that it is not healthy for adults to consume more than 300 mg. of caffeine a day. Growing teenagers can tolerate less of the drug. Several reliable studies link caffeine with the development of benign breast tumors. Caffeine also plays a part in stimulating tachycardia (irregular heart beat) and certain individuals report nervousness, irritability, and insomnia from its use.

Recently, a variety of over-the-counter pills have ap-

peared on the market that are commonly known as "look-alike" drugs. (See Look-Alike Drugs section.) Because they don't contain any amphetamines, these drugs are legal, but they do contain high levels of caffeine. A look-alike pill can contain 200 to 500 mg. of caffeine. Teenagers consume these drugs and sometimes take between 10 and 20 pills at once. At these high levels, caffeine can produce respiratory failure, and the look-alike drugs have been responsible for several deaths in the past couple of years.

Cocaine Cocaine is a white, crystalline substance that comes from the leaves of the coca bush, commonly grown in South America. Cocaine is a central nervous system stimulant that is consumed illegally by many people, including middle-class professionals.

Slang Names: Coke, flake, snow, C, leaf, cola, ski trip, blowtoot, freeze, happy dust, nose candy, Peruvian lady, white girl.

How Do Teenagers Get Cocaine? Because it is illegal to import, sell, or possess cocaine, the drug is obtained solely through illegal sources. Teenagers who use cocaine most likely get it from dealers or friends.

Cost: $100 to $200 a gram. A gram provides about ten "lines" or portions of the drug. (Gram bottles are usually little brown pharmaceutical bottles approximately one inch high and about the width of an index finger.) Maintaining even a moderate cocaine habit will cost several hundred dollars a week. Because it is so expensive, many teenagers who are habituated often become dealers or steal to get money to support their habit.

How Is Cocaine Taken? Cocaine is purchased in crushed or powdered form. This powder is snorted into the nostril through a straw, and it can be injected into a vein, though this is less common.

When cocaine is mixed with heroin (a depressant) and they are injected into the vein together, this is called "speedballing." "Freebasing" is the term used for smoking a purified form of cocaine. In freebasing the cocaine is first purified to make it stronger, and then smoked in a pipe. Speedballing and freebasing are particularly addictive methods of use.

Effects: Cocaine stimulates all central nervous system functions—heart rate, breathing, blood pressure. Cocaine users say the drug gives them increased energy, a feeling of excitement and euphoria. It can also cause insomnia and loss of appetite. A cocaine "high" usually lasts one-half to two hours, but users report feeling some of its effects for a day or two.

Dangers: Because it is usually snorted rather than injected, cocaine use, by itself, is rarely fatal. Its greatest danger is that recreational use can produce a heavy psychological addiction. When people who are dependent stop taking cocaine, they can go through severe withdrawal symptoms: hallucinations, anger, nervous anxiety, and paranoia. Using cocaine over a long period of time can also produce anxious-ness, irritability, paranoia, and hallucinations. Regular use of cocaine causes considerable stress to the nervous system. It also erodes the mucous membrane lining of the nose. Heavy cocaine users may need plastic surgery to rebuild destroyed tissue.

Another danger of the drug is that cocaine is often cut with other white, powdery substances such as sugar, talc, local anesthetics, or even Ajax, which may cause side effects or irritate the lining of the nose.

How Can You Tell If a Teenager Is on Cocaine? People on cocaine may appear excited and more talkative, but often it is difficult to tell when a person has consumed this drug. There are very few outward signs of cocaine use.

Look-Alike Drugs These are commercially manufactured drugs that look like illicit drugs and are either sold legally over the counter, or purchased legally and then resold illegally as the "real thing." They are considered legal because these drugs don't contain any federally controlled substances, such as amphetamines or cocaine, but instead consist mostly of caffeine and antihistamines.

Look-alike drugs are primarily fake amphetamines, although substances are also sold which simulate cocaine (Pseudo-caine), opium (lettuce opium), and inhalants (Rush).

Slang Names: Pseudo-caine, Rush, Lettuce Opium, Beauties.

How Do Teenagers Get Look-Alike Drugs? They are sold in record stores and head shops—stores that carry devices to hide, store, purify, or consume drugs. Look-alikes are also sold on the street as if they were illegal drugs.

Effects: The effects of these legal stimulants are similar to, but generally milder than, the effects of amphetamines. Look-alikes produce increased heart rate, blood pressure, and respiration. The user feels more talkative, has a reduced appetite, and may have nervous twitches.

Dangers: Because of the high caffeine levels in these stimulants (see Caffeine section), these drugs can cause a toxic reaction involving extreme anxiety, stomach ulcers, and possible heart problems. Teenagers, in an attempt to capture a "true" cocaine or amphetamine high, often take many times the recommended dose of these pills. In the past two years, these drugs have been implicated in the deaths of more than a dozen people.

How Can You Tell If a Teenager Is on Look-Alike Drugs? He or she will show all the symptoms of amphetamine use including loss of appetite, an inability to sleep, jitters, anxiety, and increased talkativeness. Users may complain of nausea and fatigue the following day.

HALLUCINOGENS:
The term hallucinogens is used as a classification of several illegal drugs that tend to distort or alter perceptions and a sense of reality. People who take hallucinogens see, hear, feel, taste, and smell things that aren't really there. The most common of these drugs are LSD, mushrooms, psilocybin, peyote, and mescaline. Mushrooms and peyote grow wild or are cultivated for sale, while LSD, psilocybin, and mescaline are chemically manufactured.

LSD: This is an extremely powerful drug. A single dose is measured in microscopic amounts. The drug is sold on small squares of paper (blotter acid), on gelatin squares (windowpanes), or in small pills. The actual chemical is colorless, odorless, and tasteless.

Slang Names: Fry, L, acid, mickey mouse, red dragon (in blotter form), windowpane, purple micro dot, orange sunshine, purple haze.

How Do Teenagers Get LSD? LSD is illegally manufactured and sold to teenagers through their friends or local drug dealers.

Cost: Approximately $4 to $5 a dose.

How Is LSD Taken? LSD is swallowed in pill form, sucked off blotters, or consumed in gelatin squares or in candy. Like other illegal drugs, it can be adulterated with other dangerous substances such as PCP, belladonna, or speed.

Effects: Physically, LSD produces dilated pupils and dries out the mouth. It may produce rapid heart beat, high blood pressure, nausea, low body temperature, heavy perspiration, and loss of appetite. A teenager hallucinating on LSD may experience brilliant colors or objects moving when in reality they are stationary, or have unpleasant or frightening experiences or visions. An LSD trip usually lasts about twelve hours.

After the drug wears off, it is common to feel exhausted. Some users have "flashbacks" where they reexperience for a few moments the feelings or images that occurred while on the drug.

Dangers: While LSD is not addicting, tolerance quickly builds up when the drug is taken over a period of time. Knowing this, chronic users only take LSD every other day. Physiologically there is some evidence that LSD causes chromosome breakdown, but research is inconclusive. The primary danger of LSD is its psychological effect. "Bad LSD trips" have been known to cause severe psychological and emotional damage to teenagers, which may last a lifetime. Some kids have physically harmed themselves or even committed suicide while on LSD. Even where teenagers are not self-destructive, LSD is dangerous because while on the drug kids are more likely to have accidents including car accidents, falls, burns, etc. It's not known for sure what causes some LSD experiences to be so horrible, but some people believe that they are the result of teenagers being under stress, feeling anxious, or having negative emotions before taking the drug, rather than anything to do with the drug itself. There does not seem to be a known level of overdose for LSD.

How Can You Tell If a Teenager Is on LSD or Another Hallucinogen? The person will have dilated pupils, dry mouth, and may be disoriented or seeing or hearing things that aren't really there. If the user is on a "bad" trip, he or she may be paranoid, extremely frightened or depressed, or self-destructive.

Mushrooms and Psilocybin: Psilocybin is the hallucinogenic ingredient in several varieties of mushrooms generally grown in Mexico or the Pacific Northwest, which has effects similar to LSD and mescaline. Chemically manufactured psilocybin often will contain other compounds. A psilocybin trip usually lasts for approximately six hours. Psilocybin is not addicting, but tolerance can develop. It is not possible to overdose on this drug.

Slang Names: Magic mushrooms, schrooms, los ninos.

Peyote and Mescaline: Mescaline is a chemical derived from the buttons of the peyote cactus that is grown primarily in Mexico and the southwestern United States. Mescaline is weaker than LSD, but its effects are similar. An average dose will last from five to twelve hours. It is usually taken in capsule or tablet form. It is common for a person taking peyote to have nausea and vomiting, but this doesn't happen when mescaline is taken. Like LSD, a person can't overdose from mescaline, but it is possible to experience anxiety and depression while on the drug.

Slang Names: Buttons, beans, cactus.

MDA/MDM: These are hallucinogenic compounds that come in powders and are related to both amphetamines and mescaline. In recent years these drugs have reappeared on the street in some areas. Their physical effects are similar to amphetamines, but the user experiences a mild mescaline-like high. People who use MDA/MDM report feeling panicked and severely anxious at times while on the drug. Because these compounds are amphetamine derivatives, tolerance develops rapidly and can result in overdose.

Slang names: Ecstasy, XTC.

Marijuana   Marijuana is one of the most controversial yet widely consumed illegal drugs available. The United States has the highest incidence of marijuana use among teenagers. According to the National Institute on Drug Abuse, almost one-third of all teenagers have tried marijuana and many use it regularly. The drug has been used for medical and other purposes since the ancient civilizations of Asia, Greece, and Rome. It is currently used legally in this country for symptomatic and pain relief from glaucoma, arthritis, and the side effects of cancer chemotherapy.

Marijuana comes from the leaves and flowers of the hemp plant, which grows wild and is also cultivated in many parts of the world. Most marijuana is still smuggled into the United States from Mexico, Colombia, the Caribbean, and Southeast Asia. However, in the last fifteen years there has been a steady increase in the amount of marijuana grown illegally throughout this country. Despite its illegality, or perhaps because of it, marijuana has become the fourth largest cash crop in the United States behind soybeans, corn, and wheat. Estimates are that retail sales of marijuana grown in the United States amount to about $8.2 billion annually.*

What Does It Look Like? In plant form, marijuana has long, delicate, five-fingered green leaves and small green flowers. When dried and crushed it looks much like oregano.

Street, Slang Names: Pot, weed, grass, reefers, ganja, dope, smoke. Names such as Sinsemilla, Consemilla, Acapulco Gold, Thai Stick, Maui Wowie refer to kinds of marijuana.

How Do Teenagers Get Marijuana? Next to alcohol, inhalants, and cigarettes, marijuana is probably the most easily obtainable drug available to teenagers. It is sold illegally through numerous distribution networks, often by teenagers themselves. Marijuana is available either by the joint (marijuana cigarette), or in larger quantities such as a lid (one ounce weight). Some marijuana is sold in bags or in fractions of an ounce. Many users grow their own.

Cost: $35 to $200 an ounce or more. A moderate habit could cost from $5 to $50 a week.

How Is Marijuana Taken? Most commonly marijuana is smoked in hand-rolled cigarettes called joints, or in a variety of pipes including water pipes or "bongs" (a water pipe used for smoking marijuana). It can also be eaten when baked into brownies or other foods. If the marijuana is strong, only a few puffs can make a person high for several hours.

Effects: Marijuana is not easily classified in any drug category. It is not a narcotic. It has properties of sedatives, stimulants, tranquilizers and psychedelics. The most noticeable effects of marijuana smoking are reddened eyes, increased heart rate, dry mouth, a feeling of heightened sensation, feelings of relaxation, a release of inhibitions, change in time perception, and for some people, an increase in appetite. Marijuana can also cause an anxiety or panic reaction. A marijuana "high" will last anywhere from two to four hours or longer. Because THC, the mind-altering chemical in marijuana, is stored in the fat cells of the body, the actual chemical may remain in the body for several days. Most people, however, do not consciously feel stoned after the first few hours of use. Smoking moderate amounts of marijuana daily does not seem to build tolerance to the drug and most authorities do not consider it physically addicting. "Burnout" is a term associated with long-term marijuana smoking that describes a state where the person has smoked so much marijuana over a period of time that the drug fails to produce the original high.

Dangers: While many people have positive experiences with marijuana, the drug can also produce psychologically negative reactions including anxiety, panic, disorientation, or paranoia. Recently, some researchers have reported finding carcinogenic compounds in marijuana cigarettes. There is also some evidence that the smoke may damage the lungs.

*Marc Leepson, "Marijuana Update," *Editorial Research Reports,* Congressional Quarterly, Inc. (Washington, D.C., 1982). U.S. Department of Agriculture figures for 1980.

Certain researchers conclude that the long-term smoking may affect the body's immune system, increase the chances of infertility and miscarriage, and affect long-term memory and intellectual performance.*

Much more work remains to be done before such data are conclusive, but for teenagers there are particular dangers associated with marijuana smoking. Teenagers are highly sensitive to the physiological and psychological effects of the drug. The National Institute on Drug Abuse, in a recent pamphlet to parents, states the following:

A very real danger in marijuana use is its possible interference with growing up . . . As research shows, the effects of marijuana can interfere with learning by impairing thinking, reading comprehension, and verbal and arithmetic skills. Scientists also believe that the drug may interfere with the development of adequate social skills and may encourage a kind of psychological escapism.

How Can You Tell If a Teenager Is Stoned on Marijuana? Although it is not always easy to tell when someone has been smoking marijuana, teenagers who are stoned are likely to have red eyes or complain of a dry mouth. Because there is a dreamlike effect from the drug, they may also move more slowly, and some teenagers will show signs of impaired physical coordination. Some teenagers will get the "munchies," a hungry state attributed to smoking grass. In fact, even with moderate use, it's very hard to tell. The most telltale sign is, of course, the odor of marijuana.

Nicotine In terms of personal health, smoking tobacco is probably the leading drug problem in this country. Smoking among teenagers is as serious a problem as with adults, though recent studies show that smoking among high school seniors dropped significantly between 1977 and 1981. The National Institute on Drug Abuse reported: "We are inclined to attribute this change to a long-term increase in young people's health concerns about smoking and to a shift in peer norms regarding the acceptability of this behavior."†

Teenagers smoke for a variety of reasons. In a recent study in the San Francisco area, adolescents reported that they smoked to "relax, win friends, lose weight, and show their independence."‡

Nicotine is the addictive drug in tobacco, but it is not the only harmful substance contained in a cigarette. Tars and carbon monoxide are also capable of doing great damage to the body.

Where Do Teenagers Get Cigarettes? Because it is illegal to sell cigarettes to minors, many teenagers at least initially smoke their parents' or friends' cigarettes and later find older friends who will buy cigarettes for them. Stealing cigarettes has become more difficult because they are almost always kept behind store counters.

Cost: About $1 per pack.

Effects: Nicotine is highly addicting, both physically and psychologically. Smoking three or four cigarettes a day for a week can create physical addiction. A stimulant, nicotine increases heart rate, blood pressure, and respiration.

Dangers: Smoking is responsible for a variety of respiratory and cardiac problems including shortness of breath, heart damage, lung irritation, emphysema, kidney dysfunction, strokes, and cancer of the lungs, mouth, esophagus, pancreas, urinary bladder, and larynx. Babies born to teenagers who smoke weigh less and are more likely to develop problems as infants.

Withdrawal from smoking may result in dizziness, headaches, cramps, nervousness, fatigue, tremors, depression, and increased appetite.

PCP or Phencyclidine PCP is a synthetically manufactured drug that was originally used as an animal tranquilizer, but that never had a legal use in humans because of its adverse psychological effects. Today, illegally manufactured PCP is very popular among teenagers because it is somewhat cheaper than other drugs and because it is so easy to obtain. The drug is relatively simple to synthesize and is manufactured in home laboratories and sold on the street at a large profit. Although it is found in a variety of forms, most PCP comes in a cigarette that has been dipped in the substance and then rolled in aluminum foil.

Slang Names: In cigarette form: Kool, Superkool, Sherman, Sherm; on mint leaves: angel dust; in liquid form: juice; in marijuana: lovely; in crystalline form: crystal, rocketfuel.

How Do Teenagers Get PCP? The drug is purchased illegally from friends or drug dealers.

Cost: $20 to $25 a cigarette. One cigarette can supply several teenagers with a PCP high, although it is not uncommon for one person to smoke a whole PCP cigarette.

How Is It Taken? PCP is usually smoked, either in cigarettes dipped in PCP juice or in mint or marijuana leaves that have been sprayed with PCP and then rolled into a cigarette. Less popular methods involve snorting it in powder form, swallowing it as a pill, or injecting it directly into the vein.

Effects: This drug is highly unpredictable. It can act at the same time as a stimulant, a depressant, and also as a mind-altering agent. A PCP "high" usually lasts four to six hours. Because it is an anesthetic, PCP users generally feel no pain and many experience numbness and muscle rigidity. The drug can cause hallucinations and delusions, and a person on PCP may hear a high-pitched buzzing sound, which comes and goes. The drug causes a rush of blood to the surface capillaries making users feel hot. PCP affects memory and causes slurred speech, and affects time and space judgments.

---

*Marc Leepson, "Marijuana Update," *Editorial Research Reports,* Congressional Quarterly, Inc. (Washington, D.C., 1982), pp. 108–110.

†Johnston, Bachman, O'Malley, "Highlights From Student Drug Use in America, 1975–1981" Rockville, MD: (National Institute on Drug Abuse, 1981).

‡Los Angeles *Times* (April 19, 1982).

Some PCP users disrobe and have been found walking naked through the streets. The eyes develop nystangmus or jerky movements.

PCP users are extremely volatile. They may behave calmly one moment and shift into violent rage the next. Not everyone who takes PCP experiences these symptoms, but it is entirely unpredictable which user will behave in a bizarre manner or at what point a person on PCP might begin to act bizarrely.

Dangers: Because of its anesthetic properties PCP users can injure themselves or others without ever experiencing pain or comprehending their violence until the drug wears off. Many users hear voices telling them to do strange or self-destructive things. People have broken out of handcuffs at the cost of breaking all the bones in their wrists, walked through plate-glass windows or jumped out of windows, burned themselves or others, cut off parts of their body, or drowned. On the West Coast it has become popular to take the drug before gang fights. At high doses PCP can cause convulsions or cardiac arrest.

PCP is stored in the fat of the body and is released in stressful situations resulting in flashbacks for up to two years after the drug was taken. People who have used the drug regularly (three or more times a week for three months or more) may experience prolonged psychotic symptoms, slurred speech, loss of memory, and difficulty concentrating, even after they stop taking PCP. They also continue to have moments of bizarre and violent behavior.

In her book, *Drugs, Kids and Schools,* Diane Tessler wrote:

> The general public wonders why kids so willingly take the nightmare drug. Users have explained that it blanks out all feeling. Emotional and physical pain are no longer realities. For some [teenagers] not feeling one's body and environment are considered to be desirable effects . . . Whatever PCP is, it's a grab-bag drug. One time, it's intense sound and color perceptions; the next, depersonalization; another, convincing voices telling you to kill and mutilate. Of all drugs ever known, this one has the most frightening potential.*

PCP users can become very paranoid and violent. If you have someone in your home who is under the influence of this drug, don't try to "talk them down." Instead, remove other people from the area, give the person a blanket, and leave him or her alone. Also, don't try to physically restrain someone on PCP, but call the police if it is necessary.

How Can You Tell If a Teenager Is on PCP? The person will smell of formaldehyde or ether. Typical signs of PCP use also include jerky eye movements; muscle twitches or muscle rigidity; loss of concentration and recent memory; poor muscle coordination; agitation and aggressiveness; in-

appropriate, sudden, and intense emotional changes, i.e., laughing one minute, paranoid and angry the next; distortions of size and body image; stuttering or slurred speech.

Statistics on Drug Experimentation Among High School Seniors in the United States, 1981. The following percentage of seniors have tried these drugs at least one time in their life.*

Alcohol	93%
Tobacco	71
Marijuana	60
Stimulants	32
Inhalants	17
Cocaine	17
Tranquilizers	15
Barbiturates	11.3
Quaaludes	10.6
LSD	10
Opiates (other than heroin)	10
PCP	8
Heroin	1.1

EATING DISORDERS

Eating disorders are one of the most alarming and rapidly growing problems among teenagers, particularly teenage girls. They include a whole range of behaviors from eating compulsively as a way to cope with stress or difficult emotions to the more threatening problems of obesity, anorexia and bulimia.

Our society fosters eating disorders. We place tremendous emphasis on being thin—being thin represents success, glamour, strength of character, and sophistication. Diet and weight are a national preoccupation. Estimates are that some twenty million Americans are on a "serious" diet at any given moment. Dieting has become a multibillion-dollar industry, which includes diet books, diet doctors, diet clubs, diet foods, diet medicine, and diet spas.

Though in recent years we also have become more health conscious, what is considered fashionably thin is not based on any medical standards. In fact, the ideal weight, as exemplified by actresses and fashion models, has dropped in the last few years to between 10 and 20 percent less than what is considered normal body weight by medical authorities.

At the same time that being thin is so important to us, our increased affluence has heightened our interest in and our consumption of food. All over the country, particularly in cities, we've seen a dramatic rise in the number of restaurants, gourmet take-outs, specialty food shops, cooking classes . . . What you eat and where you eat have become symbols of status. As with alcohol, advertising encourages

*Diane Jane Tessler, *Drugs, Kids and Schools* (Glenview, Ill.: Scott Foresman, 1980).

*Johnston, Bachman, O'Malley, "Highlights from Student Drug Use in America, 1975–1981"; National Institute on Drug Abuse (Rockville, Md, 1981), pp. 13–18.

and glamorizes this consumption. Women are especially vulnerable because traditionally they are the ones expected to be involved with food and food preparation. The message to women is: "Prepare delicious, gourmet meals for your family and friends, but don't eat any of it yourself!"

Teenagers, particularly girls, are caught in the middle. This is a time when they are very involved in the most demanding self-scrutiny. They are acutely aware of the standards we have for thinness and beauty, yet the demands of their own rapidly growing bodies create in them huge appetites and strong cravings for food.

Teenagers have never been known for their sensible diet; they consume quantities of junk food—hamburgers, pizzas, french fries, sodas, candy bars . . . They and their friends raid the refrigerator; they go out for pizza and Coke; they share gossip over a hot fudge sundae. Parents comment: "It seems like my kids are always eating."

> My son's always eating. There's never enough food around to satisfy him. And then he spends so much money on lunch and candy bars, he's always complaining he's broke.

As we've noted elsewhere, most teenagers are dissatisfied with at least some aspect of the way they look. Many of them consider themselves overweight. Teenage girls, in particular, often become alarmed as their bodies begin to fill out and assume more womanly proportions. Even girls who are very thin as children have to adjust to larger hips and a more rounded rear end. One study in the Los Angeles public schools found that 60 percent of a random sample of two thousand eleventh-grade girls described themselves as overweight, although most were within normal weight ranges. Forty-four percent of the girls said they were usually or always on a diet. Within this group, the most preferred methods of dieting were fasting, diet pills, and vomiting*:

> At my daughter's school all the girls are on diets. Every week it's a different one. A group of them will go on the Scarsdale, then they'll do a juice fast, then it's the protein powder.

> My daughter is always telling me she's fat. She will stand in front of her bedroom mirror before a date and cry and tell me how ugly she looks. It's horrible because she really means it.

Faced with those feelings and with conflicting pressures, many teenagers get into a pattern of binging—eating huge amounts of starchy or sweet foods and then following that with periods of fasting, rigid dieting, or more drastic measures like vomiting:

> Allison dieted the whole summer before she went into high school. When school started in the fall, she got a lot

*Hoffman, David, Ph.D., *Psychological Overview of Eating Disorders.*

of attention from boys and I think it scared her. I think that's why she started gaining all the weight back.

> I think the way Emily handled the pressure to be grown-up like her older sister was to stop eating. She was having troubles in school, in her social life and had pressure to please her parents.

These adolescents have one striking characteristic in common: they use food to cope. Like people who use drugs or alcohol, certain teenagers use eating, or not eating, or eating and purging as a way to cope with feelings of loneliness, anxiety, fear, anger, and frustration. Most of us occasionally eat out of these motives—eating can sometimes provide the comfort we need. But for the child who has an eating disorder, this ritual takes on a different level of importance. The obese teenager gets very upset if he doesn't have a candy bar before going out with his friends; the anorectic is terrified of eating altogether and sees *not* eating as the only way to cope with her problems and have any self-worth; and the bulimic will spend the hours studying for an exam alternately binging and then inducing vomiting in an effort to handle the stress. Very recent reports indicate that certain teenagers who have not developed these specific illnesses have, by their dieting, stopped their growth and delayed puberty.

SPECIFIC FOOD ABUSE PROBLEMS

Obesity:

Despite the ongoing diet craze and the multitude of regimens that are used to control weight, there is a rise of obesity in this country and there are many obese adolescents, particularly young women.

We define obesity as enough excess weight to endanger physical health. No one is exactly sure what causes obesity but it is probably a combination of social and genetic factors. Aside from the physical consequences, for teenagers the most disturbing aspect of this problem is the emotional pain it causes them. Obese teenagers are generally withdrawn, self-conscious, self-hating and not likely to participate very much in life.

Obese kids often deny that they have a problem and resist their parents' attempts to intervene or help them. The resistance usually is a reaction to the tensions that have developed in the family:

> For years my husband and I have been trying to help our son with his weight problem. He's gone to summer camps for overweight children, I've taken him to the doctor for pills and even hormone shots. He's sixteen now and I finally decided not to talk to him anymore about what he's eating or how much.

> My daughter was first anorectic and then when she finally started to gain weight, she got to be fifty pounds overweight. I think part of that was our fault. We made such a big deal over the whole subject.

Bulimia:

Bulimia is a medical term that literally means "ox hunger" or "insatiable hunger." It is used to describe a pattern of behavior in which a person, usually a girl or woman, consumes a large amount of food, perhaps several thousand calories, sometimes in less than two hours. This is followed with a "purge," which could include self-induced vomiting or the use of a laxative, diuretic or amphetamine; stringent dieting; fasting; or compulsive exercise. Though most people associate bulimia simply with self-induced vomiting, many bulimics will employ other purging methods and will use more than one technique.

Bulimics binge and purge alone, which is why bulimia has been labeled the "secret syndrome." Some estimates suggest that 15 to 20 percent of the female college population is involved at least occasionally with this behavior, and that 10 percent of these women are habitual bulimics.

The majority of bulimics are women and teenage girls. Bulimia often begins during a diet, as a way to eat forbidden foods without gaining weight. Later, the pattern becomes a way to cope with difficult emotions. Bulimics binge and purge characteristically when pressures mount up; when frustrations with studying get too great; when they feel angry toward their boyfriends or rebellious toward parents; when they are dateless and feeling lonely on a Friday or Saturday night:

> Laura became bulimic while she was dieting. That, combined with the stress of school, her job, quitting smoking, her boyfriend—was just too much for her. She was overwhelmed. She had lost weight and had gotten this neat boyfriend and she was terrified if she gained any weight, she would lose him.

> My daughter recently told me that when her bulimia was the worst, she would plan her secret Friday night binges. She would borrow the car and go around to all the different all-night markets and eat cookies and ice cream, bags full of stuff, riding around in the car. She would eat all her favorite foods and then would come home and force herself to throw up. Sometimes she'd even stop at gas stations to vomit and then go and eat some more.

> As the bulimic's illness progresses, life revolves more and more around the need to find places and times to binge and purge. School, social life, recreation, or job all become secondary:

> During the time Jennifer was eating and throwing up she stopped going out with her friends. She stayed at home a lot. She wouldn't go out on dates. I knew she was depressed but I didn't know what was going on.

Repeating vomiting over a period of time leads to serious health problems. Girls develop tooth and gum decay (from the gastric juices in the stomach and intestines), swollen salivary glands, and tearing of the esophagus that can lead to internal bleeding. Vomiting can create a hormone imbalance causing a potassium deficiency that produces muscle cramps, and irregular heartbeat, and in rare cases, heart attacks.

The psychological consequences of this illness are equally destructive. Though most girls may not get to the stage where they experience physical symptoms, virtually all teenagers who vomit regularly experience remorse and self-hate:

> My daughter has no self-esteem and it kills me to watch her. She's a beautiful girl, very bright, but she spends so much time hating herself. When she was heavier she hated herself. Now that she's thin, she still hates herself. It doesn't matter what weight she is, she still hates herself.

These girls constantly fear food. The harder they try to control their intake through purging the more out of control they feel. Bulimics are convinced they could not maintain their current weight without vomiting or other purging, and they feel enormous fear, guilt, and desperation about it. They resist seeking help because they are worried that the end result of getting help will be a weight gain:

> I was so shocked when my daughter told me she was bulimic. She said she was sick and needed help. She had been trying to tell us for a long time but she was afraid because she thought we would be angry and force her to gain weight.

> After a few sessions of therapy my daughter admitted she was sick and out of control and needed help. At first she refused to eat even a bite of food that she would keep in her body. It took urging to get her to take a protein wafer. I told her to eat whatever she was comfortable with but these days, when she discovers she's gained a few pounds, she gets hysterical. I come in and she says, "Don't come in and look at me, I'm fat." She weighs one hundred pounds.

How Can You Tell If Your Child Is Bulimic? Since bulimics are usually so secretive, you may not at first notice any big difference in their behavior, particularly not in their eating habits:

> My daughter had never done anything behind my back—I thought. That's why I was so shocked when I heard about the bulimia. She told us she would throw up ten to twelve times a day. It was going on right under our nose and I didn't see it.

> In January Mindy started vomiting with regularity. We were unaware of it at first but we noticed she seemed exhausted all the time. She started missing school. She was skipping meals but she was binging on huge amounts of food. She had all kinds of schemes for getting the food in the house and getting the containers out.

There are a few signs to watch for: large quantities of food may be missing from the refrigerator or cupboards. You may notice unpleasant odors in the bathroom from purging. You may observe that your daughter seems more tired, secretive, depressed, withdrawn, or agitated than usual. It is possible that her knuckles will be raw or bleeding from putting her finger down her throat to induce vomiting.

Anorexia:

Anorexia nervosa is a medical term used to describe an eating disorder in which a person starves herself past slimness to the point of emaciation. It is a serious disorder because the physical complications it causes can be life-threatening and also because anorectics are so often unwilling to admit they have a problem and to seek help. Estimates are that 10 to 15 percent of anorectics die from starvation or the complications arising from near-starvation. They may lose as much as 25 percent of their original body weight. They may stop menstruating and ovulating, and as the disorder progresses, they will show signs of malnutrition: mental confusion, feeling cold all the time, fatigue, loss of hair, skin problems, dizziness. . . . Many anorectics require hospitalization. Though the cure rate for teenagers who are identified and treated within the first few months is very high, it is much more difficult to permanently cure those who have had anorexia for a long period of time.

Anorexia is most likely to occur in teenage women between the ages of twelve and eighteen. Estimates are that 90 percent of anorectics are female. Like bulimia, anorexia usually starts with a diet—with the desire to take off extra pounds:

> If I have anything to say to other parents, it's that they should be very careful and watch their child if she goes on a diet. I could kick myself from here to tomorrow for not monitoring Jamie's diet more carefully, especially when she started fooling around with diet pills. It is so easy to get out of control, and then these girls wind up really hurting themselves.

Anorectics are normally not overweight to begin with but they have an intense fear of obesity, a distorted body image, and they will often claim they are fat even after they've become emaciated. They resent the alarm and concern of others. One seventy-pound girl identified her friends' concern as jealousy because she was skinnier than they were.

At the same time, anorectics are very preoccupied with food. They often collect recipes, count calories, and prepare food for other family members. They feel hunger but systematically deny themselves food. In essence they attempt to control their lives through controlling their food. They imagine that if they could only get thin enough, their problems would disappear.

How Can You Tell If Your Teenager Is Anorectic? The most obvious sign of anorexia is that your teenager loses large amounts of weight. This is particularly alarming if she is thin to begin with. Teenagers who are anorectics will toy with their food but not eat; they will exercise compulsively, sometimes running up and down stairs to burn off calories; and they will often withdraw, spending time alone rather than with friends. They may report feeling weak or cold a lot of the time. Some anorectics will also vomit, fast, and take laxatives:

> When Nina was at her thinnest she was pretty crazy. She would rush home from school, go for a three-mile bike ride, do push-ups, sit-ups—you name it. In between, she would spend time in the bathroom looking at her stomach in the mirror and saying how disgustingly fat she was. She was getting all A's in school, but she was staying up all night studying. Sometimes she would be up at night because she had trouble sleeping.

Which Teenagers Are Most Likely to Develop Eating Disorders? As we mentioned earlier, because cultural pressures on women are so great, food abuse tends to occur primarily in teenage girls. Teenage boys are more likely to be self-destructive with alcohol or drugs:

> I have two children. At one point my boy was out in the backyard growing marijuana while my girl was sneaking food and hiding it under her bed or stealing from supermarkets.

Although many adolescent girls have anorexia and bulimia, there are many more who never develop these disorders but who spend all of their teenage years obsessed with food and dieting, hating their bodies, and using food as a way to cope with feelings. They may be overly concerned with body perfection and have tremendous fear of being overweight. Their entire self-esteem will rest on how much they weigh. They may feel "good" when they eat little and "bad" when they eat fattening foods.

This pattern is in itself psychologically damaging. Our children don't have to develop bulimia to feel guilt and remorse about eating; to feel like failures if they can't attain or maintain a certain weight; and to feel that being accepted and appreciated rests on how thin they are.

Many anorectics and bulimics come from middle- and upper-middle-class homes. Bulimics are usually bright, highly motivated young women with career ambitions, who are anxious to please others, particularly their parents. They tend to set unrealistic standards for themselves. Many of these girls have in their minds an ideal weight, and when they can't achieve or maintain it they panic.

Anorectics are often described as model children, "the quiet girls, the overachievers, the best, brightest, sweetest, most obedient and most cooperative."* Anorectics are described as being more passive than bulimics and although both deny their problem, anorectics are more likely to delude

---

*Steven Levenkron, *The Best Little Girl in the World* (New York: Warner Books, 1979).

themselves, even to the point of denying they are losing weight at all.

There are a number of opinions about the psychological make-up of those girls who are at risk or who actually become anorectic. Some people believe that these girls are literally trying to starve themselves back into a more childlike body. Another theory is that anorectics have failed to achieve independence from their parents and particularly their mother. Or anorexia may be a way to gain control over the family and to express anger and rebellion. Though some of these characteristics apply to some anorectics, there are also girls for whom none fit.

A feature common to both anorectic and bulimic youth is that over half of them seem to come from families in which at least one parent is very involved with food. That parent is often dieting, worrying about getting fat, and very controlling about food:

I'm not skinny and I'm not fat. I'm very conscious of my weight and am concerned about my looks. I feel guilty about my daughter's anorexia because I get upset myself when I gain a pound. I didn't do anything on purpose, but I myself am a product of a home where my mother always wanted me to be thin.

I've never had much of a preoccupation with food or a weight problem. Ironically, since this disease started, I've been overeating. It's almost like I'm carrying it for her. My husband, though, has a tremendous weight problem and preoccupation with food and dieting. Years ago, when he was trying to lose weight, he would eat a big meal and then go to the bathroom and vomit. He didn't binge in secret like Janice, but when he overate he would vomit. Today he is still sick from it. She may have gotten the idea from him, but she denies it.

Some teenagers who develop anorexia or bulimia have a very dependent relationship with one or both parents. They come from families where, for whatever reason, it's difficult for both parents and their teenagers to let go. So the conflict of independence versus dependence gets played out through the eating disorder. Anorexia and bulimia become a way for teenagers to control themselves and their families and to assert their independence:

Liz is growing away from the family. She'll be eighteen soon and I think part of her really wants to be out there on her own. But another part is still clinging to the family. Also, she and her father are very mad at each other. He's furious at her for having this disease, and the more furious he gets the more she binges. The anger's coming out in other areas—she spends lots of nights with her boyfriend and that goes against my husband's morals.

What Can We Do?   As parents we must look first at ourselves and our own behavior around food. As in the case of alcohol and drug abuse, the strongest message we give our children comes from how we act. For many of us, this may not be easy to control. We may have spent years in the grip of this weight-diet problem ourselves. Though our behavior may not necessarily be harmful to us, we end up teaching our children that weight and diet are extremely important issues in life. For a young person who may not yet have too clear a sense of who she is, this is a powerful message. What may be only a preoccupation for us can become a serious physical and psychological problem when absorbed by our teenager. In order to help our child, we may have to make changes in our own thinking and our own way of relating to food:

Since the episode with Becky's anorexia I think differently about dieting. I'm not so rigid about my weight. I don't intend to get fat, but in the counseling group I had to look at how I control myself all the time and how I control my family.

When I was on a diet, I didn't let the kids eat any sweets. We all had to eat carrots and celery. Then I would break my diet and start binging again and I would buy junk for the kids—I guess because I felt guilty about eating it myself. Now I don't take my kids on and off my diet with me anymore.

We can act as a buttress for our children against the status quo. We can explain to them how superficial and rigid it is to think that being thin is the only goal in life. We can help our kids see that whatever today's ideal is of what is beautiful, it will change, pointing out that twenty-five years ago the "ideal" was a lot heavier. In any case, few people are naturally built as thin as today's models and actresses.

Our children need our help to resist the pressure to look a certain way and weigh a certain amount. Though it may seem that our opinion doesn't count for much, it's important that we keep telling our child what we think is beautiful about her appearance and that we point out her unique and lovely qualities. The chances are that we are heard by our teenagers more than we think and that we are helping them put their priorities in perspective. If trying to achieve or maintain a specific weight results in severe emotional or psychological or physiological upset for our child, then its important to help her work at accepting herself a few pounds heavier than her arbitrary goal:

I finally got my daughter to see that there wasn't any way she was going to be a size seven. We went to our pediatrician and he showed her her growth charts since she was a baby. Everyone in our family is big—big bones, big feet. I kept telling her that in a few more years lot of girls will be as tall as she is. She's not fat. It's just that she developed early.

Finally, without judging their behavior or trying to force them to change their patterns, we can help our children become more aware of the habit of consuming food in an effort to deal with emotions:

My daughter and I have worked out this plan where, when

she would get upset and start to go for food, we had a list of other things she could do—like jog or write in her journal or talk to me or talk to her girlfriend. It didn't always work but at least it made her conscious of what she was doing.

There is a lot more talk these days about exercise and having a good diet, and many teenagers are aware of what constitutes nutritionally sound eating. Even so, they often refuse to take responsibility for their own eating. Many girls diet by fasting and then get so hungry that moderate eating is impossible. We can help by explaining that teenagers need to develop sane eating habits, not simply because a balanced diet is good for them but because the consequences of a bad diet and bad habits can be disasterous physically as well as emotionally.

If Your Teenager Has an Eating Disorder.   As we have noted, many teenagers during these years are preoccupied with weight and looks. They have bad eating habits, go on crazy diets, and even binge periodically, yet they eventually grow out of this behavior on their own. When an eating problem is severe, however (frequent vomiting or rapid, marked weight loss), it's generally more complicated to make a change in behavior. Eating disorders all involve secrecy, denial, and withdrawal, and for most teenagers *they do not go away by themselves.* Moreover, the longer your teenager is involved with food abuse, the harder it becomes to break the pattern.

The most important step in helping your teenager is your own willingness to recognize that there is a problem in the first place. Often parents may detect something is going on with their child and food but they are not really convinced that anything dangerous is happening. It is easy not to take this problem seriously. Everyone eats and all of us have our own individual eating habits. So it is common to overlook a peculiarity that may lead to trouble later. We may even feel confused or fearful, yet do nothing. We may tell ourselves that the problem is not like drug or alcohol abuse. It is, though. Food abuse can be just as damaging emotionally and physically as any other substance abuse:

> Susan was on a merry-go-round where she couldn't stop binging and vomiting. She felt like this ritual of hers was her only friend. She was terrified to give up vomiting and yet she felt totally trapped. Even now, after the therapy, she still reserves the right to binge and vomit when the pressure gets too great.

Our responses to this kind of behavior can include everything from anger and embarrassment to horror and guilt. Some parents view their child's disorder as adolescent rebellion: "She's doing this just to spite us." Usually the causes involve defiant behavior as well as psychological disturbance:

> In some ways, I think Alice's disease is a last-ditch effort to form a relationship with her father. He is a very egocen-

---

HOW TO HELP YOUR TEENAGER LOSE WEIGHT AND MAINTAIN A WELL-BALANCED DIET*

1. *Increase physical activity.*
The most pronounced difference between overweight kids and kids who are in the normal weight range is that normal range teenagers are considerably more active than are their overweight counterparts. Parents can help by initiating family activities such as walks before or after meals, and weekend family outings which include some sort of physical activity (bicycling, hiking, swimming, etc.).

2. *Be a good role model for your teenager.*
Teenagers who have problems with weight or food are helped greatly by seeing parents who have put their own feelings about the issue of weight and diet and eating in perspective, who eat a well-balanced diet, and who are neither obsessed with being too thin nor involved with eating as a way to cope with emotional ups and downs.

3. *Help your teenager deal with emotional problems.*
Kids who have weight or food problems use food as a way to cope with feelings. Parents can help their children by increasing communication, and by helping their teenagers devise ways other than eating to deal with problems (e.g., writing down feelings, beating pillows to get out anger, running, or other physical activity, etc.). It is also important to help your son or daughter practice releasing his or her feelings *before* they build up inside.

4. *Avoid becoming the policeman of your teenager's diet.*
Don't let him or her put you in that position, and avoid commenting on your son or daughter's eating habits in front of other people.

5. *Reward small steps toward behavior change.*
Small steps might include your child substituting fruit for a sweet at dessert, or cutting down on the amount of junk food consumed in a week. Behavior change is a much more valid measure of progress than is a number on the scale. In fact, if the scale has become very important in your teenager's life, or yours, as a measure of self-esteem, consider throwing it out.

6. *Acknowledge to your child that losing weight and keeping the weight off are difficult problems.*
Many people have weight problems, and as we all know, it is not easy to lose weight!

*Suggestions courtesy of David Hoffman, Ph.D. Center for Health, Behavior and Nutrition.

tric person, very occupied with his career and his own needs. Just at this time, when she needs him the most, he's so angry with her he is turning his back on her. He feels it's a self-inflicted disease that is hurting the whole family, and he's really become hysterical. He goes to pieces over it and screams at her when she vomits, "Go ahead and vomit, you pig. You're stinking up the whole house." He ripped the bathroom door off the wall and then ripped her scale out of the bathroom. None of this stopped her from vomiting.

Eating disorders are a secret, self-punishing pattern of behavior. Breaking that pattern involves not only our recognition of the situation but our child's as well. If our teenager is able to admit to herself and to her family that she has a problem with food, that in itself is a step toward recovery:

Our daughter went to hear a lecture on bulimia and she decided she had to tell us. I had a feeling she was vomiting but I kept denying it to myself. I didn't want to see but she finally forced me to.

Where these problems are not too advanced, a change in family attitude may be enough to help the teenager change her behavior. This is particularly true with bulimia. Sometimes a teenager can enlist the support of other family members to help her talk about her tensions at the moment when she feels the urge to abuse food. But where the pattern is well-established, outside help is frequently necessary. This is particularly true for anorexia because the problems underlying that disturbance are often complicated.

There are many types of treatment for eating disorders and a number of facilities have been started around the country during the past few years to treat people with these problems. (See Resource section.) Treatment can include individual or group therapy; self-awareness techniques, including keeping a journal of moods and diet and learning how to use a binge as a key to self-knowledge; nutritional counseling; and behavior modification. Another approach is using self-help groups such as Overeaters Anonymous (OA). OA is a self-help program fashioned on the Alcoholics Anonymous model, which serves as support for people who have problems with food. One advantage of OA is that there are groups in most cities in the United States and in some areas there are specific groups for teenagers and also for bulimics.

An essential component of treatment is mutual support. It is very helpful for teenagers who have these problems to meet together, share experiences, exchange phone numbers, and give each other encouragement:

Liz goes once a week for therapy with other kids who are anorectics or who have food problems. The girls have a buddy system and they call each other in the middle of the night if they're feeling upset. They really help each other.

Getting help can involve not only treatment for our teenager but some kind of support or counseling for ourselves:

At first I was so wrapped up in getting Joanna help and my husband under control, but finally, I was falling apart at the seams and I started in therapy myself. I needed to get out of the middle of this. I've been through a lot in my life but this has got to be the worst.

Family therapy has been very helpful with many adolescent eating disorders. As we have noted, for teenagers, anorexia and bulimia can often be the outward sign of aggressive and defiant attitudes. Whether we like it or not, our child's problems around food are also a family problem, and this sort of therapy can help us work through some of the tensions and conflicts.

In addition to family therapy, an emotional support group for parents can be useful. Many parents have found it extremely valuable to talk to other people who are going through similar crises. Alanon is a self-help group for families and friends of alcoholics that, in some parts of the country, also includes families of food abusers. Although the specific problems of drug or alcohol abuse are different from food abuse, parents of teenagers with drug and alcohol problems and parents of teenagers with eating disorders both need support in setting limits, in expressing their feelings, and in recognizing that they alone cannot solve these problems for their child:

When my daughter was anorectic I finally said to her that if she didn't get hold of herself, she was going to end up in a hospital. I told her she needed to make a choice. Did she want to be sick for the rest of her life? Because I couldn't help her anymore. There was nothing more I could do and I had to take the risk to let her go. So now I consciously stay out of her problem, but the suffering I do myself I wouldn't wish on anybody.

Finally, one day, I had to say to myself, "I am a father who has a daughter who is fat." I don't like it but she's not going to die from being too fat. I can't make her thin. I realize my wife and I couldn't do anything about Susan's weight at that time. It hurt me a lot to see her anguish and her self-involvement, but I had to come to grips with the fact that her being fat was not the worst tragedy in the world. It wasn't like she was dying of leukemia.

BOOKS AND RESOURCES
Drugs and Alcohol

Brecher, Edward, *Licit and Illicit Drugs*. Boston: Little Brown, 1972.
Informative and easy-to-read report by the Consumers Union that provides an excellent, critical overview of the drug problem in America. It's major drawback is that it doesn't contain up-to-date information on drugs, especially marijuana.

Cretcher, Dorothy. *Steering Clear: Helping Your Child Through the High-Risk Drug Years*. Minneapolis, Minn: Winston Press, 1982.
Informative, reasonably written guide for parents with special emphasis on setting limits and instilling a sense of responsibility.

Delaine, John K. *Who's Raising the Family? A Workbook for Parents and Children*. Available from Wisconsin Clearinghouse, 1954 East Washington Ave., Madison, Wis., 53704.
Excellent workbook designed to help parents deal with their concerns and frustrations about their children's drug and alcohol abuse. Presents drugs as part of a larger picture and suggests practical exercises for parents and children to do together.

Editorial Research Reports. Published by Congressional Quarterly, Inc., 1414 22nd St., N.W. Washington, D.C. Accurate, current information. Some past reports are "Marijuana Update," "Caffeine Controversy," and "Teenage Drinking."

Fort, Joel, M.D. *The Addicted Society: Pleasure-Seeking and Punishment Revisited*. New York: Grove Press, 1981.
Controversial analysis of drugs in our society and how they relate to teenage problems. This book is very critical of federal and state law enforcement agencies and the advertising industry. Very readable.

Jackson, Michael, and Bruce Jackson. *Doing Drugs*. New York: St. Martin's/Marek, 1983.
Candid portrayal of teenage drug use and abuse for parents and teens, written by a father and son team.

Moses, Donald A., and Robert E. Burger. *Are You Driving Your Children to Drink? Coping with Teenage Alcohol and Drug Abuse*. New York: Van Nostrand Reinhold, 1975.
Explores possible causes of substance abuse and provides valuable information on the use and abuse of alcohol and drugs. Particularly helpful in identifying the signs of drug and alcohol abuse and available options for help.

National Institute on Drug Abuse. Pamphlets are available free of charge from: National Clearinghouse for Drug Abuse Information, P.O. Box 416, Kensington, Md. 20795.
"Drug Abuse Prevention for You and Your Friends," Up-to-date information on commonly used drugs; "Drug Abuse Prevention for Your Family," Pamphlet for parents; "For Kids Only: What You Should Know About Marijuana," Written for kids twelve to fifteen years old; "For Parents Only: What You Need to Know About Marijuana," "Parents, Peers, and Pot," Strategies and guidelines to prevent drug abuse for parents. Flyers on inhalants and PCP.

Tessler, Diane Jane. *Drugs, Kids and Schools*. Glenview, Ill.: Scott Foresman and Co., 1980.
Practical strategies for educators and parents to open communication and deal with drug use and abuse. Full of basic information, exercise activities, and resources.

Woodward, Nancy. *If Your Child Is Drinking . . .* New York: G. P. Putnam's Sons, 1981.
Helpful book for parents on recognizing and dealing with a child's drinking problem.

For Teenagers

Childress, Alice. *A Hero Ain't Nothin' But a Sandwich*. New York: Avon, 1982.
Story about a thirteen-year-old living in Harlem who is hooked on drugs.

Go Ask Alice. New York: Avon, 1972.
The diary of a fifteen-year-old middle-class girl who becomes involved with drugs.

Hentoff, Nat. *Does This School Have Capital Punishment?* New York: Delacorte, 1981.
A teenager is falsely charged with possessing drugs at school.

Scoppetone, Sandra. *The Late Great Me*. New York: Bantam, 1980.
Story of a seventeen-year-old girl who is an alcoholic, and how she copes with her disease.

Snyder, Anne. *My Name Is Davy and I Am an Alcoholic*. New York: New American Library, 1978.
A teenage alcoholic tells his story.

Resources
Substance Abuse HOTLINE: Families Anonymous, an organization for parents of children who are substance abusers, has a 24-hour nationwide referral service: (213)989-7841

or write to them at
P. O. Box 528
Van Nuys, Calif. 91408

Narcotics Anonymous: (213)372-9666 or check locally

Alcoholics Anonymous: check local phone book

ALANON self-help
P.O. Box 182
Madison Square Station
New York, N.Y. 10159
For families and friends of substance abusers

National Clearinghouse for Alcohol Information
P.O. Box 2345
Rockville, Md. 20853
Write for list of local alcohol treatment programs.

National Federation of Parents for Drug-Free Youth
P.O. Box 57217
Washington, D.C. 20037
Write for information on how to start a local parent group.

National Institute on Drug Abuse
P.O. Box 2305
Rockville, Md. 20852
Write for free books for parents.

Eating Disorders

Burns, Marilyn. *Good For Me: All About Food in 32 Bites.* Boston: Little Brown, 1978.
Useful guide for adolescents and their parents on food and what it does for us.

Chernin, Kim. *The Obsession: Reflections on the Tyranny of Slenderness.* New York: Harper & Row, 1981.
Nicely written analysis of society's increasing demand that women be thin.

Levenkron, Steven. *The Best Little Girl in the World.* New York: Warner Books, 1979.
Moving account of a young woman's struggle with anorexia nervosa.

O'Neill, Cherry Boone. Starving for Attention. New York: Continuum Publishing Co., 1982.
Story of Pat Boone's daughter's struggle with anorexia nervosa. Sympathetic and sensitive account.

Orbach, Susie. *Fat Is a Feminist Issue II.* New York: Berkley Books, 1982.
Presents a step-by-step program to conquer compulsive eating and gain control of your life. Second edition recommended.

For Teenagers

Bershad, Carole, and Deborah Bernick. *Bodyworks: The Kids' Guide to Food and Physical Fitness.* New York: Random House, 1981.
Nicely written and readable guide for teens on food and physical fitness.

Blume, Judy. *Blubber.* New York: Dell, 1974.
Fiction. Another one of the well-received books for pre-teens by this author.

Danzinger, Paula. *The Cat Ate My Gym Suit.* New York: Dell, 1980.
Fiction. Story of an overweight teenager.

Design For Health. (Workbook, 1979) Order from Project Outside/Inside, Somerville Public Schools, 81 Highland Ave., Somerville, Mass. 02143.
A wonderful book for teenagers on physical fitness, weight loss and gain, and emotional health.

Hautzig, Deborah. *Second Star to the Right.* New York: Avon Books, 1982.
Fiction. Story of a teenage girl's battle with anorexia.

Josephs, Rebecca. *Early Disorder.* New York: Farrar, Straus, Giroux, 1980.
Fiction. Sensitively written story about a young girl's problem with anorexia.

Resources

Many large medical centers have Eating Disorder Clinics. Call a large hospital in the city nearest to your home and ask for the psychiatric department. They should be able to refer you to local programs.

American Anorexia Nervosa Association, Inc.
133 Cedar Lane
Teaneck, N.J. 07666

Center for Health, Behavior and Nutrition
16260 Ventura Blvd., Suite 600
Encino, Calif. 91436
David Hoffman, Ph.D., Director

Eating and Weight Disorder Clinic
Henry Phipps Psychiatric Clinic
Johns Hopkins Hospital
600 N. Wolfe St.
Baltimore, Md. 21205

Eating Disorders Project
Michael Reese Medical Center
Psychosomatic and Psychiatric Institute
29 Ellis Ave.
Chicago, Ill. 60616

Eating Disorders Research and Treatment Program
New York State Psychiatric Institute
Columbia Presbyterian Medical Center
722 W. 168th St.
New York, N.Y. 10032

NAANAD
(National Association of Anorexia Nervosa and Associated
   Disorders)
P.O. Box 271
Highland Park, Ill. 60035

Overeater's Anonymous
World Service Office
2190 West 190th St.
Torrance, Calif. 90504
(213)320-7941
OA also has groups for anorectics and bulimics

UCLA Eating Disorder Clinic
Neuropsychiatric Institute
760 Westwood Plaza
Los Angeles, Calif. 90024

INDEX

sexuality, 9–12, 63–94
  anxiety about, 70–71
  books and resources on, 91–94
  discussions about, 38–39, 65–69
  fear of, in parents, 11
  of parents, effect of children on, 11
  parents' embarrassment about, 65
  societal pressures and, 10
sexually transmitted disease (STD), 42, 63, 64, 65, 66, 71, 83, 84–91
  asymptomatic carriers of, 85, 88
  complications arising from, 87–91
  diagnosis of, 86–90
  homosexuality and, 87
  prevention of, 86–90
  symptoms of, 86–90
  transmission of, 86–90
  treatment of, 86–91
  see also specific diseases
single parents, 11, 13–14
skin, changes in, 41
sleep habits, 35, 51, 53
smegma, 41
"special time," 26
sperm, 39, 40
spermatids, 40
spermatogenesis, 40
sponge, contraceptive, 75
spontaneous erection, 35
stimulants, 108–10
stomach trouble, 54, 108
stress, 52, 87
substance abuse, 97–122
  books and resources on, 120–22
  communication about, 103
  see also alcohol; drugs; eating disorders
suicide prevention, 58
support:
  for children, during pregnancy, 77–78
  for children, during puberty, 65
  for parents, 25–26, 55–56, 82
  for parents of homosexuals, 82
suppositories, contraceptive, 76
sweat glands, 41
syphilis, 84, 85, 86, 89

tachycardia, 109
talking back, 28–29
tampons, 46
teenagers, *see* adolescence
television, communication problems and, 27

testicles, 40, 41
  cancer of, 42
  infections of, 90
  undescended, 42
therapy, 54, 82
  family, 55, 56, 119
  group, 54, 56, 119
  individual, 56, 119
touching, 26
toxic shock syndrome, 46
tranquilizers, 108
trichomoniasis, 84, 90
truancy, 29, 52, 54, 101
Tuinal, 106
tumors, 47

undescended testicles, 42
unhappiness, in adolescence, 23
urethra, 42
  infections of, 42, 89, 90
urination, painful, 88, 89, 90
urine test, for pregnancy, 78
uterus, 39, 44, 46, 47
  perforation of, 76

vacuum suction abortion, 79
vagina, 39, 40, 46, 47
  discharge from, 88, 89, 90
  infections of, 89–90
  irregular bleeding from, 46–47, 76
Valium, 108
vas deferens, 40
VDRL, 89
venereal disease, *see* sexually transmitted disease
vitamins, prenatal, 78
voice changes, 35, 36, 41, 51
vulva, 44

weight:
  gain or loss in, 53, 86, 88
  shifting distribution of, 44
wet dreams, 35, 40, 51
withdrawal (drug and alcohol), 105, 106, 107, 108, 109, 112
withdrawal (during intercourse), 76
withdrawal (emotional), 4, 52, 54, 84, 101, 116

yeast infections, 90

zygote, 39, 46

ABOUT THE AUTHORS

RUTH BELL is co-author of *Our Bodies, Ourselves*; *Ourselves and Our Children*; and the principal author of *Changing Bodies, Changing Lives*. She lives with her family in Los Angeles, California.

LENI ZEIGER WILDFLOWER is a health education specialist and teenage counselor. She lives in Santa Monica, California.